SAGE was founded in 1965 by Sara Miller McCune to support the dissemination of usable knowledge by publishing innovative and high-quality research and teaching content. Today, we publish over 900 journals, including those of more than 400 learned societies, more than 800 new books per year, and a growing range of library products including archives, data, case studies, reports, and video. SAGE remains majority-owned by our founder, and after Sara's lifetime will become owned by a charitable trust that secures our continued independence.

Los Angeles | London | New Delhi | Singapore | Washington DC | Melbourne

Riots and after in Mumbai

Thank you for choosing a SAGE product!
If you have any comment, observation or feedback,
I would like to personally hear from you.

Please write to me at **contactceo@sagepub.in**

Vivek Mehra, Managing Director and CEO, SAGE India.

Bulk Sales

SAGE India offers special discounts
for purchase of books in bulk.
We also make available special imprints
and excerpts from our books on demand.

For orders and enquiries, write to us at

Marketing Department
SAGE Publications India Pvt Ltd
B1/I-1, Mohan Cooperative Industrial Area
Mathura Road, Post Bag 7
New Delhi 110044, India

E-mail us at **marketing@sagepub.in**

Get to know more about SAGE

Be invited to SAGE events, get on our mailing list.
Write today to **marketing@sagepub.in**

This book is also available as an e-book.

Riots and after in Mumbai
Chronicles of truth and reconciliation

Meena Menon

Los Angeles | London | New Delhi
Singapore | Washington DC | Melbourne

Copyright © Meena Menon, 2018

All rights reserved. No part of this book may be reproduced or utilized in any form or by any means, electronic or mechanical, including photocopying, recording or by any information storage or retrieval system, without permission in writing from the publisher.

First published in hardback in 2012
This paperback edition published in 2018 by

SAGE Publications India Pvt Ltd
B1/I-1 Mohan Cooperative Industrial Area
Mathura Road, New Delhi 110 044, India
www.sagepub.in

SAGE Publications Inc
2455 Teller Road
Thousand Oaks, California 91320, USA

SAGE Publications Ltd
1 Oliver's Yard, 55 City Road
London EC1Y 1SP, United Kingdom

SAGE Publications Asia-Pacific Pte Ltd
3 Church Street
#10-04 Samsung Hub
Singapore 049483

Published by Vivek Mehra for SAGE Publications India Pvt Ltd, Phototypeset in 10/13.5 Goudy Oldstyle Std by Diligent Typesetter, Delhi and printed at Sai Print-o-Pack, New Delhi.

Library of Congress Cataloging-in-Publication Data Available

ISBN: 978-93-528-0614-0 (PB)

SAGE Team: Manisha Mathews, Sandhya Gola and Rajinder Kaur
Cover photograph: Paul Noronha

I would like to dedicate this book to my sister Mukta and my friend Dilip Samel, my grandparents Unni Shankara Warrier and K. Sarada, and my uncle K. K. Menon, whose adventurous life will always inspire and amuse me.

CONCOMITANTLY: DECEMBER 6

Now
This city is no longer mine
It was only yesterday that you told us
That this country belonged to us
Tell us now, is this country really ours?
The walls of my own house charge upon me
They want to assassinate me
Digging up dead bodies from the past the enemies are busy
Playing the politics of chastisement

Dhasal, Namdeo. 2007. *Poet of the Underworld: Poems 1972–2006*, Selected, introduced and translated from the Marathi by Dilip Chitre. Navayana Publishing.

CONTENTS

List of Abbreviations	ix
Preface	xi
Areas Covered, Period of Research, and Sources of Information	xix
Acknowledgements	xxi
Introduction	xxv

1.	The City of Gold	1
2.	Cow Protection, Temple, and Mosque Disputes Go Way Back: A Chronicle of Communal Riots in Bombay City	22
3.	Jogeshwari Riots: Old Wounds, New Ghettos	83
4.	Extended Ghettos: Naya Nagar	108
5.	Displacement and Polarization	121
6.	Loss of Livelihood	166
7.	Perceptions of Justice	208
8.	Conclusion	222

Appendix	243
Bibliography	249
Index	255
About the Author	263

LIST OF ABBREVIATIONS

AICC	All India Congress Committee
AIDS	Acquired Immune Deficiency Syndrome
ATS	Anti-Terrorism Squad
BA	Bachelor of Arts
BBC	British Broadcasting Corporation
BCom	Bachelor of Commerce
BEST	Bombay (later Brihanmumbai) Electric Supply and Transport Undertaking
BJP	Bharatiya Janata Party
BMC	Bombay Municipal Corporation, later Brihanmumbai (Greater Mumbai) Municipal Corporation
CA	Chartered Accountant
CIC	Chief Information Officer
CID	Criminal Investigation Department
CM	Chief Minister
CPM	Chief Presidency Magistrate
C. P. Tank	Cowasji Patel Tank
CrPc	Criminal Procedure Code
CRC	Community Resource Centre
CSDS	Centre for the Study of Developing Societies
DCP	Deputy Commissioner of Police
EPW	*Economic and Political Weekly*
FIR	First Information Report
FPJ	*Free Press Journal*
IPC	Indian Penal Code
MCOCA	Maharashtra Control of Organised Crimes Act
MHADA	Maharashtra Housing and Area Development Authority
MLA	Member of Legislative Assembly
MLC	Member of Legislative Council
MMR	Mumbai Metropolitan Region

MNS	Maharashtra Navnirman Sena
MP	Member of Parliament
NCP	Nationalist Congress Party
NGO	Non-governmental Organization
OUP	Oxford University Press
PSP	Praja Socialist Party
PWD	Public Works Department
RDX	Research Department Explosive
RP Act	The Representation of the People Act
RSS	Rashtriya Swayamsevak Sangh
SIMI	Students Islamic Movement of India
SSC	Secondary School Certificate
SAHER	Society for Awareness, Harmony and Equal Rights
STF	Special Task Force
TADA	Terrorist and Disruptive Activities (Prevention) Act
UP	Uttar Pradesh
VHP	Vishwa Hindu Parishad
VSNL	Videsh Sanchar Nigam Limited
WRAG	Women's Research and Action Group
YUVA	Youth for Unity and Voluntary Action

PREFACE

The book is based on the research for the SARAI Independent Fellowship from the Centre for the Study of Developing Societies (CSDS), 2007, titled 'Recovering Lost Histories: Riot Victims, Communal Polarization of Mumbai, Its Impact on People and Perceptions about Communities'. The main focus was on the riot victims and the city of Mumbai, which has changed in obvious and not-so-obvious ways since the post-Babri Masjid demolition riots of December 1992 and January 1993. Divisions between Hindus and Muslims have become deeper, and ghettos have sprung up in new places. I spent some time looking at how the city has changed and how people have lived through the difficult times since the riots. Mumbai's social fabric was torn apart, and very little has been done to punish the people guilty of heinous crimes in those two months.

When I started out to research the lives of riot-affected people of the 1992–93 violence in Mumbai, the premise was very simple. It was to go back and see how they had coped with their lives after the riots that took place in the aftermath of the Babri Masjid demolition on 6 December 1992. Some common threads emerged in the interviews of the people I met—people sought refuge in their own community, they suffered trauma which was not really addressed, they lost their livelihoods and they were alienated. These riots and the previous ones had been creating a schism in Mumbai that was reflected in the attitudes towards, and the understanding of, the Muslim community, which was being constantly vilified for owing allegiance to Pakistan, for causing terror and for being 'anti-national'. How did these divisions creep up over the years, what were the factors that led to this mistrust and stereotyping were some of the questions that bothered me at first.

Officially 900 people were killed in mob rioting and firing by the police, 2,036 were injured (*Report of the Srikrishna Commission*, Volumes 1 and 2, 1998) and thousands of people were forced to move out to relief camps that were mostly being run by individuals and NGOs. The riots clearly intensified the divide between the two communities and created a process of further ghettoization. I traced some families of which many have moved from their original houses at the time of the riots and are now living in other areas. The riots also led to many people going to live in the extended suburbs of Mumbai or in the neighbouring Thane district. New colonies were created by this migration, which in the course of time developed their own identity and culture. These areas are now labelled as 'terrorist' hotbeds, and many people accused of 'anti-national' crimes are picked up from these localities, such as Mumbra in Thane district and Naya Nagar in Mira Road, just outside the city. What an irony this is!

Some of the Muslims picked up were suspected to be working for Pakistan-sponsored terror groups, of which a few were let off after being questioned, while the others are still under trial. The Indian security agencies have been at the receiving end of a proxy war by Pakistan, which has lead to the Indian Muslims, too, being targeted because of the perception created that it is the 'Muslim' terror that poses the gravest threat to India and that there is no differentiation between the individuals and the community. The serial bomb blasts on 12 March 1993, which stunned the city after the riots, were unprecedented and led to comparisons between the two events, as we shall see. A see-saw contest between blasts and riots was set off, and with every riot and every blast, suspicion and distrust increased. By going back to the riots, by meeting the people who suffered it, by trying to understand the history of riots in this city, and by looking at the whole issue in the context of nationalism, Hindutva and secularism and what it means, I hoped to understand some of the complexities of the situation. That is, in a nutshell, what I have tried to do. This book is as much an exploration as a journey; it does not aim to offer any answers, but actually raise more questions.

I went backwards from the 1992–93 post-Babri Masjid demolition riots to look at the history of violence between Hindus and Muslims in Bombay/Mumbai, and the archives reveal interesting details about the communal situation which worsened during the Partition. Today it is common to hear the word 'ghetto' and to think of Muslims as the 'other' and 'terrorists'; in fact, many Muslims are denied houses because of who they are; for them jobs are hard to come by and the sense of alienation is evident. The popular perception about Muslims is that 'all Muslims are not terrorists but all terrorists are Muslims'. The situation became worse after the Babri Masjid demolition on 6 December 1992 and the riots in Mumbai in 1992–93—the worst it has possibly ever seen. The riots were followed by the serial blasts in the city on 12 March 1993, which killed 257 people, injuring 713. Anger spilled out against Muslims, and many people told me (at that time I was a reporter with *The Times of India*, Mumbai) that Muslims were never the victims of the riots; that they were in fact the aggressors and the blasts proved that. The government appointed the Srikrishna Commission to investigate the riots, which came up with an extensive document that has been all but shelved, while the serial blasts accused were arrested under the *Terrorist and Disruptive Activities (Prevention) Act* (TADA), now repealed. The state conducted a highly publicized and prolonged trial which began on 30 June 1995, and resulted in 100 convictions including death sentences (*Indian Express* web edition, 18 May 2007).

The uproar over the lack of justice for riot victims and their families became sharper after that. After the riots, the Dadar police station registered a total of nine cases against the Shiv Sena mouthpiece *Saamna* and its editor Mr Bal Thackeray, who is also the founder of the Shiv Sena. Six cases ended in acquittal, while three were closed. Though applications were filed against the acquittal orders, the Bombay

High Court, while dismissing the civil applications on 23 February 2007, observed that no ends of justice would be served by digging up the old cases after the expiry of seven years, that they would only revive the communal tension (Government of Maharashtra affidavit to the Supreme Court, 16 January 2008). The difference was obvious. Terror will be punished with death, but rioters need not worry. Old wounds need not be reopened. So deep was the belief that the riots were in fact a war against Muslim invaders that the Shiv Sena assumed the role of the heroic avenger and along with the Bharatiya Janata Party (BJP) went on to win its first ever assembly elections in Maharashtra. The Sena says that the riots were spontaneous and if it wasn't for the Sainiks, the Hindus would have been decimated. After the riots, which split the city like never before, perceptions about Muslims have hardened. The repeated bomb blasts, too, have worsened the situation. Soon after another terror strike in suburban local trains on 11 July 2006, the Mumbai police put up posters everywhere titled 'Mumbai Unbreakable', cautioning its numbed citizens to be brave and alert. Mumbai is often called a resilient and an unbreakable city, but its famed resilience has been tested too many times and is wearing thin.

Since July 2007, there has been an effort by various human rights organizations and other groups to revive the cases of Mumbai riots and implement the *Srikrishna Commission Report*. The police registered 2,267 cases during the riots and made nearly 9,000 preventive arrests (*Memorandum of the Action Taken Report*, Government of Maharashtra) of which 5,103 were Hindus, 3,456 Muslims and 414 others. About 1,371 cases were closed in 'A Summary' as true but undetected. First, a Special Task Force (STF), formed in 2000 to act on the recommendations of the *Srikrishna Commission Report*, reviewed these cases and later this was re-examined by a committee headed by the then Director General of Police, Maharashtra. About 112 cases were re-investigated. Of this, in eight cases fresh chargesheets were filed (Government of Maharashtra affidavit to Supreme Court, 16 January 2008).

Politicians who indulged in the worst kind of propaganda were responsible in a large part for the murder and mayhem. Yet these people were let off mildly. After 15 years of the riots, Madhukar Sarpotdar, Shiv Sena leader and former Member of Parliament (MP), was convicted under Section 153A of the *Indian Penal Code* on 9 July 2008 for his speeches during the riots. Sarpotdar, who passed away, was the first and only politician who has been handed out a year's simple punishment and a fine of ₹ 5,000. The police also played a role during the riots that cannot be forgotten. Few were actually punished for some really heinous crimes. The Srikrishna Commission listed 31 policemen who actively participated in riots, communal incidents or incidents of looting, arson and so on. One of them was a former Joint Commissioner of Police (Crime), Ram Deo Tyagi, against whom victims fought a long-drawn-out case, which ended in Tyagi's acquittal along with other policemen in the famous Suleiman Usman Bakery case.

The affidavit (Government of Maharashtra affidavit to Supreme Court, 16 January 2008) says that in the case of 31 policemen indicted by the Srikrishna Commission, 10 were punished after departmental inquiries, 11 were found not guilty and 1 died. The state government, in 2001, had filed a case against 18 policemen in the Suleiman Usman Bakery case, but 9 of them, including Tyagi, were discharged in 2003 by the trial court. The affidavit says that the law judiciary department is re-examining whether a revision appeal can be filed in the high court.

Meanwhile, in response to a victim's challenging the discharge of Tyagi, the Bombay High Court upheld the lower court order as just and legal and cleared him and eight other policemen accused of forcibly entering and killing nine people in the Suleiman Usman Bakery firing on 9 January 1993. This case was examined by Justice Srikrishna, and he said, 'The Commission is of the view that the story of the police does not inspire credence' (*The Hindu*, 5 December 2009).

Justice Mridula Bhatkar's order of 16 October 2009 upheld that the trial judge has rightly observed that the firing in the bakery was unnecessary. 'Indeed it was a cruel and atrocious act on the part of the police. In the case of the communal riots, a humane and sensitive approach is expected', she says. 'However it should be within the legal framework. Howsoever be the serious or heinous offence, an innocent cannot be put to trial', the order continues. The court held there is no sufficient evidence against Tyagi and others that they either had common intention to murder the inmates in the bakery or have committed or abetted the offence of criminal trespass.

Despite promises, the government did not appeal against the discharge. It was left to another victim of firing, Noorul Huda Maqbool Ahmed, a madrassa teacher near the bakery. He has now decided to approach the Supreme Court (*The Hindu*, 5 December 2009).

However, there was more disappointment in store and Tyagi and the others accused were absolved of any blame for the killings. On 4 July 2011, the Supreme Court in its order dismissed the special leave petition by Noorul Huda Maqbool Ahmed. Justices V. S. Sirpurkar and T. S. Thakur in their order stated:

> The description in the statements is that some persons were shot dead by the police. In all the statements the act of shooting and killing is attributed to the police without identifying them. Some of these statements are of those who were injured. In short, in all the statements, the only act attributed to the police who entered the Suleiman bakery was of firing at the persons and inmates and some of the inmates dying due to that. There is not a single statement identifying those policemen who fired or suggesting that those who did not fire committed any other mischief by beating by rifle butts, etc. All the statements referred to the order of the police to take out the hidden weapons.

The apex court held that

> [T]he statements, even if they were to be believed completely, would only provide material against those who actually fired the gun shots. Under such circumstances, if admittedly the respondents (Tyagi and the other policemen) did not fire a single bullet, it cannot be said that they had a common object to kill

the innocent insiders in Suleiman Bakery or the Madarsa and Mosque attached thereto. We are quite convinced that the Trial Court and the revisional court were not wrong in relying on this very material circumstance that none of the respondents, though armed, fired a single bullet.

The Maharashtra chief minister decided (in 2007) to create four special courts to try the 253 pending cases related to the riots. A total of 894 chargesheets were filed in courts (Government of Maharashtra affidavit to Supreme Court, 16 January 2008). The affidavit says that the Maharashtra government decided on 22 August 2007 to form a high-level committee chaired by the additional chief secretary (home) to review the pending riot cases. The committee examined the pending cases and selected 16 to be expedited through the special courts, apart from reviving 93 dormant cases. In addition, 41 absconding accused were arrested, who were involved in 24 pending cases. In 539 cases of the riots, the accused have been acquitted or discharged. Of these, 379 were scrutinized and 50 identified for further action.

According to the latest figures from the home department (7 May 2010), 202 cases were sent to the fast-track courts, and many of them are in progress. Of the 900 dead (as listed in the *Srikrishna Commission Report*), 575 were Muslim, 275 were Hindus, 45 were unknown and 5 others. The causes and the resulting number of the deaths are police firing 356, stabbing 347, arson 91, mob action 80, private firing 22 and others 4. About 1,105 Muslims and 893 Hindus were injured. Out of 173 missing persons, a total of 65 legal heirs were given ₹ 2 lakh each, and legal heirs of 49 persons were not traced (Government of Maharashtra affidavit to Supreme Court, 16 January 2008).

After the riots abated somewhat, the then Prime Minister, P. V. Narasimha Rao, constituted a judicial commission of enquiry to probe the events, and by a notification dated 25 January 1993, the Maharashtra government, then headed by the Congress Party, formed a commission to be headed by Justice B. N. Srikrishna with five points as terms of reference.

About 2,125 affidavits were filed before the Commission, of which 2 were from the government, 549 by the police and 1,575 by members of the public. The government changed in March 1995 and the Shiv Sena–BJP combine, which came to power, expanded the terms of reference of the Commission to probe the circumstances and the immediate causes of the serial bomb blasts of 12 March 1993.

The Commission started recording evidence by 29 June 1993. However, the saffron coalition disbanded the Commission on 23 January 1996, justifying that the Commission was taking too long and its report would reopen old wounds. Protests followed this decision, petitions were filed and though the government at the Centre changed, the then Prime Minister, Atal Bihari Vajpayee, advised Maharashtra Chief Minister Manohar Joshi to revive the Commission and it was done on 28 May 1996.

The recording of evidence was resumed from 24 June 1996 and ended on 4 July 1997. A total 502 testimonies were recorded, and 9,655 pages of evidence received, apart from 2,903 documents. In all, 26 police stations and their jurisdictions were covered by the Commission. The *Srikrishna Commission Report* was submitted on 16 February 1998 after a High Court order, and in his epilogue, Justice B. N. Srikrishna, who laboured over the *Report* for five years, quoted the Shankaracharya: 'The same God resides in you and me: why then be needlessly angry with me.'

AREAS COVERED, PERIOD OF RESEARCH, AND SOURCES OF INFORMATION

Areas Covered

South Mumbai: Mazgaon, Thakurdwar Tulsiwadi

West Mumbai: Behrampada, Naupada

Central Mumbai: Kurla, Ghatkopar, Sion, Chunabhatti, Antop Hill, Bainganwadi, Govandi

North Mumbai: Jogeshwari, Goregaon, Malad, Kandivali, Naya Nagar (Mira Road)

Period of Research

February 2007 to November 2009

Sources of Information

Archival material from the Department of Archives, Government of Maharashtra and Elphinstone College, Mumbai, as well as newspaper reports, first-hand interviews, reports on the riots, books on communal violence, writ petitions, people who did relief work during the riots or lived here at the time and who were directly or indirectly affected, non-governmental organizations (NGOs) and activists. Some of the material has been published in the form of articles in *The Hindu*.

ACKNOWLEDGEMENTS

First of all, I would like to thank the Centre for the Study of Developing Societies (CSDS), New Delhi, for awarding me the SARAI-CSDS Fellowship in 2007, which enabled me to do a research on the lives of riot victims in Mumbai. I am grateful for the encouragement and support of Mr N. Ram, editor-in-chief, *The Hindu*, for both the fellowship and the book. I also thank Kalpana Sharma, my former bureau chief at *The Hindu*, Mumbai; Darryl D'Monte, former resident editor, *The Times of India*; and *The Hindu* rural affairs editor, P. Sainath, for their constant support and encouragement. In addition, I was encouraged by Shuddhabrata Sengupta, Vivek Narayanan and others at the CSDS when I made my presentation in New Delhi to try and publish a book. I am thankful to them for their support. I also wish to thank my former colleague Ranjit Hoskote, with whom I first discussed the idea of writing about the Mumbai riots, not knowing at that time where it would lead.

This work would not have been possible without many people who went out of their way to help me and who gave me so much time in the most patient and unselfish manner. Some helped me track down people I could meet and others assisted with documents and vital details, while some discussed the project with me and suggested ways of improving it. I would specially like to acknowledge the valuable help and contribution of Pappu Qureshi and Fazal Ali Shaad for sharing a wealth of information and taking time out to help me meet people; Shakil Ahmed for helping with legal papers, updates on riot cases and contacts; Rasheeda Bi and Ayub Sheikh who helped me in Behrampada; Cynthia Correa, Santosh Bhogte, Sitaram Shelar and Gita Bane from Jogeshwari who were wonderfully patient in tracking down people. Pappubhai in particular has worked extensively during the riots in documenting cases, and thus he and Fazal Ali Shaad have the most amazing network and are still in touch with many of the affected people. I would also like to thank Arif Naseem Khan, Minister for Minority Affairs, Maharashtra, who put me in touch with many people including Mukim Sheikh. I am also grateful to Samar Khadas, Muzaffar Hussain, Virochan Raote, Dr Arif Khan, Sheikh Yunus Sheikh Musa, Huma Khan, Fatima Khadas, Farhan Hanif, Khatun Bi, Razia and Noorjehan formerly with Women's Research and Action Group (WRAG), Teesta Setalvad, Vagish Jha, Professor Imtiaz Ahmad, Bipan Chandra, Zoya Hasan, Manohar Joshi, Ravindra Waikar, Sunil Harsshe, and many others for their help and time. I have to acknowledge the help of Sudhakar Ramchandra Duduskar, P. D. Thombre and staff from the Department of Archives, Maharashtra state government at Elphinstone College, Mumbai, for their help in tracking down documents connected with my research; The Asiatic Library, Mumbai, for permitting me to copy documents for the research and the staff, as well, for specially helping me find books and papers; Additional Chief Secretary (Home) Maharashtra government, Chandra Iyengar; and Sumit Mullick, writer and Principal Secretary (Protocol), Maharashtra government. Dipak Rao went out of his way to share many documents and details in a very generous manner, and his help has been invaluable. Most of all this work would not have been possible without the extensive help and cooperation from the people I interviewed, who gave me so much time despite their constraints. I am indebted to them for their time and sharing of experiences, which were not always happy.

A number of journalists have written extensively about the riot-affected people and their lives, and tracked the various developments with great commitment and engagement which has been inspiring. Nikhil Wagle, Jyoti Punwani and Teesta Setalvad, among others, played an active role in focusing on the riots, engaging with communities affected, continuing to write about the victims and cases and keeping the issue alive.

I am grateful to all my friends for their faith in me and their support. I also wish to acknowledge the camaraderie and sense of purpose of my colleagues at *The Times of India* during the riots in 1992–93, and I will always remember those difficult times we went through. Above all, my husband Venkat (Ravi) Iyer has been a huge pillar of strength and my strongest critic in this venture, and this work would not have been possible without his support. I also thank my brother-in-law Shankar, my mother Girija Menon who has always let me choose my path, my aunt Madhavikutty Menon and my mother-in-law Jaya Seetharaman.

INTRODUCTION

THE 1992–93 RIOTS AND AFTER

When I first heard Mahmood Mamdani, writer of *Good Muslim Bad Muslim*, talk of Truth and Reconciliation and the South African Experiment, and the way in which it could be a model for other communities in conflict, I wondered how it could be applicable here in India. Then again in a talk at the Press Club in Mumbai, in 2009, he elaborated on how it was the second-best option for the South Africans to get on with their lives not in acrimony but in a spirit of togetherness. This did not mean, however, that everything was forgotten. There was an attempt to identify and acknowledge the issues that drove the violence, and then look for answers in South Africa (interview in *The Hindu*, 17 January 2009). Often the best alternatives may not work they seem to have realized.

The way out of a violent conflict cannot be more violence. This is amply clear from what is happening around the world, be it in Kashmir, in Palestine, in Afghanistan or in Iraq. In India too with its long history of communal riots, well before the Partition, while there are efforts to understand the violence, reconciliation has been a rather painful process. While there have been many attempts to bridge gaps between violence-affected communities, there has been no real political process to bring them to any sort of middle ground. There is very little truth and no reconciliation at one level but at a more personal level, in the minds of people, some reconciliation has taken place, allowing them to move ahead with their lives. Even after the Godhra massacre, families of victims spoke about the need for peace. Families who lost their loved ones in the Godhra train fire did not support the revenge taken in their names (Punwani 2002: 69).

Writing about the Partition, Urvashi Butalia (1998: 365) says, '... for the community of survivors, the remembrance ritual works at many levels. It helps keep the memory alive and at the same time, it helps them to forget. They remember selectively, in order to forget.' Justice remained illusory; after years passed, people ceased to expect it. In the interviews, some of them referred to the demolition of the Babri Masjid and what it had really achieved: large-scale displacement, divisions and a hardening of the communal mindset. The temple is not yet built, the mosque lies in ruins and people's lives are shattered. Apart from the daily struggle for life, the story of many Mumbaikars is one of shattered dreams and restricted choices. The riots touched everyone in some way and the scars remain, hidden in the daily hustle and bustle. Some look for the elusive justice to punish the guilty, some are getting on, some have rebuilt their businesses and some have raised families. The shadows of those days always remain in the background—now misty, now sharp. The mosaic of stories adds to the city's complexity.

'The 1992–93 riots were the worst the city has ever seen, and left 900 persons dead. For most of Mumbai's residents, the city changed forever after the riots' (Punwani 2003: 237). And again Punwani writes:

> There have always been Hindu 'parts' and Muslim 'parts' of Bombay. However, after 8 January, 1993, at the peak of the violence, many Hindus for the first time realized what it meant to belong to the majority community; virtually the entire city was theirs to roam as they chose. (Punwani 2003: 238)

INTRODUCTION

Punwani writes about the 1984 riots which seem to have faded out of public memory. This was in many ways a precursor of the future.

> Somehow, the impression remained that the 1984 riots had remained confined to a few 'sensitive spots' though they had spread all over the city. The most infamous incident in those riots took place in a slum colony called Cheetah Camp, where eight Muslims were shot dead without provocation. (Punwani 2003: 241)

> However, the 1984 riots were the turning point for a lot of young Bombayites who had grown up in the 70s believing that their city was truly a microcosm of India, with no place for regional chauvinism. The riots proved that Bombay was a microcosm, but of urban India, where the two principal communities lived in separate ghettos, with little intermingling, their myths and suspicions about each other intact, easy prey to communal propaganda. (Punwani 2003: 242)

After the 1992–93 riots, which created displacement of an unprecedented scale, the polarization worsened. Sushobha Barve (2003: 106) says, 'Hindus living in predominantly Muslim areas and Muslims in predominantly Hindu areas became insecure after the turn of events and moved out to other neighborhoods.'

Barve has written in detail about the efforts in Dharavi in bringing about peace, and the work of the *mohalla* committees (local area committees) in bridging the gap between two riot-scarred communities with some success. She cites the case study of Imamwada in south Mumbai, where dialogue between the Hindu and Muslim communities and the police initiated by the *mohalla* committee helped solve tricky disputes. 'In Imamwada, community policing and partnership with the community and the problem solving approach were successfully utilized' (Barve 2003: 217). Barve (2003: 219) concludes that '[t]he (mohalla committee) movement has given Mumbai a mechanism that can be activated at a short notice and can assist the police in defusing tensions and maintaining peace with public support in a crisis'. After the riots, the *mohalla* committees worked well for a while before the police took over and things started disintegrating.

However, spurred on by former Mumbai Police Commissioner, Julio Ribeiro, the movement is still continuing under the Mohalla Committee Movement Trust, which was established in 1994 by Mr Ribeiro and another former Mumbai Police Commissioner, Satish Sahney. Virochan Raote has been working since 2006 as a volunteer in Mumbai in mobilizing *mohalla* committees that have become defunct in places. Earlier these committees handled community issues, were an interface between police and the public and organized sports events; now they handle more routine issues. People are disinclined to be active in areas where they perceive there is no tension. Virochan thinks that the communal mindset that existed during the riots is no longer there, but people are still communal in their thinking.

While I was researching this book, Farooq Mapkar, a security guard who had gone to pray on 10 January 1993 to Hari Masjid, a mosque in Central Mumbai, was acquitted of rioting and murder charges. A special court for riot cases headed by Additional Sessions Judge R. D. Jadhav pronounced Mapkar innocent on 18 February 2009, nearly 15 years after the original chargesheet was filed. He was actually a witness to the police firing in Hari Masjid, which killed seven persons. He was shot in the back and yet the police filed a case against him and 50 odd others, accusing them of rioting, murder, attempted murder and rioting with deadly weapons. Since then Farooq, both a victim and an accused in the firing, had been running around for justice. He fought a long battle for acquittal, helped by his lawyer Shakil Ahmed. He has even managed to get the high court to order a CBI inquiry in 2008 into the excesses by police officers who fired in Hari Masjid. In cases such as Tahirbhai Wagle's, whose son Shahnawaz was killed by the police, nothing has happened; only statements were recorded, and that too after 15 years. The police filed a chargesheet against Shahnawaz and the case is pending. The government has clarified that no evidence was brought forward to show that the boy was killed by the police, despite the adverse remarks in the *Srikrishna Commission Report*. As such, the investigation has been closed and the government averred that the policeman from Byculla Police Station, Inspector Wahule (named in the *Srikrishna Commission Report*), is not responsible or related to the killing of Shahnawaz (Government of Maharashtra affidavit to Supreme Court, 16 January 2008).

According to Omar Khalidi (2006), Mumbai probably has the largest number of Muslim labourers in the country as the nation's commercial capital. Within Mumbai lies Dharavi, Asia's largest slum. Made up of ramshackle corrugated tin sheds, it is home to more than 600,000 people with a high proportion of Muslims. Muslim businesses were burnt down in the 1992–93 riots. Muslims in the informal sector too suffered discrimination from the hands of textile mills. Even then they were considered a security risk and there was a policy not to hire Muslims for daily wage labour in the mills (Khalidi 2006: 201). As small traders or businessmen Muslims flourished in Mumbai and the south part was a case in point.

The riots of 1992–93 targeted these very Muslims and destroyed their livelihoods. Many had to shut down their businesses and move out, but some like Abdul Sattar of Suleiman Bakery, a business which was over 70 years old, on Muhammed Ali Street chose to stay back despite the odds. The daily wage earners or the small traders and businessmen were the ones who lost out and almost never recovered their balance, for instance the timber shops in Ghatkopar or the cloth merchants in Behrampada. What the riots did was to create such fear and insecurity among Muslims that many of them moved out, they left the city or moved to ghettos within the city, sometimes forming new ghettos. Both Hindus and Muslims shared a common feeling of distrust. Like the textile mills which refused to employ Muslims before the Independence when there were riots, people were hesitant to give them jobs or let them stay in their buildings. Even today people are recovering without much help and are more or less abandoned to their fate.

Mumbai suburbs has a Muslim population of 1,488,987 or 12.4 per cent of the total population, while Mumbai city has a population of

734,484 or 36.6 per cent Muslims. Maharashtra has 10.6 per cent Muslims according to the *Social, Economic and Educational Status of the Muslim Community of India, A Report* (chaired by Justice Rajendra Sachar), 2006, quoting 2001 census figures. The literacy rate is 80.5 per cent in Mumbai suburbs, and for women the figure is 75.2 per cent. In Mumbai city, it is 80.5 per cent total and 77.5 per cent for women.

Since long, there have already been areas which have predominant Muslim populations in parts of south, central, western and eastern Mumbai. Post riots, there has been a major sense of insecurity among the victims, both Hindu and Muslim, and their decision to move out of 'mixed' localities (where both Hindus and Muslims live) has been influenced by this fear. There are many definitions of ghettos but primarily it is a poor section of a city inhabited by people of the same race, religion, or social background, often because of discrimination. In the past it often referred to the Jewish quarter, especially in European cities. Ghettos imply many things, such as restriction, discrimination and a lack of freedom of movement. It also reflects the helplessness of its people who huddle together for reasons of safety or security.

After the riots,

> ... Mumbai had in fact set an example of close teamwork between the NGOs and the government in distribution of relief and rehabilitation work. Each week, all the concerned government officials, headed by the relief and rehabilitation secretary of the Maharashtra government, met the representatives of the NGOs. Farida Lambay vice principal of Nirmala Niketan college of Social Work, coordinated the work from the citizens side. Different areas were allotted to the NGOs to avoid duplication of work. (Barve 2003: 146)

However, she adds, 'What was not satisfactory was the economic rehabilitation of the victims. As a nation we are not good at seeing the rehabilitation process through to completion. The victims are left to fend for themselves' (Barve 2003: 147).

Going back and learning about the lives of riot-affected people for me was an important part of understanding how they coped with so much trauma and injustice. It will also lead to an understanding of the new equations between communities. In this book, I am revisiting some victims of the riots, and their detailed stories explain their situation and their place in the city which they will never leave. As Tindall (1992: 23) sums up, though in a different context, 'Bombay is still, for many of them, the place where they most want to be. For some, even, it is home, the inescapable zero place however much assaulted and changed.'

Going Back

Why after so many years are you going back to those times? This was a question I was asked by many people, who clearly thought I was wasting their time. In fact, a couple of people I tried to interview scolded me for carrying out useless research which would benefit no one. One of them said, 'What is the use of your research? You will write about it for a while and then everyone will forget. How can you help in anyway?' In fact this person refused to help me with my work and I sensed great hostility. I do not blame him or any of the others who reacted this way. I think in many ways the current social tensions, the continuing bomb blasts and the targeting of the community have made people edgy and hostile and insecure.

Along with many others, as a journalist, I covered the riots and bomb blasts in 1992–93, and at that time met many of the victims and travelled to the riot-affected areas in the city. For journalists who covered the riots, it was a terrible experience in many ways. The sound of gunfire; the sight of yellowing bodies of young men piled up in hospital corridors; the gaping wounds; and the pall of smoke, silence and death that hung over the city for days is unforgettable. As soon as the riots abated, the city was shattered by the serial bomb blasts of 12 March 1993. The charred bodies, the panic, the mangled mess on the streets that day will always stay with me. A lot of what happened then has stayed with many of us, and we feel the need to revisit some of those events in the past and the people it affected. These events cannot be allowed to hang loose as a fragment of history. I feel they have to be recovered and represented in a way that helps people make important linkages with the past and present. The riots and the serial blasts changed perceptions and reinforced stereotypes about communities.

After the riots there was a tendency in some sections of the media and even in the popular conscience that Muslims deserved the riots, they deserved to be treated badly, killed or burnt. It all happened in 'their' areas, people said. They were responsible for the riots, many felt. In contrast, the attitude towards the Shiv Sena was one of appreciation. Many people told me that the Sena had saved the Hindus. Otherwise the Muslim hordes would have swamped the city and carried out a Hindu genocide.

During the course of my research I was determined to meet the Bane family, which as many journalists have pointed out was the face of Mumbai's second phase of rioting in January 1993. It was the fire in Gandhi *chawl* (mistakenly reported everywhere as Radhabai *chawl*) on 8 January 1993 that sparked off the bloody second phase of rioting. The Shiv Sena and its mouthpiece *Saamna* screamed revenge as those who were killed in the fire were Hindus, families from the Konkan, typical migrants to Mumbai, who were living in the *chawl*. The Konkan migrants are the core of the Sena's support base and for some of its members to be so brutally killed horrified the city which was soon held to ransom by rampaging mobs seeking revenge for the 'Hindu' deaths.

Naina Bane managed to escape with two children from the roof of her house, which was locked from outside. As she lay in hospital fighting severe burn injuries, the city was destroyed. *Saamna* and its editor, Shiv Sena chief Bal Thackeray, exhorted revenge for the six who were killed, including Naina's parents Sulochana and Rajaram Bane and four others including a handicapped girl. It was an event that spread shockwaves in the city and many people till this day remember the riots only as an aftermath of the horrific Gandhi *chawl* incident. They seem to forget that already in December the city had witnessed riots which had killed over

200 people. Public memory has become selective over the years. People choose to remember what they associate with as riots in those days. The six deaths become the reason for every kind of mayhem in the city.

Naina was promised so much by the Shiv Sena and many political parties. But today she and her family, her sisters and two brothers, are no better off than other victims of riots. The fact that once they were the face of the Mumbai riots has been forgotten by everyone, and they are left without any support. They neither have a house of their own nor jobs, and their suffering is their own. In suffering and death there is a strange equality. And that is why an initiative by Congress leader Muzaffar Hussain in Naya Nagar makes so much sense. In his bit to promote communal harmony, Muzaffar has set up a common burial ground and crematorium to prove that death has no religion and no one can escape it (personal Interview with Muzaffar Hussain).

The serial blasts which were perceived as a 'revenge' for the riots, added to the polarization. Families of the victims of the blasts had to contend with the shock and severe trauma of losing their loved ones. In fact Vinayak Devrukhkar who lost his brother and sister in the 12 March 1993 blasts became numb and cold when the verdict was announced by the designated court in the blasts case (personal interview, 2007). Tears still roll down his face when he remembers that day when he lost his siblings. A bitter Vinayak joined the Shiv Sena after that hoping for justice. The city has so many of these scars, which it bears seemingly lightly. The scars of those years have created deep divisions, and in tracing the complexities involved some important truths may emerge. Far from being an 'unbreakable city', it is in reality one with many fissures, often glossed over. Mumbai has become an 'unreal' city of sorts for many victims who live in the past. It has become a city of their memories more than anything else, something that helps them survive the harsh reality.

On 26 November 2008, 10 highly trained men wreaked havoc in a few hours in Mumbai, killing 166 innocents. After the 60-hour siege and the trauma which numbed the city, people were worried. Would there be riots? How do these incidents affect the social fabric? Soon

Pakistan emerged as the brain behind the attack, unprecedented in brazenness and brutality. On 6 May 2010, Kasab was sentenced to death for his crimes by a special sessions court in Mumbai. There was much celebration and distribution of sweets. People thought that terrorism was conquered, mistakenly so. Around that time a young Pakistani was held in the United States for planting a bomb in a car at Times Square in New York. The cycle of revenge seems endless. The hate that is planted cannot be so easily conquered.

After the 26 November terror strike, Muslim groups came out strongly against terror, and refused to give space in their burial grounds for the nine dead terrorists who were buried secretly by the government in January 2010. Once again the Muslims had to reiterate their nationalism and patriotism and proclaim their allegiance to the Indian flag. The alienation of Muslims has led to increased number of ghettos, and these are perceived as trouble spots and remain under the scanner every time there is trouble. People in these ghettos are then targeted in many ways such as by not being issued passports or being arrested every time there is a terror attack or a blast. I have mentioned Naya Nagar near Mumbai, an area where the riot-affected Muslims fled to after the riots. During the 1993 riots, Behrampada was targeted as a Muslim criminal den but police investigations revealed little organized criminal activity. The Sena went to town about the nefarious activities in Behrampada and the criminal intent of its residents, but as the chapter on Behrampada shows these were the very people brutalized by violence.

Mumbai was perceived to be a cosmopolitan city, it still is in many ways, but not so in other ways. The city too has been affected by dominant ideas of communalism and nationalism, leading to division and strife. The hope is in the minds not made up yet, giving the city that faint tinge of togetherness and cosmopolitanism.

The Riots, Ram Temple and Shiv Sena

In the preliminary chapter of his report of inquiry into the Mumbai 1992 and 1993 riots, Justice (Retired) B. N. Srikrishna wrote after 'painstakingly wading' through logbook entries of wireless communication from the police on 6 and 7 December 1992:

6th December 1992

Trouble appears to be brewing in the city even before the demolition of the Babri Masjid and percolation of the news. The chronology of events on that day

0010 hours—155 people gather near Ambedkar Garden at Charni Road and there is trouble near Bharat Care in Chembur at 0045 hours

1134 hours—There is trouble reported near Bombay municipal corporation building Darga, Lohar Chawl and Bharatiya Janata Party at different places in the city.

1233 hours—A crowd of 300/400 holds a meeting opposite Shiv Mandir Dadar

1400 hours—A crowd is reported near Elphinstone Bridge in Bhoiwada jurisdiction

The Babri Masjid is demolished at about 1230 hours and the news of this event is widely publicized by the electronic media, particularly BBC news.

1640 hours—A cycle rally of 200/300 persons is taken out by the local leaders of Shiv Sena in Dharavi jurisdiction. This rally passes through several communally sensitive and Muslim predominant areas in Dharavi and terminates at Kala Killa where a meeting is held and addressed by the local activists of the Shiv Sena. Provocative speeches are made at this meeting.

From 1952 hours onwards crowds gather at various places in South Mumbai and at 2110 hours stone throwing is reported at Jogeshwari. By 2334 hours there is an arson attempt at Pydhonie and firing near Minara Masjid and by midnight there is firing and stone throwing.

The events of that Sunday gave little indication of the prolonged violence that was to paralyse the city, the worst since Bhiwandi in 1984 which spread to parts of Mumbai as well. In less than a span of two months the city which never sleeps was desolate and funereal, mourning its dead with simmering anger and anguish. Much before the actual demolition of the Babri Masjid, the nation and even Mumbai was whipped into a feverish frenzy over the building of the Ram temple at Ayodhya. Rath yatras, Ram shila pujas and public collections marked the high pitched mobilization by the Sangh Parivar with the promise of *Kar Seva* at the Babri Masjid itself, a holy deed to redeem oneself.

However, this was not the first time Ayodhya was chosen as a target of Hindu revivalism. The first attempt to exploit the issue of Ayodhya, writes Jaffrelot (1999: 91), was in the 1800s.

> To the Hindu Mahasabha, Ramjanmabhoomi (the birth site of Ram in Ayodhya, Uttar Pradesh) was undoubtedly a symbol which could be manipulated in such a way as to provoke a massive mobilisation of Hindus. A temple is said to have stood on this holy site and was supposedly demolished in 1528 at the order of Babur, the founder of the Mughal dynasty, in order to build there a mosque, the Babri Masjid ... However, a conflict surrounding the site erupted in the 1850s. It seems that in 1853 Bairagis (Hindu ascetics) who claimed that the Babri Masjid was built on Ram's birthplace attacked the mosque. From the mid 1850s prayers were offered at a platform outside the mosque and it was here that in 1883 a pandit demanded that a temple be built, which was refused by the British authorities because of the proximity of the mosque. (Jaffrelot 1999: 92)

But, in 1949, two years after Independence, in December someone placed idols of Ram Lalla and others in the mosque, setting off a well-documented chain of events (see Jaffrelot 1999: 93). That a faraway mosque's fate would be so closely connected with violence in Mumbai was unthinkable and no one in the city in their wildest dreams would imagine the brutality of those days. Much like what happened in Gujarat 10 years later, Mumbai had become a theatre of carnage. People left in hordes fearing for their lives and the city was riven, leading to bloodshed. Many who left have not come back and persons are reported missing till this day.

While the first phase of rioting in December in Mumbai was mishandled by the police, which was widely accused of having a communal bias against Muslims, it was in the second phase that the Shiv Sena as pointed out by Justice Srikrishna took the lead and fuelled violence. The Sena with its large network of *shakhas* or branches and its grass-roots organization network was swift in its ploy of revenge. The Sena leaders claimed that this was a spontaneous reaction to Muslim attacks. Though the Sena has never had a good rapport with the Rashtriya Swayamsevak Sangh (RSS), the idea of *shakhas* or local units is very similar in some ways. The Sena which launched itself as a nativist organization to protect Marathi interests soon travelled on the path of Hindutva and built its popularity on the hatred of the others, in this case, south Indians, migrants and Muslims. Mumbai already had its share of organizations such as the Hindu Sabha, and prominent citizens were a part of these groups, but there was no such mass mobilization. The city which was a haven for migrants was sought to be shaken by the Shiv Sena which wanted a distinct Marathi and even Hindu identity enforced on it. For many in Mumbai Thackeray was a demigod, a saviour from the onslaught of the migrants and job seekers and a real '*Hinduhridaysamrat*'.

However, before its anti-Muslim stand, Thackeray had associations with a number of other parties and people. Bal Thackeray's Sena supported the Praja Socialist Party (PSP) in the municipal corporation election in Bombay in 1968, whose leading lights included Socialist leader Madhu Dandavate. Later, in 1973, the Sena teamed up with the Muslim League for the corporation elections. Raj Thackeray's photobiography on Bal Thackeray has photographs of a young Thackeray addressing a League meeting before a podium draped with the green flag of the League with the crescent moon and star. In 1981, veteran Communist Party of India (CPI) leader S. A. Dange and a staunch critic of the Sena was a special invitee to a party meeting in Mumbai. Thackeray had close links with George Fernandes and a host of political leaders including Sharad Pawar and Vasantrao Naik, former chief ministers of Maharashtra. A decisive change in political ideology came after the Sena's alliance with the Bharatiya Janata Party (BJP) in 1984; then Thackeray addressed meetings of the Vishwa Hindu Parishad (VHP) as well. After the Babri Masjid demolition, Thackeray said that if the Babri Masjid was demolished by Shiv Sainiks, he was proud of them (Thackeray 2005).

The Sena's alliance with the BJP in 1984 gave it the political edge it needed and finally the combine came to power in 1995 assembly elections. While remaining a regional party, the Sena used Hindutva to garner state-wide appeal which propelled it to the forefront of the political playing field. To locate the Sena in the larger context of Hindutva and Hindu nationalism is important, even though it had no real national ambitions or aspirations but its ideology and aims were very much those of the Sangh Parivar and Veer Savarkar and later the BJP. Bal Thackeray who referred to politics as ringworm had no qualms in propelling the party to a political endgame, using violence and a threat of Muslims who were supposed to invade and decimate Mumbai.

The Shiv Sena actively took part in the Ram Janmabhoomi movement (though Sena leader and former Chief Minister Manohar Joshi in a personal interview says it was not so active), and Mr Thackeray met L. K. Advani during his visits to Maharashtra several times. Sainiks were proud to have been on top of the Babri Masjid when it was brought down, giving the party that feeling that it was part of a large Hindu monolithic community in the country. Along with the Sangh Parivar, the Sena too celebrated the fall of the Masjid before it went aggressively to enforce its supremacy in the violence that followed the demolition. Well before this it had already arrived as a party that adopted Hindutva as we can see in the section on the rise of the Sena. The Sena too went on to the protection of the Hindu religion, culture and Hindu nationalism. Its raison d'être was to save the 'Marathi *manoos*' from being deprived of jobs initially, but later took on a larger religious and political dimension.

INTRODUCTION

The history of the communal riots between Hindus and Muslim in the then Bombay Presidency since 1893 shows that sectarian hatred and whipping up of passions was not alien to the city. With the launch of the Cow Protection Movement in keeping with other parts of the country in 1887, the Bombay Presidency also witnessed a flurry of activities seeking a ban on cow slaughter and public meetings to mobilize opinion. This had created considerable tension, which culminated in the riots of August 1893. The 1900s saw a series of riots again stemming from religious issues such as tombs or temples or religious processions. The events happening elsewhere in the country had its impact in Bombay as well and the onset of Partition, the communal award, and the demand of the Muslim League for a separate country, the RSS's opposition to this, the Congress vacillation, all created a volatile atmosphere of strife which continued up to Independence and beyond.

The Shiv Sena was formed in 1966, with cadres spread all over the city which could be mobilized in an instant. In the agitation over the Maharashtra–Karnataka border issue, the Sena brought the city to a standstill in February 1969, forcing the then government to bring in the army. The party thrived on threats and intimidation and aimed at ending the communist unions in the city, becoming a handy tool for industrialists. However, as Jayant Lele points out, it was in 1992 that the Shiv Sena achieved a state of mass mobilization which had not been seen before. As he notes in his essay (Lele 1996: 185):

> During the January 1993 riots in Bombay, the Shiv Sena once again displayed its muscle power. This time the mobilization of its troops had some distinctive features. It was far more systematic than ever before, in its organization, in the targeting of its enemy and in the total dehumanization and brutality of its methods. The rise and fall in the Shiv Sena's prominence in the political events of Bombay–Maharashtra has often been described in terms of waves of popularity and decline. The distinctive features of the events of 6–11 January 1993, however, require that it not be treated as 'just another communal riot'.

> The blatant claim of responsibility for the orchestration of the riots without reprisal, and open threats of further violence if necessary, by the leader of the Sena, indicate the dramatic changes that have occurred in the climate of political legitimacy since the sixties. For the first time in Bombay's history, people were fleeing en masse from the city; over 200,000 are reported to have abandoned their possessions and their livelihoods to escape attacks of the Sainiks. That these included Muslim and non Muslim Maharashtrians, raises some questions about the authenticity and efficacy of the Shiv Sena's espousal of the 'Hindu' cause and about the concept of hindutva itself. (Lele 1996: 185)

Lele also explains the Sena's bent to Hindutva and the portrayal of Muslims as the other.

> ...the Sena's initiation of and participation in anti Muslim riots has followed a similar pattern. In each case, it has tried to persuade its constituents that the tradition of tolerance and passivity of Hindus has made them vulnerable to the aggressive and conspiratorial actions of Muslims, that Muslims are the dominant element in the world of crime and that they have increasingly become a menace to national security because of their primary loyalty to Islam and thus to Islamic nations. It has thus managed to portray itself as a righteous vigilante organization, always on the alert to protect Hindu communities from this menace. (Lele 1996: 202)

Though the nativist ideal attracted many people to the Sena, it also acquired an anti-Muslim stance early on. Hindutva came in handy for a party which wanted to create a quick and acceptable enemy, initially south Indians and later Muslims, and bringing back the days of Maratha glory under Shivaji Maharaj. Jayant Lele (1996: 199–200) points out:

The Shiv Sena's decisive turn to hindutva came in 1984 when it established its political alliance as a dominant partner with the BJP. At the time, signs of loss of its popularity in the Bombay region had become visible. Even among lumpenized youth it had to share its influence with a number of other competing forces. At the same time the declining hegemony of elite Marathas had led them to look upon militant Hinduism as a possible alternative ideology to help re entrench their dominance over an increasingly differentiated and self conscious group of subaltern castes. A strong sense of disenchantment with traditional forms of politics had permeated all sections of youth. Within Bombay the appeal of the anti South Indian Maharashtrianism had dramatically weakened.

The Sena took the militant Hinduism much further than anyone else in the past in this region.

The militant pro Hinduism of the Shiv Sena is also not new to Maharashtra. Militant Hindu nationalism had reared its head in the late 19th century, but nowhere had it formed a mass movement as in Maharashtra. The cult of Shivaji in Maharashtra expressed itself in violent opposition to the Muslims. Tilak introduced the Ganapathi festival in 1893 to keep this spirit alive, and to revitalise Maharashtrian chauvinism by introducing not only traditional sacred symbols, but also such militant activities as training in the art of defence. In Maharashtra, Hindu nationalism—the revering of the Gita and the exaltation of Shivaji—and anti Muslim feeling rolled into one composite whole. (Gupta 1982)

In Bombay/Mumbai, the Cow Protection Movement was one of the reasons for creating tensions. After that there were disputes over mosques, temples, prayer timings, etc., and every time there was violence, the two communities went a little further away from each other. After

Independence, in Maharashtra, some major riots took place in 1967 in Malegaon, Bhiwandi, Jalgaon and Mahad in 1970 and later in 1984 in Bhiwandi and Mumbai, but it was in 1992 that the division became very serious. The serial bomb blasts of 12 March 1993 only served to create further suspicion. Comparisons between the riots and the blasts flew thick and fast, and the Srikrishna Commission had its terms of reference enhanced. The Indian National Congress was the party in power when the notification was issued, but in the state assembly elections in 1995, a Shiv Sena–BJP coalition came to power. The *Srikrishna Commission Report* says, 'Consistent with its public utterances, the Shiv Sena–BJP government desired the Commission to go into certain aspects of the serial bomb blasts which occurred on 12th March 1993 in the city of Bombay.'

The terms of reference were expanded after March 1995, and the Commission now had additional tasks: The circumstances and the immediate cause of the incidents commonly known as the serial bomb blasts of the 12 March 1993, and whether the riots and the blasts were linked and whether they were part of a common design.

The Commission issued a public notice in newspapers calling upon all members of the public to disclose by affidavit any information they may have in connection with the blasts. Apart from affidavits of senior police officers, the only affidavit filed pursuant to the notice was of 2 August 1995 by an advocate Prabhakar Pradhan who submitted that he had casually bumped into someone who claimed that the serial bomb blasts were the handy work of Central Intelligence Agency of United States, and not the outcome of the revenge of Muslims. The Commission felt the content of the affidavit was speculative. However, the Commission said,

> One common link between the riots of December 1992 and January 1993 and the Bomb blasts of March 12, 1993 appears to be that the former (riots) appears to have been a causative factor for the latter. There does appear to be a cause and effect relationship between the two riots and the serial bomb blasts.

INTRODUCTION

Another common link is that some of the accused who were involved in substantive riot-related offense were also accused in the serial bomb blasts case, though their number is only three or four.

Tiger Memon, the key figure in the serial bomb blasts case and his family had suffered extensively during the riots and therefore can be said to have had deep rooted motive for revenge. It would appear that one his trusted accomplices, Javed Dawood Tailor alias Javed Chikna, had also suffered a bullet injury during the riots and therefore he also had a motive for revenge. Apart from these two specific cases, there was a large amorphous body of angry frustrated and desperate Muslims keen to seek revenge for the perceive injustice done to and atrocities perpetrated on them or to others of their community and it is this sense of revenge which spawned the conspiracy of the serial blasts. This body of angry frustrated and desperate Muslims provided the material upon which the anti national and criminal elements succeeded in building up their conspiracy for the serial bomb blasts.

There is no material placed before the commission indicating that the riots during December 1992 and January 1993 and the serial blasts were part of a common design. In fact this situation has been accepted by Mahesh Narain Singh who was heading the team of investigators who investigated into the serial bomb blasts case. He also emphasizes that the serial bomb blasts were a reaction to the totality of events at Ayodhya and Bombay in December 1992 and January 1993 and the Commission is inclined to agree with him.

I have quoted in detail this aspect of the *Commission's Report of Inquiry* to draw attention to the argument of revenge and the Sena–BJP's attempts to subvert the gravity and extent of the violence after the Babri Masjid was demolished. The final report of the Commission submitted in February 1998 was rejected by the Sena–BJP government, which felt the police were secular and non-communal and the government had done everything to stop the riots. But its observations vis-à-vis the blasts are important. The government was unhappy that while accepting the common link between the riots of December 1992 and January 1993 and the serial blasts, the Commission had rejected the idea of a common design.

> In spite of such an overwhelming evidence, the Commission does not accept that this was a part of a common design. Government can never agree with this conclusion of the Commission. In fact, the government is taken aback that the Commission has not given adequate importance to the serial blasts although 257 innocent people were killed in a dastardly manner, 713 were injured and a huge loss of ₹ 27 crore was caused. It is strange that the Commission did not take adequate note of such unprecedented, horrifying and totally opprobrious and barbarous incidents. The Commission had devoted 600–650 pages of the original report for detailed analysis, minute examination, prolonged discussion and sharp observations about the riots. Government is surprised that the Commission has chosen to dispose of terms of reference (related to the blasts) within three to four pages in a frivolous and cursory manner. (Memorandum of Action to Be Taken by Government on the Report of the Commission of Inquiry)

The government conveniently chose to forget the equally 'horrifying, opprobrious and barbarous incidents' which paralysed the city for the best part of December 1992 and January 1993, and over which some 600 pages were devoted in the report of inquiry. All this set the tone for the future in different ways. The see-saw battle of who started it first, the classic 'which came first' debate ensued. The background to the riots of 1992–93 in Mumbai was the Ram Janmabhoomi movement and the demolition of the Babri Masjid. As Justice Srikrishna has meticulously recorded, the protests started on the 6 December 1992 itself. After the riots and blasts of 1992 and 1993, every time there is a blast, the revenge motive is raked up. After the Gujarat violence too reports suggested that young men were sent to Pakistan for training for revenge. Muslims are arrested, and let off as in the case of the Ghatkopar blasts in Mumbai, and some trials continue forever. This is not to say the guilty must not be punished or that there is no role of Muslims in terror activities. The targeting of the community as a whole is reinforcing stereotypes and making it more vulnerable.

The role of the Sangh Parivar and the aim of a Hindu Rashtra cannot escape the lens either. There is a lot of talk of action and reaction, spontaneous reaction and revenge, but it eludes the truth. The people behind the blasts whether based at Pakistan or local terror groups have to be identified and punished. Terrorism cannot be used as a weapon for tarnishing an entire community. Now there is evidence to link the right-wing groups to bomb blasts as well. The Sangh Parivar may object to the use of the term 'saffron terror' as articulated by Union Home Minister P. Chidambaram in Parliament (*The Times of India*, Mumbai, 26 August 2010), but these are the very people who have popularized the terms 'Islamic', 'Muslim' or even 'green' terror, and maintain that 'all terrorists are Muslims'. It was only after the Malegaon blast arrests of Sadhvi Pragya Thakur Singh and an army officer that even the BJP said that terror has no colour.

The tendency to present the riots as part of a common design is another attempt to divert from the truth. What was the common design in the Babri Masjid demolition, the violence and the blasts? Nothing, as Justice Srikrishna Commission had pointed out. The common design is elsewhere—in the movement to forge a Hindu national identity and target a common enemy—Muslims or Christians. This endless talk over 'spontaneous reaction' and 'action and reaction' is meaningless again because it does not explain why there was a movement to build a temple and then the creation of a frenzied nationwide support for it, or why there was violence before and after it. It can only be understood in the light of the agenda of the Sangh Parivar which in its attempts to further the cause of a Hindu Rashtra mobilized people on the issue of the Ram temple. The eruption of Vedic rites and sending purified bricks for the Ram temple at Ayodhya acquired a nationwide frenzy, and as Jaffrelot puts it, 'the synchronization of all these rituals across India corresponded to Benedict Anderson's very exact definition of the nation as an "imagined community"'(Jaffrelot 1999: 401). 'For the RSS and its affiliates, the rewriting of the history of Ayodhya was entirely consistent with the parallel effort to reinterpret the myth of Ram as a supreme hero' (Jaffrelot 1999: 402).

The evolution of a strong Hindu nationalism stigmatizing the other, using traditional symbols as the cow, religious festivities and processions gained ground since the late 19th century. Nationalist identities and communal concepts are serving to estrange communities from each other. As Aloysius (1998: 225) rightly concludes,

> What these two stalwarts (Gandhi and Periyar) from the two polarities of the sub continent's dichotomous political awakening feared so much in 1947 appears to be increasingly becoming a reality in our body politic: the rise of communal— nationalism (communal with reference to not only other religious communities but also the mass of lower castes) of a brutal kind, and on the other hand multiple reactions to it, ethnic nationalisms and group ideologies threatening the very existence of the new nation state.

Earlier Riots and Cow Protection

I also realized I knew very little about Bombay/Mumbai's past history of riots, and decided to look at the history of communal violence between Hindus and Muslims in the Bombay Presidency. The starting point was 1893, a significant year in more ways than one. The riot of 1893 was in the backdrop of the Cow Protection Movement which was launched in Bombay, in keeping with similar activities elsewhere in the country.

Pandey (2008: 174–75) details the rise of the Cow Protection Movement in northern India and the riots in various parts of the United Provinces, which spread to Calcutta and Bombay. 'All this served further to harden feelings and sharpen a widespread and growing sense of Hindu–Muslim antagonism' (Pandey 2008: 175). He quotes John McLane saying, 'As McLane puts it, a trifle overdramatically, for 1893, 'it seemed momentarily as if two nations were emerging in many parts of India' (Pandey 2008).

McLane (1977) was not far from wrong. Pandey (2008: 176) points to the growing aggressiveness of the Cow Protection Movement as it advanced from the 1880s to the 1890s and from Punjab and the Central Provinces to eastern UP and Bihar. As in Bombay, here too the societies were established to set up homes for sick or old cattle, and to propagate the religious and other reasons for protecting the cow (Pandey 2008: 176). The Cow Protection Movement continued after the Independence too; the RSS was to launch petitions in 1952 for prohibiting cow slaughter (Jaffrelot 1999: 113) and later the VHP in 1966 and the Jana Sangh in 1966–67 used it to mobilize the Hindu vote.

> Among Hindu organizational efforts, the most widespread and dramatic was made by the Cow Protection movement. Its unparalleled success in north India can be attributed to at least two important characteristics: first, its platform appealed alike to orthodox, traditionalistic and reformist Hindus; and second, its organizational structure united urban centers and their rural surroundings. (Freitag 1989: 606)

Discussing the movement in north India, Freitag observes that,

> Dayananda Saraswati formed the first Gaurakshini Sabha in 1882 and soon after published a book on the subject as well. The cow was a powerful symbol to call into play, for not only was it sacred in itself but its by products played essential roles

in most Hindu rituals. Moreover, it allowed more Westernized Hindus to defend an important facet of Indian life in terms deemed legitimate by the Western world, for the cow occupied as well a pivotal position in the agrarian economy. (Freitag 1989: 606)

She refers to the Arya Samaj which apart from the Cow Protection Movement mobilized Hindus.

Though the most influential 'Hindu' organization of the period, Cow Protection was preceded and accompanied by other organizational efforts among Hindus. The most prominent of these, though not in U.P. the most influential, was the Arya Samaj. Supported in the main by professionals who were educated in English and attempting to reformulate their indigenous traditions to withstand Western criticism, the Arya Samaj had first taken root in 1877 in the Punjab. Soon exported to the cities of U.P. as well, its adherents there remained small in number and moderate in tone until after the turn of the century. Yet its impact was doubtless felt beyond its numbers, for it abrasively proffered a radical vision of Hinduism, one which emphasized monotheism and the Vedas and condemned idolatry. Supported, moreover, by upwardly mobile urbanites, it formulated a view of religion which treated the individual as the basic unit of action. (Freitag 1989: 604)

Cow protection and Hindu revivalism formed the base of a religious resurgence which laid the base for the future nationalism. Aloysius says, 'The history of the nineteenth century is not only the history of Indian nationalism but also of the birth and development of modern Hinduism as the womb that later delivered the political progeny' (1998: 102).

In the 1900s what started out as a common nationalist movement, started splintering with different communities gradually voicing different aspirations. Violence was a continuing factor over the years over temples, tombs, processions and even after the Partition, the divisions continued. In Bombay/Mumbai the rise of the Shiv Sena added to the existing pantheon of right-wing groups, and its provocative articulation of Hindutva placed the Muslims as the other. For the Muslims who stayed back in India, there was nowhere to turn to after the Partition and they had to continually prove their allegiance to the country. As Aloysius (1998: 224) analyses, '[t]he conclusion is inevitable: nationalism succeeded but the nation failed to emerge'.

The efforts of the Cow Protection Movement in north India in the late 1800s led to riots. In his book, D. N. Jha says the cow became a tool of mass political mobilization when the organized Hindu cow protection movements, beginning with the Sikh Kuka (or Namdhari) sect in the Punjab around 1870, and later strengthened by first Gorakshini Sabha in 1882 by Dayananda Saraswati, made this animal a symbol of the unity of a wide-ranging people, challenged the Muslim practice of its slaughter and provoked a series of communal riots in the 1880s and 1890s. Although attitudes to cow killing had hardened even earlier, there was undoubtedly a 'dramatic intensification' of the cow protection movement when in 1888 the North West Provinces High Court decreed that the cow was not a sacred object. Not surprisingly, cow slaughter very often became the pretext of Hindu–Muslim riots, especially those in Azamgarh district in 1893 when more than 100 people were killed in different parts of the country. Similarly, in 1912–13, violence rocked Ayodhya and a few years later, in 1917, Shahabad witnessed a disastrous communal conflagration (Jha: 19).

In his paper on the Basantpur riots in Bihar in 1893, Anand A. Yang says,

> Collective violence always has some structure. Even the most 'spontaneous' clashes between Hindus and Muslims grew out of situations which provided the occasion for the disturbances. Disputes over sacred spaces and processions, for example, frequently prompted rioting. The latter especially were 'ready targets for communal violence . . . (because its) members . . . are

immediately identifiable, available, and particularly threatening members of a community'. Furthermore, processions were potentially explosive situations even as they performed an integrative function because 'the very mobility of the sacred space surrounding a procession, while providing an element essential in fostering communitas, also posed some crucial problems. These occurred primarily when one religion's sacred space overlapped another'. (Yang 1980: 580)

There is then little that is accidental in these violent outbursts and innocuous as it may have seemed, the Cow Protection Movement was far from that, as Yang points out.

> Although initially at least the message of cow protection was phrased in eclectic terms, increasingly the issue was seen as defining people's relationships and activities. Under the Sabha's influence, many everyday routines took on a different order. In many villages, Muslims were refused access to wells. In some areas 'the pots in which the village Kandhu ["grain parcher"] had parched the corn both of Muhammadans and Hindus alike were now ordered to be broken. New and unpolluted pots were prepared . . . while individual Mussalmans were put to the somewhat new experience of parching their own corn'. (Yang 1980: 588)

In the various movements of that time there was a commonality as Pandey (2008: 93, 94) says,

> In all of these movements, one could say, politics appears in the form of religion, religion is at the same time politics. 'Sanskritization' and 'Islamization' were means of asserting an identity, demanding rights and self-respect, and they challenged the existing social order even as they encouraged religious orthodoxy and 'improvement'. Towards the end of the nineteenth

century, movements such as these among the lower and intermediate castes of eastern U. P. and western Bihar received a considerable fillip owing to the Cow Protection Movement, which challenged the rights of Muslims to sacrifice cows as a central part of their religious obligation.

The Roots of Hindu Nationalism or Communalism

A communal identity did not even exist in the ancient and medieval periods of Indian history, as Romila Thapar, Harbans Mukhia and Bipan Chandra (1981: 40) have pointed out, and as Bipan Chandra (Thapar et al. 1981: 8) further says: 'There is ample evidence from the sources of ancient period to suggest that religious sects and groups in pre Islamic India did not identify themselves as Hindus and as a unified religion.' Again,

> It is significant that today when we write about this period [from seventh to thirteenth century AD] of history we bracket together the Arabs, the Turks and the Persians and describe them all by the single term, 'the Muslims'. Yet until the thirteenth century, the word Muslim is rarely used in the sources to describe these various peoples. The sources of this period do not use a religious terminology but refer to them in a purely political manner. (Thapar et al. 1981: 8)

> Significantly, even in the 17th century when great popular uprisings took place like the Maratha uprising, the Sikh and the Jat uprisings, and these led to enormous conflicts between the Marathas and the Mughal state, etc., they did not lead to communal riots at the social level even in the worst days of Aurangzeb's 'tyranny'. (Thapar et al. 1981: 37)

Bipan Chandra argues that '[i]t would be no exaggeration to suggest that a communal historical approach has been, and is, the main ideology of communalism in India. Take away that and hardly anything is left of the communal ideology' (Thapar et al. 1981: 39). Communalism and the writing of history had a major contribution to play in the evolution of nationalism and religious identity and were used to bond disparate groups within communities into strong religious groups with a common political agenda and identity. Even the cow which assumed so much significance in Hindu revivalism did not enjoy such a pride of place in Vedic tradition as D. N. Jha has pointed out.

> The veneration of the cow has been converted into a symbol of communal identity of the Hindus and the obscurantist and fundamentalist forces obdurately refuse to appreciate that the cow was not always all that sacred in the Vedic and subsequent Brahmanical and non Brahmanical traditions—or that its flesh, along with other varieties of meat, was quite often a part of haute cuisine in early India. (Jha: 20)

In the formation of the Arya Samaj in the late 1800s, in response to the proselytization of Christian missionaries, lay the roots of what would eventually become a more focused and formative Hindu nationalism of the early 1900s. Jaffrelot says the origins of the Hindu nationalist movement

> ... lie in the socio religious reform of the nineteenth century when, in order to resist the European administration and missionary offensive, organisations like the Arya Samaj invented a Vedic Golden Age. This ideological construction enabled them to regain self-esteem, defend their threatened identity and demonstrate how the values of the dominant power could be adopted with advantage. (Jaffrelot 1999: 76, 77)

Pralay Kanungo (2003) quoted Robert Eric Frykenberg, who comments, '"the Hindu community" is the twin of "India" as a state, both were constructed about the same time. He mentions three parallel processes—institutional, ideological and socio-political—which significantly contributed to the shaping of the modern religious community known as Hinduism' (Kanungo 2003: 103). Apart from the use of the word 'Hindu', the all-India census of 1871 introduced a 'vocabulary of communal, social and religious categorization. It gave a concrete meaning to the term "Hindu" which was a vague label till then' (Kanungo 2003: 103). While the Orientalists were fond of referring to the ancient Hindu civilization, 'the third most important process was mobilization of local resistance to conversion movements initiated by Christian missionaries in the eighteenth century' (Kanungo 2003: 104).

A point also made by Christophe Jaffrelot (1999: 11), who says:

> Hindu nationalism was constructed as an ideology between the 1870s and the 1920s ... Hindu nationalism derives from socio-religious movements initiated by high caste Hindus such as Arya Samaj. This organisation, founded in 1875, was to a large extent set up in reaction against the British colonial state and Christian missions. Its primary concern was to maintain the basic elements of the traditional social order and culture of the Hindus while adapting that tradition to take account of certain aspects of western society. This endeavor implied both the stigmatization and the emulation of those who threatened Hindu society.

Before this, Jaffrelot explains:

> A Hindu consciousness apparently found its principal expression in the seventeenth and eighteenth centuries in the empire of Shivaji and then in the Maratha confederation. In 1720 Brahmins took over the latter kingdom, in which they had formerly served as chief ministers (Peshwas—a name they retained when they became the ruling dynasty) and military chiefs. These two political institutions were formed in Maharashtra in opposition to the Mughal empire and in the name of

Dharma. [However they do not represent nationalist constructions, as argued by Jayant Lele, nationalism being a later development]; the slaughter of cows, which the Muslims sometimes offered as a sacrifice was thus forbidden there. But the conquests of the Marathas in the direction of the Gangetic plain 'did not imply the existence of a sense of religious war based on ethnic or communal consciousness'. They resulted from a motivation that was ritual in character- to restore to the Hindus certain holy places, like Varanasi, which were revered throughout India as a whole. In fact, as Christopher Bayly emphasizes, it is almost impossible to detect the presence of any communal identity before 1860. (Jaffrelot 1999: 5)

Two key issues emerge from Jaffrelot's research—first is that the modern Hindu identity emerged after the missionaries entered India, and second there was also a need to create some changes in Hinduism to make it a more reformative religion in response to Christianity and colonialism. This is what the Arya Samaj set out to do but 'The Arya Samaj of Dayananda was not, however, a proponent of Hindu nationalism' (Jaffrelot 1999: 17). The Arya Samaj also started the *shuddhi* programme which was meant to convert people into Hinduism and counter missionaries. On the other hand, the Hindu Sabha which was formed in Punjab 'displayed a proto Hindu nationalism', says Jaffrelot (1999: 18). 'The Punjabi Hindu Sabha, like its counterpart in the United Provinces (modern Uttar Pradesh [UP]) and the Hindu Mahasabha (literally the Great Hindu Association)—the national confederation which had been formed in 1915—worked to provide a collective defence of the socio-political interests of Hindus' (Jaffrelot 1999: 19). Later the *shuddhi* or mass purification programmes and *sanghathan* which unified Hindu groups into a movement would be the provocation for many of the riots in India.

Referring to Muslim revivalist trends, Yunas Samad says, 'However, it was the shuddhi and sanghathan campaign of the 1920s (started by Hindu activists in the wake of the Khilafat Movement) that prompted Muslims to initiate similar programmes, such as tabligh (propaganda) and tanzim (organisation, and accentuate these revivalist trends' (Pandey and Samad 2007: 78).

Tanika Sarkar's (2001) book on the Hindu middle class in the late 19th-century Bengal at a point when they were turning to Hindu cultural nationalism says,

> The rhetoric of Hindu nationalism gradually came into its own in the decades after 1857. As the panic of the revolt receded and colonial repression began to be cast in unmistakably racist and authoritarian terms, the Bengali intelligentsia was faced with the moral implications of its own complicity with alien rule, and beset with doubts about the progressive potential of such complicity. (Sarkar 2001: 142)

In her trenchant analysis of Bankim Chandra Chattopadhyay, where she discusses his last five years of work and his three historical novels on Hindu–Muslim antagonism including *Anandamath* (first published in 1882), Sarkar says,

> This phase of Bankim's work is considered a decisive component of Hindu revivalism, and indeed it provided vital resources for late twentieth century Hindutva and its RSS leadership. I prefer to treat this phase more as constituting a link between nineteenth century Hindu revivalism in Bengal—whose Hindu supremacist agenda was not primarily turned against Muslims or Islam—and the hard, aggressive Hindutva politics that started organizing itself in the 1920s on an exclusively and explicitly anti-Muslim platform. (Sarkar 2001: 165, 166)

Again discussing Bankim's song *Vande Mataram*, she says,

> The song, which remains a powerful imaginative resource for the Hindutva project, complicates and widens notions of a

binary opposition between peaceful traditional Hinduism and violent Hindutva. Bankim's militant bhakti lets go of nothing, its language is supple and inventive enough to effect many movements between opposites—which is today considered by VHP thinkers to be the essence of Rama bhakti. (Sarkar 2001: 180)

Importantly she locates the ideas of Hindu conjugality at the very heart of militant nationalism in Bengal (Sarkar 2001: 191). The *Age of Consent Bill 1891* which sought to raise the age of consummation of marriage of a girl from 10 to 12 caused a furore. The barbaric deaths of young girls dying after intercourse was perfectly passable since it kept up the *garbhadhan* tradition according to Hindu *shastras* that girls should 'cohabit with their husbands on the first appearance of their menses and all Hindus must implicitly obey the injunction' (Sarkar 2001: 224). 'The politics of cultural recognition turns out to be a fundamentalist defence of internal power structures—patriarchy, caste, class—rather than a systemic critique of these' (Sarkar 2001: 234).

As an extension of this, Sarkar says: 'Communalism is part of a process in which modern political concepts draw many of their valences from the realm of sacred meanings' (Sarkar 2001: 272). She also suggests that communalism inserted itself into, and drew its life from, two modern forms of *bhakti*: *deshbhakti* and *Rambhakti*. Of this duo, *deshbhakti* is a reflectively new form of devotion, while *Rambhakti*, an older tradition, was refigured through new usages during the anti-colonial movements (Sarkar 2001: 272).

While conjugality and a Brahminical concept of the women in the domestic domain, as mothers, housewives or goddesses were important aspects of Hindu revivalism, they were not in the forefront of the RSS till much later.

The RSS used the aura of Ram as well as the aura of the Goddess by founding its first shakha on the day of Vijay Dashami, when Ram is supposed to have received the blessings of the mother goddess in his war against the demon. Nationalism had already fused these two forms of bhakti. With Hindutva the inspiration was initially male centred: the RSS is an exclusively male organisation and until the 1990s women were not allowed into its political movement. In fact a women's wing was only founded in the RSS eleven years after the organization's own foundation. (Sarkar 2001: 280, 281)

However, women, as even L. K. Advani (2008) says in his autobiography *My Country My Life*, formed a large part of the support for the Ram Janmabhoomi movement. In her analysis of Sadhvi Rithambara, who campaigned in the meetings leading up to the Babri Masjid demolition, Sarkar says:

Rithambara's voice brings back the call for desh, the feminized sacred force. Yet she dedicates the country itself to Ram—'yah des Ram ka hai, yah parives Ram ka hai' [This country belongs to Ram, this environment belongs to Ram]. Rithambara gives this divine hierarchy an earthly counterpart. As a sanyasin she embodies shakti within herself. But she also calls Hindu men to action, to vengeance—'vir bhaiyo jago!' [brave brothers, awaken!] ... she uses emasculation and eunuch frequently as tropes while relying on images of combative masculinity. Women are also invoked, and there are things for them in her speech: anecdotes about other brave women; images drawn from food and cooking; homely and humorous tales referring to domestic concerns; domestic politics played out among daughter, mother and sister-in-law. There are heroic images too which women can identify, and Rithambara reverently refers to matrishakti—the shakti that specifically resides in the mother goddess and, by extension, in mothers. Women must internalize the Ramjanmabhoomi agenda, they must fill their hearts with anger and take their place in the struggle. She leaves them in no doubt about what role they should play. Their hearts angry, their bodies hard with the desire to avenge, they must produce sons who will kill Muslims. (Sarkar 2001: 283, 284)

A militant Hindu nationalism then which was present well before the close of the 1900s, developed further in the early 20th century with the formation of the RSS in 1925 by Keshav Baliram Hedgewar. 'The RSS took on several features of the Indian terrorist societies, including a military style of training recruits and a certain religiosity' (Jaffrelot 1999: 35). The upper-caste Brahmin-dominated RSS was antagonistic to Gandhi's idea of Hinduism and his support for the lower classes.

Jaffrelot (1999: 25) goes on to say:

> More instrumental than anyone else in bringing about this qualitative leap was another Maharashtrian Brahmin, Vinayak Damodar Savarkar, the former head of a terrorist group and a future president of the Hindu Mahasabha (1937–42). His work *Hindutva: Who is a Hindu?*, first published at Nagpur in 1923, is a basic text for nationalist 'Hinduness' (the generally accepted translation of 'Hindutva').

Hedgewar's successor Madhav Sadashiv Golwalkar enunciated the true ethos of the organization. Golwalkar radically rejects the idea of a multi-ethnic nation; as suggested in the following paragraph:

> The foreign races in Hindusthan must either adopt the Hindu culture and language, must learn to respect and hold in reference Hindu religion, must entertain no ideas but those of glorification of the Hindu race and culture ... or may stay in the country, wholly subordinated to the Hindu nation, claiming nothing, deserving no privileges, far less any preferential treatment—not even citizen's rights. (We, or our nationhood defined.) (Jaffrelot 1999: 56)

INTRODUCTION

With the formation of the RSS in 1925, the VHP in 1964 and the Bharatiya Jana Sangh, which later morphed into the BJP on 5 April 1980, the Sangh Parivar was complete. The dream of the Hindu Rashtra of the RSS would be achieved by the Jan Sangh first and later the BJP. Kanungo (2003: 90) refers to the 'massive upsurge of community consciousness and identity politics all over the world in recent years'.

> As the pace of modernization accelerates, the individuals are increasingly seeking to escape from individualism towards a more community based identity. Every major philosophy of the present time considers individual alienation and cultural dislocation as important problems of man and society. The RSS which has been championing the cause of a Hindu community since the 1920s has also intensified its ideological propaganda during the last decade on the themes of 'Hindu identity', Hindutva (Hinduness) and Hindu Rashtra (Hindu Nation). (Kanungo 2003: 90)

The BJP co-opted part of the Janata Party's programme, and 'This decision was confirmed at the meeting in Bombay when Vajpayee proposed as the party's creed "Gandhian socialism" and "positive secularism"'. He went to great lengths to present the former as a cooperative third path that was particularly close to the Jan Sanghi tradition because of its decentralizing and social reformist implications. As for the latter, Vajpayee emphasized that it was different from Congress secularism, which he claimed was biased in favour of minorities in order to create 'vote banks' (Jaffrelot 1999: 315, 316).

The RSS took the agenda of cultural nationalism even further which climaxed in the spread of its group organizations in Gujarat, Madhya Pradesh and Orissa and the violence it unleashed there. Along with Muslims, Christians were also perceived as the other, with their loyalties not in India but in some faraway lands to the Pope or in Mecca, as the case may be.

With the Vishwa Hindu Parishad (VHP) the RSS whose leader, Golwalkar, was present both at the foundation of the organisation and at the Allahabad meeting—had opened up a new front, one that conforms to our interpretation of Hindu nationalism in terms of a strategy of stigmatization and emulation. Its ideology is constructed by means of a very precise rationale that is defined by three principal characteristics: first, being subjected to a real or imagined external threat, Hindu militants stigmatized it and developed strong feelings of vulnerability and hostility towards the 'threatening Other'; second, they undertook to reform their community, borrowing cultural features from the aggressor to which they attributed the latter's strength; and third, such reform is experienced or presented as a return to the past, from which they could extract pride to legitimize this imitation of the Other. This process of imitation, whereby the VHP used the adversary's own weapons against it, was well illustrated by the dispatch of 'counter missionaries' to the tribal zones of the North-East affected by Christian proselytism. (Jaffrelot 1999: 201, 202)

That the Sangh Parivar would permeate Indian society would be seen over the years, and its spread was systemically evolved from the grass-roots level in the form of shakhas or branches, schools, training workshops and the aim was to reach a wide array of people from different classes and communities. After the initial accusation that it was a higher-caste organization, the RSS and later the BJP tried to draw the poorer communities like *adivasis*, which it terms *vanvasis*, backward classes and scheduled castes into their fold. As Pralay Kanungo (2003), describes it after the BJP, 'carrier of Hedgewar's legacy', occupied the seat of power at Delhi for the third time.

> The Congress which supposedly inherited the Gandhian legacy, has been convincingly defeated in the race to control state power. This is not to make any comparison between Gandhi

and Hedgewar, but to recognize that an organisation which started with only five persons in 1925, has spread its tentacles into every possible sphere of India's civil society, including the political. Hedgewar maybe unknown to the Indian masses, but his creation—the RSS has become a household name. Its ideology—Hindu Rashtra—which remained peripheral during India's freedom struggle, has come to occupy centre stage. (Kanungo 2003: 13)

Kanungo's study of the origin and evolution of the RSS, says that the

The Montague Chelmsford reforms of 1919 brought religion more pervasively and passionately into Indian politics and exacerbated communal animosity. While a section of Hindus began to characterize themselves as 'the dying race', their Muslim counterparts saw a grave danger for the Muslim community. Mahatma Gandhi, however, always emphasized Hindu Muslim cooperation and successfully mobilized them in his non cooperation movement against the British. But soon after he withdrew the movement, Hindu Muslim relations soured and communal riots broke out with alarming frequency and intensity. Now communal suspicion and clashes replaced inter communal cooperation. Competitive communal mobilizations like shuddhi and sangathan among the Hindus, tabligh and tanzim among the Muslims further deteriorated Hindu Muslims relations. (Kanungo 2003: 36)

The Khilafat Movement initiated by Gandhi was also a tool for RSS founder Hedgewar, who was a follower of Tilak, to beat the Congress with. 'Hedgewar regretted that Indian Muslims had proved themselves "Muslims first and Indians only secondarily": when the Khilafat demand was given up in Turkey, they withdrew from the allied movement for national independence and displayed "Muslim fanaticism"' (Kanungo 2003: 41).

The Shiv Sena too, though not part of the Sangh Parivar as such, was very much part of this Hindu identity creation which it seeks to formulate through a show of strength, its pro-Hindu stand and its opposition to Muslims. It questions the Muslims and their 'pro Pakistani' tendencies and says that they should be asked to leave the country, though it lets 'nationalist' Muslims stay back. The Sena and the Sangh Parivar seek to stigmatize the 'other' and ride on a premise that Hindus are in grave danger.

Kanungo also makes special mention of Bal Gangadhar Tilak:

> ... for he not only attempted to draw the outline of a Hindu nation, he also actively and effectively mobilised the Hindus to crystallise Hindu identity; secondly, Hedgewar and his political guru Moonje were ardent followers of Tilak. The ideology of the RSS undoubtedly took its cue from Tilak. (Kanungo 2003: 107)

Tilak's views on the 1893 riots have been mentioned in Chapter 1. He made sure that the Ganpati festival became a public celebration, and with the Ganpati and Shivaji celebrations, Tilak mobilized religious and political sentiments. Kanungo (2003: 108) writes that 'the RSS has certainly borrowed from Tilak the technique of militant mobilisation to assert and consolidate Hindu identity. It also emphasizes, like Tilak, the importance of demonstrating one's strength in a charged communal atmosphere.'

Kanungo (2003: 178) makes the important point that

> ... responding to the changing dynamics of Indian politics the RSS has changed the course of its political journey—from moderate, pragmatic, and accommodative to militant rigid and intolerant. It also used the Ram Janmabhoomi agitation to promote its political mobilization through an innovative use of Hindu cultural and religious symbols, thereby wrapping its political agenda in a cultural cover.

The attempt to change accepted Hindu practices by the colonial powers drew a backlash from the community, which tried to reinvent a glorious past to justify its ideals. As Aloysius (1998: 104) says:

> Faced thus with real and supposed onslaughts on its monopolistic dominance, and having tried different forms of meeting the challenge such as reforms, and revivalism the Brahminic ideology finally settled upon an adequate strategy by reincarnating itself as pan-Indian political-national Hinduism. The agency through which this transformation was brought about was the small circle of upper caste communities usually centred around the Brahmins in different parts of the country, undergoing the multiple processes of accommodation, unification and empowerment through imperial patronage.

He says, the emergent 'Hinduism was at once Brahminical as well as national. Nationalism and nationalist consciousness was the context in which the ideology of sacred and secular hierarchy transformed itself into, and articulated itself as Hinduism' (Aloysius 1998: 104).

From Banaras to Bombay/Mumbai

Over 80 years before the first riots between Hindus and Muslims were recorded in Bombay in August 1893, Banaras in 1809 witnessed clashes over a temple, a precursor to the gamut of violence over religion which was only to intensify in the next century. The progression of violence then was one indicator of where things were headed in the prelude to the Partition and into the reasons why colonial India would not be free as a composite whole. While much of the violence took place in north India, the city of Bombay too had no small role to play as we shall see in Chapter 1. How did this violence and the religious/cultural movements shape the course of the future? 'Cultural identity takes a political form and differentiation between "we" and "they" gets sharper and more concrete. Cultural identity is transformed into communal identity and community consciousness becomes communal consciousness', says Kanungo (2003: 91).

As Pandey (2008: 220) puts it:

> The relevant question for the historian of nationalism is perhaps this: How was the imagined political community of the future (commonly described by the late nineteenth century in the vocabulary of nationhood) being constructed by Indian nationalists at different times? The answer, I would like to suggest, is that it was not, in the earlier stages of the national movement, constructed in the way in which we in India have begun to 'think' the nation since the 1920s and 1930s.
>
> Before that time, the nation of Indians was visualized as a composite body, consisting of several communities, each with its own history and culture and its own special contribution to make to the common nationality. India, and the emerging Indian nation, was conceived of as a collection of communities: Hindu+ Muslim + Christian + Parsi + Sikh, and so on.
>
> Sometime around the 1920s this vision was substantially altered, and India came to be seen very much more as a collection of individuals, of Indian 'citizens'. The difference between these two positions was quite fundamental: and it is my contention that it was in the context of the change from one to the other that the concept of communalism was fully articulated. In other words, communalism and nationalism as we know them today came to acquire their present significance in the 1920s or thereabouts, to a large extent in opposition to one another, and in response to far reaching changes that were occurring in the national movement as well as the way in which Indian nationalism was being constructed.

Claims to temple land, playing of music before mosques and cow slaughter took pride of place in disturbances across the country, and

Cow Protection became a focal point not only from saving ageing and sick animals but also to impart a religious angle and fervour to the act. Pandey (2008: 163) writes:

> Regarding Cow Protection, Rafiuddin Ahmed notes that the question of the ritual slaughter of cows came to occupy centre-stage in the politics of the late nineteenth century 'not so much because Muslim loved to sacrifice cows as because militant Hindus (and one might add) the colonial regime made it an issue'. 'What used to be a quiet and private ritual', he notes further, 'now came to be celebrated with public éclat as an ostentatious response to the Hindu challenge'. McLane describes the movement for cow protection as a 'species of sub-nationalism' that sought to shape and define the community in terms of the 'supremacy of Hindu custom' and thereby, excluded Muslims from the 'primary community or nation'. [sic]

However, as Pandey points out, 'neither "nationalism" nor "communalism" was quite so easily "made" or so triumphant as historians and others have sometimes assumed ... By the early years of this century, the sense of religious (as of caste) community was far more widespread and more keenly marked than ever before' (Pandey 2008: 204).

In the 1980s, the Congress secularism started showing its true colours, and this was helped mainly by Prime Minister Indira Gandhi's new found devotion to religious matters and also the encouragement of Sikh militant Sant Bhindranwale to weaken the Akali Dal in Punjab. In Jammu and Kashmir too Ms Gandhi played the Hindu card to counter the National Conference. A worse period was to come after the assassination of Ms Gandhi and the anti-Sikh riots that were instigated by the Congress, destroying its secular image. The handling of communal riots after 1980 too showed a marked reluctance on the part of the state to act against the culprits (Jaffrelot 1999: 333). Prime Minister Manmohan Singh has since described the anti-Sikh riots as a blot, but done little else to render any justice.

The Shah Bano case and the passing of the *Muslim Women (Protection of Rights on Divorce) Act,* 1986, favoured hard-line Muslim sentiments. 'Both tendencies—the marginalization of social development in the Congress programme and the erosion of secularism—were interrelated: the party shifted from populist promises, which the Indian electorate treated with less and less respect, to communal categories to attract support' (Jaffrelot 1999: 336).

A particularly significant issue was raised in early 1986 when a district and sessions Judge in Faizabad ordered that the Uttar Pradesh government should unlock the gates of the Babri Masjid/Ram Janmabhoomi temple thus enabling devotees to offer darshan and puja in the disputed structure ... Shortly afterwards Rajiv Gandhi's government came forward with the Muslim women (protection of rights on divorce) Bill, which showed a surprising readiness to conciliate orthodox Muslim opinion. (Jaffrelot 1999: 369, 370)

Once again the same cries of threats to Hinduism were raised, especially after the Shah Bano affair and the conversions to Islam in Meenakshipuram in 1981. A series of events followed with the VHP's Sadhu Sansad being called the Dharma Sansad. 'The perceived threat from Christianity, Islam and even Sikhism, whose ecclesiastical hierarchies were playing an increasingly public role, probably explains the Hindu nationalists' desire to create an equivalent role for Hinduism' (Jaffrelot 1999: 352). 'It was only natural that the Ayodhya issue would be raked up with the Dharma Sansad demanding the "liberation of the site at Ayodhya" its first meeting in 1984' (Jaffrelot 1999: 363).

Jaffrelot analyses the choice of the Ram temple as a focal point of mobilization. As we have seen 'Ram bhakti' played a central role in the Sangh Parivar's religio-political nationalism.

The creation of an issue like the Babri/Ram Jamnabhoomi would have been of little benefit to the BJP had it not been brought to the attention of the greatest possible number of people, and shrewdly dramatized. This was the task of the Hindu nationalist networks. (Jaffrelot 1999: 383)

The movement to mobilize support for the Ram Temple left in its wake a series of violent events all over the country, which started from Kota, Rajasthan:

> ... the first riot of the 1989 cycle of communal violence took place in Rajasthan, Kota, a frontier strict adjacent to Madhya Bharat. After 33 years of intercommunal harmony, rioting broke out there on September 14, 1989 causing 15 deaths and ₹ 7.5 million worth of damage. As in 1956, when last there had been violence in the town, the immediate cause of the riot was the festival of Anant Chaturdashi but this time it was anti Muslim slogans ... The Ram Shila (or bricks) procession left a bloody trail in Madhya Pradesh, Uttar Pradesh, Gujarat and Bihar where nearly 1000 people were estimated to have been killed. (Jaffrelot 1999: 396, 398)

Many movements to mobilize Hindus for the Ram Temple were in evidence after 1984, and linked to these were demands for cow protection and a ban on cow killing. The most significant one was Advani's 'Rath Yatra'. In 1990, L. K. Advani's 10,000 km Rath Yatra throughout the country was 'a movement [that] marked the culmination of the strategy of ethno-religious mobilization. For the first time, a political leader used propaganda of an overtly Hindu nationalist character throughout eight of India's states' (Jaffrelot 1999: 418). The Ram Jyot Yatras also led to violence in 1990 in Rajasthan, Karnataka, West Bengal and Andhra Pradesh, the worst was Gujarat (Jaffrelot 1999: 419, 420).

For Advani, the Ayodhya movement in many ways was the continuation of the spirit of Somnath where a temple was built post-Independence.

I regard the Ayodhya movement as the most decisive transformational event of my political journey. As every student of India's contemporary history will attest to, its impact on our society and polity—indeed, on our sense of national identity—has been tremendous. Destiny made me perform a certain pivotal duty in this movement, in the form of the Ram Rath Yatra from Somnath to Ayodhya in 1990. (Advani 2008: 341)

Jaffrelot (1999: 421) talks about the Kar Seva and the cult of martyrdom, as the building of the temple now had assumed ultra-religious tones and those who volunteered were given an exalted status. Figures on the kar sevaks killed in action while making their way to Ayodhya were touted to be around 100, though the reality was much lower.

For many Hindus the shooting of kar sevaks was to have a profound psychological effect. The feeling of Hindu vulnerability had now been transformed into exasperation against the political authorities, which were seen as inexplicably reluctant or at least inefficient in making Muslims see reason. Anger was channelised against Muslims themselves, even though most of them kept a low profile during the episode. (Jaffrelot 1999: 422)

The Ayodhya issue had a strong attraction for many young people, women and men from all over the country. Advani believed it was cultural nationalism.

Thus, the Ayodhya issue no longer remained limited to construction of the Ramjanmabhoomi temple. Rather it became the symbol of a struggle between genuine secularism and pseudo secularism. It also provided the context for a sharply polarized debate between two opposite conceptions about the source of India's nationhood and national identity: the unifying concept of cultural nationalism and the dividing concept of anti Hindu nationalism. (Advani 2008: 367)

This clearly endorses all that has been said about the Ram Janmabhoomi movement and the centrality of Ram to the debate. Secularism was being redefined, and all those who were not in favour of a temple were the embodiment of 'pseudo secularism'. Advani also says the comparison between the Ram temple and the Babri Masjid is outrageous (Advani 2008: 366). 'In contrast the Babri Masjid had no religious significance whatsoever for Indian Muslims. If Muslims are entitled to an Islamic atmosphere in Mecca, and if Christians are entitled to a Christian atmosphere in the Vatican, why is it wrong for Hindus to expect a Hindu atmosphere in Ayodhya' (Advani 2008: 366). This echoes the thoughts of his mentors such as Golwalkar.

It was not only Ram but the birthplace of Ram which became an important and crucial aspect of the struggle. Sarkar talks of

> [t]his 'spatialization' of the object of devotion i.e. the sacred as a specific place or space which needs to be recovered through a struggle, moves the struggle for sacred birthplace—not of the people, but of Ram. In the video cassette Bhaye Prakat Kripala, the map of India has a green blinking light to indicate the birthplace of Ayodhya. If Christianity has its Bethlehem and Islam its Mecca, the green light of Hindutva shines with saffron favour upon Ayodhya. The techniques of propagating Hindutva are frequently borrowed paradoxically from the very religions that are being opposed. (Sarkar 2001: 283)

Secular Nationalism

However, in the countdown to the Independence, there was an attempt at forging secular nationalism, going beyond community concerns which changed dramatically.

> Forty years after Partition and Independence, questions of the defence of *custom*, of *established religious institutions* (including

buildings), of the *rights of religious communities* have again assumed an overwhelming importance in the politics of India. On all sides, Indian politics today is marked by renewed and exaggerated claims along these lines; and we face an increasingly strident demand for recognition of what is called the essentially Hindu character of India, Indian civilization and Indian nationalism. At this juncture, it is necessary to reiterate that no such thing as India, Indian civilization or Indian nationalism was given from the start, from the dawn of history as it were. All of these were constructed through the manifold exertions of millions of men and women, and constructed (or reconstructed?) to a large extent during the colonial period and in the struggle against colonialism.

The cry of Hindu nationalism in this particular form—of India as essentially the land of the Hindus—is part of the discourse of communalism that came to the fore in the 1920s. Before that, Indian nationalists had sought to emphasize the fact that India was more than only, or primarily, Hindu. (Pandey 2008: 259, 260)

Earlier things were different.

Along with the attempt to mobilize a wider Hindu community (and a wider Muslim community) in the later nineteenth and early twentieth century went an attempt—in places involving many of the very same men and women—to build up nationalist feeling and nationalist associations that went beyond the confines and concerns of the religious community. Bayly's close study of politics on the Allahabad region between 1880 and 1920 illustrates the point very well indeed.

This study draws our attention to the early development of a secular tradition in Allahabad's nationalist politics, built up around the towering personality of Ajudhia Nath Kunzru, the 'only leader of national standing' in the local Congress until his death in 1892, and inherited at a later stage by Motilal Nehru and his allies—widely described as 'friends of Muslims'. But Bayly's work underlines at the same time another, at least equally important dimension of this early nationalist activity.

The author points to the close connections of the radical Congress leadership of the 1910s with 'Hindu sectional interest groups' that had been active for some time before then. He writes of the 'strong conservative' and 'revivalist' strain in local nationalism during its early years, and illustrates this by referring to the work of the Prayag Hindu Samaj (founded 1880) and the regional Madhya Hindu Samaj (founded 1884), both of which later constituted electorates for the annual sessions of the congress. The annual sessions of the Madhya Hindu Samaj were held concurrently with the Indian National Congress until 1891 or 1892, he notes: and the Samaj's concerns reflected the 'whole drift of official policy during the 1880s, which encouraged people to think beyond their localities ... in the agglomerate categories of Hindu and Muslim'. The overriding issues were the propagation of the Hindu (i.e., Devanagri script) and protection of cattle. (Pandey 2008: 205, 206).

Aloysius (1998: 113, 114) points to the fact that

[m]ost members of the Congress were also members of different religio-cultural organizations—the Cow Protection society, Hindu Sabhas, Arya Samaj etc.—and passed from one onto the other without any sense of contradiction ... In fact this is now the secularity and 'nationalness' of the Indian nationalist movement in general, and of the Congress in particular, was maintained.

However, all that was to change. Aloysius (1998: 140) explains that the

> ... multiple religio-cultural traditions of the subcontinent were now seen as part of a single coherent religion—Hinduism—which was emerging with all the regular trappings of organised religions such as Islam and Christianity. The intelligentsia, both within and without the political movement repeatedly felt compelled to define the Hindu person and the context of Hinduism. Their definition invariably revolved around Vedic Brahminic ideals, icons and codes of behaviour as represented in the Dharmashastras. The culture of the subcontinent was defined and described as Hindu culture and Hindu civilization, and in explicitly political contexts, as Indian culture and civilizations.

Naturally this upper-caste ideal had little room for class or caste concerns and veered towards a unified Hindu Brahminical ideal. As Aloysius (1998: 114) says:

> The traditionalist organizations in which many Congressman participated actively stood, more or less openly, for the re establishment of the Brahminical order of society; they had more effective contacts with the mass and rural organizations to exercise social control, and restrain them from 'aping the west', which only meant demanding change towards egalitarianism. The main thrust of the trio—Bal, Lal and Pal, of Annie Besant and later of Gandhi—was an unambiguous articulation outside the formal forums of Congress, in favour of maintaining tradition, and yet these were the men who were guiding the destiny of the nation through the leadership of the movement. The pervasive and persistent theme of their socio-cultural world view is that of going back to tradition, which in the context meant social slavery for the lower-caste masses.

INTRODUCTION

Just as patriarchal concepts were not challenged, the social order too was not sought to be shaken in the confines of the national movement for Independence. Finally it came down to the fact that 'Questions relating to the relocations of power within society, the emancipation of lower castes, the removal of agrestic bondage etc., became "social questions" and had to be firmly kept out of the movement' (Aloysius 1998: 120). Simplifying the diverse nature of the country's religions, culture and tradition into a monolithic Hindu entity, and that too a Brahminic one, threw the Congress open to criticism. Aloysius (1998) quotes Periyar:

> Coming down heavily on the Congress brand of nationalism which sought to restore to dominance all forms of religious superstition, Periyar indicated in his inimitable popular style the kind of nationalism he had in mind.
>
> If we consider, on what must depend the nationalism of a nation, minimally, the people of a nation, without having to sell or bargain their mind or conscience, should be able to eke out their livelihood. More than this there are several other nationalisms; knowledge should grow; education is needed; unity is needed; self effort is needed; genuine feelings are needed; cheating one other for a living should not be there; lazy people should not be there; slaves not be there; untouchables and those who cannot walk on public streets should not be there; like these several more things should be done. (V Annaimuthi, ed. 1974, volume 1: 372, in Aloysius 1998: 153)
>
> Before all these, however, nationalism requires the total abolition of caste and its discrimination based on birth. (V Annaimuthi, ed. 1974, volume 1: 371–88, in Aloysius 1998: 153)

Aloysius, quoting B. B. Misra, accurately pinpoints the twin birth of nationalism and communalism to occasions when the government moved away from its patronage of Hindu upper castes. In the process, however, he attributes altruistic motives to the colonial government and this need not have been the case for it is more consistent to argue that the imperialist motive has all along been to achieve profit and permanence and that their tactics had been shifting to this end (Aloysius 1998: 108).

Changes in the Nationalist Movement

Benedict Anderson (1991: 6) defines

> [n]ation as an imagined political community—and imagined as both inherently limited and sovereign. It is imagined because the members of even the smallest nation will never know most of their fellow—members meet them, or even hear of them, yet in the minds of each lives the image of their communion.

In the imagined community then lays the seeds of the diverse aspirations to notions of a separate nationhood. In colonial India, the strong current of religious differences and divisions shaped those cultural identities, among other things, which was finally articulated in the division of India into separate nations. As Anderson (1991: 12) says:

> Needless to say, I am not claiming that the appearance of nationalism towards the end of the eighteenth century was produced by the erosion of religious certainties, or that this erosion does not itself require a complex explanation. Nor am I suggesting that somehow nationalism historically 'supersedes' religion. What I am proposing is that nationalism has to be understood by aligning it, not with self-consciously held political ideologies, but with the large cultural systems that preceded it, out of which—as well as against which—it came into being.

While the Hindu community was mobilized by Cow Protection Movement and Sanskritization on the one hand, the Muslims, on the other hand, too reacted. Pandey (2008: 228) says: 'In (Maulana) Mohammed Ali's well known words, the problems facing the Muslim leader in India at the turn of the century was that he could but be aware of belonging to two circles which were not concentric—that of Islam and that of Hindustan.'

Like the *Sachar Committee Report*, which detailed the condition of the Muslim community in India in 2006, the *Hunter Committee Report* on Muslims way back exposed the sharp differences in terms of the socio-economic conditions of Muslims. Pandey (2008: 228) says:

> There were other reasons, too, for the difference in Hindu and Muslim positions. From the time that W W Hunter's Indian Mussalmans was published in the 1870s, the belief had gained ground that the Indian Muslim community as a whole had fallen behind the Hindus in education, recruitment to government service, advancement in 'modern' industries and other economic activities, and, consequently, in social and political position as well as in a more general self confidence. In an age when far sighted political leaders were expected to service Community and well as Country, any public worker who professed interest in the 'Muslim community' would have to do everything possible to lift the community up by its bootstraps. That is precisely the task Syed Ahmed Khan would seem to have set himself in the period after the 1860s; and the same concern appears to have molded the vision of other major Muslim leaders of Northern India who followed in his wake.

Aloysius (1998: 89) also notes that with 'Khilafat and cow slaughter occupying the centre stage of nationalist politics under the leadership of Gandhi in 1920s, a distinct Muslim-nationalism in preference to the political nation along with the non Muslim masses, had certainly started its career'.

While Muslim nationalism of a different kind rose with the Khilafat Movement, the Ali brothers and Gandhi who stood together soon parted ways over the question of civil disobedience. The devolution of power starting with the Morley–Minto Reforms in 1919, the Montague–Chelmsford Reforms in 1932 and the Simon Commission also paved the way for the Partition. From the Morley–Minto/Montague–Chelmsford reforms which gave Muslims separate electorates to the end of the Khilafat Movement in 1923, the Muslim community was increasingly alienated. As Page explains (1982: 36):

> The Montague Chelmsford reforms also changed the nature of all India Muslim politics. Before 1920, Muslim political organisations at the all India level had been in the hands of the Muslims of the United Provinces, Bihar and Bombay. In these provinces, a Muslim educated elite had shared the political aspirations of the Hindu educated elite and had masterminded a political alliance with the Congress in pursuit of constitutional reform. Almost as soon as the government's reform proposals were formulated, however, the League leaders saw the writing on the wall.

Page (1982: 73) also says:

> From the point of view of Hindu Muslim relations, the period after the introduction of the Reforms stands out in stark contrast with the period which preceded it. During the War years, the Muslim League and the Congress worked together for constitutional reform, and after the War, Gandhi and the Ali brothers joined forces to preserve the Khilafat and to gain Swaraj. After the introduction of the Reforms, however, and particularly after the subsidence of the Khilafat and non-cooperation movements, communal unity gave way to communal antagonism, the fraternization of 1919 seemed an aberration, and many parts of North India were plunged into scenes of bloodshed and strife which were to have no parallel until Partition itself. Nor was this development merely of temporary significance. On the contrary, because it

polarized relations between the two communities in the crucial period before the Montague Chelmsford constitution was reviewed, it had far reaching implications for the future of the subcontinent.

It was the Reforms then which led to the cleavage down the line.

The Montague Chelmsford Reforms Constitution produced two main trends in all-India politics, a centrifugal trend and a communal trend. Between 1923 and 1927, every all-India confrontation with the Raj was beset by provincial pressures, and the lesson which the all-India politician learnt during these years was that either he had to bow before the pressures or to bow out of politics altogether. Particularly after 1925, the Congress Swaraj party resembled a Colossus doing the splits, one leg planted at the centre; and the Muslim League and the Khilafat Committee, though possessed of fewer organizational resources, displayed similar tendencies, as may be demonstrated by reference to the careers of the Ali brothers and of Jinnah. Of a piece with this centrifugal trend was a trend towards communal polarization. Because separate electorates were continued the introduction of ministerial responsibility set the two communities at each other's throats. Either one community effectively dominated the transferred departments to the detriment of the other, as in the Punjab, or politically depressed sections of a majority exploited communal feeling for their own regeneration, as in the United Provinces. In either case, the result was the same: Hindu was divided from Muslim at the provincial level, and all India politics soon came to be affected. (Page 1982: 142)

After the publication of the Communal Award in 1932, giving Muslims control of the Punjab and Bengal, the stage was set for a division.

In the consolidation of political interests around communal issues, the Imperial power played an important role. By treating the Muslims as a separate group, it divided them from other Indians. By granting them separate electorates, it institutionalized that division. This was one of the most crucial factors in the development of communal politics. (Page 1982: 260)

As Page (1982: 264) best puts it, 'With each stage of devolution, Indian was set against Indian, caste against caste, community against community. But as each area of government and administration was ceded to Indian control, even the Raj's closest allies were only allies for a purpose.'

While Hindu identities were sharpened with the launching of the Arya Samaj and colonial reform, Muslims leaders too realized the need to move away from a single nationhood. Aloysius draws attention to the breaking away of Jinnah, once an ardent nationalist.

As has been pointed out, the Hindu–Muslim communal problem was basically a regional problem of Punjab, Bengal and the United Provinces where the Muslim masses were near equals of the lower castes and were in majority. Within the new structure of politics, when numbers became politically significant, the caste Hindus could not bring themselves to accept their own reduced political significance. Instead of solving the problem by containing it, the Gandhi event enlarged and nationalized it and further complicated it through mystification. Antagonism grew unabated between the two communities in spite of all efforts, so much so that when Gandhi launched his civil disobedience programme, Shaukat Ali, the comrade and soulmate of Gandhi during the Khilafat years, preached against it, saying its goal was Hindu Raj. And Jinnah, once an ardent nationalist, became an inveterate advocate of a separate homeland for Muslims. (Aloysius 1998: 191)

Aloysius (1998) says the main ideologues of Muslim nationalism—Syed Ahmed Khan, Iqbal and Jinnah—all started out as staunch pan-Indian nationalists, and only subsequently turned separatists. 'The first articulations of the separatist Muslim national consciousness, by consensus, can be traced to the 1860s when Ahmed Khan's ambiguous statements were expressed when the demand for replacement of Urdu by Hindi in the U P administration was raised' (Aloysius 1998: 168).

Later, historiography, due to contemporary political compulsions, sought to apportion equal responsibility and blame to both Hindu and Muslim communalisms or exclusivist visions. But at the level of society, it was the social and cultural separatism of the dominance castes that was prior both logical and historical. Aspiration for political separatism on the part of the Muslim elite was truly a fallout of their inability to secure an honourable place within the sectarian national vision of the cultural nationalists. (Aloysius 1998: 168, 169)

Mahatma Gandhi sought to unify these fragmenting priorities which did not eventually succeed. 'Cow, Khilafat and Untouchability were the three Mantras which sought to bring down the surging bipolar political consciousness and change the emerging new alignment of social forces' (Aloysius 1998: 181).

However, this had serious consequences as Aloysius explains.

The direct result of Khilafat and Non-cooperation was to tear asunder the lower caste Muslim unity, bring the respective masses under the leadership of the traditional elite of the two communities, using the newly fabricated idiom of pan-Indian political identities, both Hindu and Muslim. (Aloysius 1998: 184)

The right wing emphasized the Hinduness of India and the need to have a nation reflecting that ethos.

Thus there arose the idea of a Hindu Raj which would reflect the glories of the ancient Hindu civilization and keep Muslims in their place, to be matched in due course by the notion of a

Muslim Raj which would protect the place of the Muslims. The Hindu-Muslim problem now became 'the question of all questions' [Gandhi]; it 'dominated almost everything else' [Nehru]. (Pandey 2008: 235)

The British and the Congress had each a role to play in this divide. Page (1982: xxii) points out the impact of the Reforms, of devolving power to the provinces without any change in the Centre.

> It was argued in Prelude that the manner in which power was devolved to the provinces without any corresponding devolution at the all India level encouraged centrifugalism. The trend was discernible after 1920; it became crystal clear after 1937. Muslim separatism was reinforced by the emergence of autonomous Muslim majority provinces and the Congress had to develop new strategies and new mechanisms to keep the nationalist movement united.

Page (1982) and Anita Inder Singh (2010) have in their detailed studies shown how the Congress and the British underestimated the Muslim League and how the 'mass contact programme' among Muslims launched by the Congress failed in 1939. Page (1982: xxii) says:

> If it was a serious mistake for the British to make the overriding principle of their programme of constitutional reform outmaneuvering the Congress, it was arguably an equally serious error on the part of the Congress to take the view that the Muslim question was a colonial creation which would disappear with Independence. To refuse to think in terms of coalitions, to attempt to undermine the leadership of the community, however conservative it may have been, by means of the mass contact movement, to insist to the end that Congress represented the whole of India may have been necessary for the rhetoric of

nationalism and bargaining with the British, but it had serious consequences for India's plural tradition.

Inder Singh (2010) too refers to the British and Congress tactics which encouraged the Muslim League.

> The question to be confronted is when and how religious feeling came to be 'politicized' to the point where partition became inevitable. The answer to this question may be sought not only in the emergence of the Muslim League with its demand for sovereign Muslim state from March 1940 and the mobilization of Muslim provincial support, but also in British and Congress tactics which contributed to the rise of the League and the solidification of its communal support. And the circumstances of a declining empire may have contributed as much to Muslim political unification as the League's appeals to the nationalism supposedly inherent in Muslim religious communalism. (Inder Singh 2010: 237)

Inder Singh (2010: 252) concludes: 'Always underestimating the seriousness of the call for a sovereign Pakistan neither the British nor the Congress formulated a strategy to challenge or to resist it. In August 1947, the Muslim League was the only party to achieve what it wanted.

Partition then made Indian Muslims more vulnerable. Mushirul Hasan (2007) writes,

> The birthplace of Pakistan on 14–15 August 1947 undermined, from the liberal and left perspective, the values of religious tolerance and cultural pluralism. The ideological foundations of secular nationalism, the main plank of the Indian National Congress in its mobilization campaigns, also weakened. For the Muslim communities that remained in India, partition was a nightmare ... the so called Islamic community in India, which

had no place in Jinnah's Pakistan, was 'fragmented', 'weakened', and left vulnerable to right wing Hindu onslaughts. (Hasan 2007: 6, 7)

The creation of Pakistan led to a human tragedy, the effects of which are still in evidence. And that very country now is believed to be responsible for the various acts of terror in India starting with the 1993 blasts in Mumbai. The chief perpetrators of the blast, Dawood Ibrahim and his henchman Tiger Memon, are reported to be seeking refuge in Pakistan; Dawood has been named on the Forbes list of the world's most wanted fugitives released in 2008. We seem to have come full circle. That the division of the country would result in the proxy war being waged by Pakistan, the festering issue of Kashmir and the hand of the Inter-services Intelligence (ISI) in most Indian terror strikes, barring the ones suspected to be planned by the Hindu right-wing groups, has created a vicious atmosphere of strife and division. When Ajmal Kasab was caught fleeing after gunning down people at Mumbai Chhatrapati Shivaji Terminus, the city bayed for his blood. There were demands for a public hanging not only from politicians of all hues but also ordinary people. So charged is anything to do with Muslims and Pakistan that nothing less than blood will do.

Pakistan and its state-sponsored terror has become another stick to beat the Indian Muslims with after the Partition.

As Muhammed Mujeeb wrote in his magnum opus The Indian Muslims, Partition did not solve their problem. On the contrary, 'they became a much smaller minority in India, physically not less but more vulnerable by the creation of the separate state of Pakistan, with their loyalties obviously open to suspicion and doubt and their future nothing but the darkness of uncertainty'. (Page 1982: xxxii)

Every time there are riots, people abuse Muslims and ask them to go Pakistan. The animosity to Muslims is interpreted by using the word

'Pakistan'—which is loosely used for any large Muslim ghetto—the term 'mini Pakistan' not only has derogatory allusions to that of a ghetto but also something that is hostile to Hindu and India's interests. Nationalism and communalism stand for a Hindu identity, a monolith, in which Muslims have no place. I will never forget the bewilderment of a taxi driver in Gujarat, driving us around after the riots in 2002, who asked me, 'will these people really drop us to the border and will Pakistan take us in'. He was genuinely worried that this could become a reality.

Mumbai has seen bloody years of violence right from 1893, as the chapter on the riots shows. That it would become the epicentre of riots and terror and so much violence was to be demonstrated in future years. In Maharashtra, animosity between the two communities resulted in riots sporadically and by the time the Shiv Sena was formed though on a nativist principle, the stage was set for more polarization. While its initial target were not Muslims, the nationalist identity was asserted some years later when it adopted Hindutva and launched a tirade against Muslims. From reclaiming places of worship, the Sena launched elaborate Shiv Jayanti celebrations where Muslims were abused and attacked. In Dhule, in 2008, a peace of 40 years was shattered by riots which started with minor incidents of stone throwing on religious processions but the fury of the riots surpassed anything the town had witnessed. Temples and mosques bore the brunt of mob fury and both sides lost out.

Along with Hindutva, terrorism has been revived by the right wing. There was little that was peaceful to begin with in the Hindu Rashtra ideology. Abhinav Bharat founded by Savarkar has been rejuvenated in a new avatar by an army officer to spring terror through bomb blasts in 2008. Nathuram Godse killing Gandhi was a terrorist act though not really recognized as such, and Godse today is a hero for many in this country. The Maharashtra Anti-Terrorism Squad (ATS) led by Hemant Karkare, who was killed on 26 November 2008, pinpointed the Malegaon bomb blast of 29 September 2008, which killed seven people, to this right-wing Hindu group Abhinav Bharat. The 11 arrested included Sadhvi Pragya Thakur Singh, and an army officer, a decorated one at that, Lt Col Prasad Shrikant Purohit. The ATS chargesheet filed on 20 January 2009 clearly says Hindu Rashtra was the aim of this group, and Purohit had founded Abhinav Bharat in 2007 for this purpose. But, well before this members of Hindutva groups had been caught red-handed making bombs, some dying in the effort but there is very little that happens once these cases are committed to trial. In fact, the Malegaon blast trial is embroiled in whether the provisions of the Maharashtra Control of Organised Crimes Act (MCOCA) should apply or not even before the actual trial can begin.

The Malegaon terror attack seems to have links with blasts in Ajmer and Hyderabad and the matter is under investigation (Smita Nair, Indian Express, 15 September 2010, Malegaon, Ajmer, Hyderabad,). In September 2008 the ATS filed a voluminous chargesheet against six members of a religious revivalist organization near Mumbai, Sanatan Sanstha, and the Hindu Janjagruti Samiti for a series of crude bomb blasts in Thane, Panvel and Navi Mumbai. In 2010, 11 members of the Sanathan Sanstha have been chargesheeted for the blasts in Goa on 16 October 2009. Writing about the Malegaon blast case, Jaffrelot (2009) says:

> The people, the places and the modus operandi are revealing of the continuity that underlines the Hindu tradition of terror, harking back to V.D. Savarkar. The young, revolutionary Savarkar had created the first Abhinav Bharat Society in 1905. The movement drew its name and its inspiration from Mazzini's 'Young Italy', but was also influenced by Frost Thomas's Secret Societies of the European Revolution, a book dealing mostly with the Russian nihilists. The movement was dissolved in 1952, but ten years back, just before finishing his term as Hindu Mahasabha president, Savarkar had created the Hindu Rashtra Dal, another militia whose mission was to impart military training to the Hindus in order to fight the Muslims, Gandhi's followers and the Mahatma himself. This movement cashed in on the work of the same institution—the Bhonsle Military School, started in 1935 by B.S. Moonje, another Nagpur-based

Savarkarite, after a European tour which had exposed him to Mussolini's Balilla movement.

Like the Abhinav Bharat of today, the Hindu Rashtra Dal attracted Hindutva-minded Maharashtrian Brahmins—especially from Poona—who found the RSS insufficiently active. Some of them also had connections to the British Army. (Jaffrelot 2009)

And so Hindu nationalism articulated at the beginning of the 20th century to assert the identity and religious proclivities of Hindus continues with the revival of bomb blasts and fresh attempts to assert Hindutva as a response to 'Islamic' terror. Only this time, there is open support for the Sadhvi and others from the Sangh Parivar, which vociferously objects to the description 'saffron terror'.

The incidents of bomb blasts perpetrated by right-wing groups are not recent. In 1992, there was a blast at the Neemuch office of the VHP. One person died and two others were injured. Incriminating material for making the bombs was recovered from the VHP office. On 22 April 2002, a bomb blast took place at Swar Mandir, Mhow, Madhya Pradesh. The four persons arrested were suspected to be RSS members.

However, it was due to the incident at Nanded, Maharashtra, on 6 April 2006 that the involvement of right-wing groups came into the limelight.

In April 2006, a powerful explosion in the Nanded home of a retired Public Works Department (PWD) executive engineer Laxman Gundayya Rajkondwar was the first indication of a possibility of a home-grown right-wing terror network. Though initially police covered it up by saying that it was a cracker explosion, investigations revealed that Rajkondwar's house doubled as a bomb-making factory. Two persons, Laxman's son Naresh and another Bajrang Dal leader Himanshu Panse, died on the spot. Four others present that night, Maruthi

Keshav Wagh, Yogesh Vidulkar (Deshpande), Gururaj Jairam Tuptewar and Rahul Manohar Pande, were grievously injured. (Menon 2008)

This was followed by another blast in Nanded in 2007 killing two persons.

The Malegaon blast trail is still being investigated and the matter is in court. 'Islamic terror' will be matched with 'Hindu terror' and the aim will be Hindu Rashtra. The means may be more violent but the end is the same.

1

THE CITY OF GOLD

The first conquest of the seven islands that made up Bombay, as it was known then, came from the sea. As Gillian Tindall (1992: 29, 30) puts it:

> The first Portuguese landing in Bombay, in 1509, was a rapacious foray.... Bombay was at that time the property of the Moslem ruler Sultan Muhamed Shah Begada, who initially repulsed the foreign invaders; but gradually, by repeated assaults, the Portuguese consolidated their holdings on the west coast. The Sultan's grandson, Bahadur Shah, was finally persuaded in 1534 to make over to the King of Portugal the seven islands plus Bassein, which was a chunk of mainland territory north of Bombay also known as Salsette.

Over 400 years later, the sea came in handy for two major terror strikes in Mumbai—12 March 1993 and 26 November 2008. The first was a series of 12 bomb blasts, and the more recent one saw the city being held to ransom by 10 armed gunmen. In the 1993 blasts, the chemical RDX was ferried from the sea for use to deadly effect, while in November 2008, the armed gunmen are said to have sailed from Karachi by boat and later by dinghy to disembark at the fishermen's colony in Colaba.

When you think of it, the city initially was a group of seven small islands, with the grey sea stretching infinitely around. Tindall (1992: 25) writes further:

> Twentieth century maps of Bombay show a tongue of land about 12 miles long (or fourteen, taking in the thinner promontory of Colaba at its tip), and about three miles wide for most of its extent: it projects alongside the mainland, to which it is linked at its northern end by causeways, like a bizarre copy of New York's Long Island. But the earliest maps of the area tell a different story. When the English received the place, variously described as 'the Fort', 'the islands' and 'the Island', from the Portuguese in the 1660s, there was not one main island, but seven, plus other islets in the harbour and certain bits of watery, semi detached mainland, which still, today, are not part of Bombay proper but are within the area currently administered by Greater Bombay.

Tindall (1992: 29) also says:

> Bombay, although one of a number of places down that stretch of the western coast of India that were known as ports from ancient times, has no early history apart from the history of the whole region.... It is sufficient to note that various Aryan Hindu invaders, the ancestors of the Mahrattas, held sway in this part of India from the third century for the next thousand years or so, that there were scattered settlements on the Bombay islands, and that power passed into the hands of Moslem invaders from Gujarat in the north at roughly the same time as

the Middle Ages were ending in Europe, as it was during this time that the first beginnings of a Moslem community from the adjacent Konkan began to establish itself among the Bombay Islands.

A third of its population comprised of Muslims then (Tindall 1992: 29). The city has always had a cosmopolitan tag because somewhere, despite so much effort at division and rife, there is a bonding. Bombay, and later Mumbai, is a tiny magnet attracting people from all over. The tightly knit bustling settlements, its traffic-snarled roads, and grey buildings extend hope like other great cities:

> Today Bombay with a density of population about four times that of modern New York, probably resembles more nearly, in social and economic ethos, the New York of a hundred years ago. Certainly it contains grinding mills, both metaphorical and actual; it contains wickedness, ruthlessness and heartlessness. But it is also for many people, including some of the poorest, a place of endeavour, activity, chances, succour, a place to seek your fortune and even find it. Battered, dirty, overcrowded and choked with exhaust fumes it may be but it is also a city of dreams. (Tindall 1992: 22, 23)

> Mumbai is known as a cosmopolitan metropolis. Though capital of the Marathi speaking state, the proportion of Marathi speaking population in Mumbai has declined from around 45 per cent in 1981 to 42.6 per cent in 1987–88. The majority of the population (57.4 per cent) of the city belongs to the non Marathi linguistic groups, Gujaratis accounting for 18.6 per cent. (Vora and Palshikar 2003: 162)

If you go closer though, you will find that cosmopolitan image-shattering—people are identified by their origin, caste, and class. Mumbai's citizens do not observe niceties when it comes to people. People are

Madrasi (if you are from the south), Gujarati, *bhaiyya* (all north Indians), or worse, *landya*, if you are a Muslim. Communally, Mumbai has been somewhat of a trouble spot, though not as much as some other places in north India. The city saw its first Hindu–Muslim clash in 1893 (Maharashtra State Gazetteers Department 2001: 192, 193) and since then, there is a steady attempt to polarize the city on these lines. There is a worsening of relations, making people huddle together for safety.

Tindall (1992: 45) writes about:

> ... the 'founding father of Bombay', Gerald Aungier who encouraged settlement from elsewhere, and made plans for each religious or racial community to have its own official representatives. A French physician Dellon, who visited Bombay during the years of Aungier's rule, wrote admiringly of it as a city where they grant liberty to all strangers of what religion or nation soever to settle themselves, and exempt them from all manner of taxes for the first twenty years.

One of the communities was the Banias, who were given their own burning grounds by Aungier. The city then was a city of refuge as it still is today, but communal riots created a refugee status for many of its citizens within its protective confines.

The Muslims of Bombay or Mumbai are not a homogeneous community.

> Although distinguished from Hindus, Parsis and Christians, the Muslims of Bombay city were by no means a single entity. As a prominent Muslim pointed out in 1908, 'the most essential fact to be learnt about the Mahomedan community of Bombay is that there is no such community. There are various communities in this city which profess this religion.' The 1901 Census listed some fourteen different categories of Muslims in the city with a further category 'unspecified' and the list might be even further refined. (Masselos 2007: 15, 16)

Amongst Muslims we can discern three divisions. First there are business communities like Bohras and Momins who migrated to the city during the colonial period. Second, there are the Konkani Muslims who came in search of source of livelihood, and third there are North Indian Muslims who have acquired greater significance in recent years. In colonial days, the Mumbai Muslims were divided between the Muslim League and the Congress. After Partition, the League gradually became insignificant. Muslims basically looked towards the Congress as their protector. (Vora and Palshikar 2003: 163, 164)

The chapter by Vora and Palshikar notes that after the riots, the Muslims shifted allegiance to the Samajwadi Party, which has its roots in UP.

The Bombay of old had clear demarcations, as evident from Mariam Dossal's writing:

By the 1840s, Bombay island covered an area of eighteen square miles. The European quarter or 'Fort', located in the southern part of the island, was protected by ramparts or town walls which extended from Apollo Bunder in the south to Bazaar Gate in the north. (Dossal 1996: 16)

Dossal gives an idea of how the city looked like in those days:

From its inception, Bombay, like other British colonial towns, had been divided into the 'Fort' or 'White Town' or European quarter and the 'Black Town' or Indian quarter. The two were physically separated by an esplanade or open maidan. (Dossal 1996: 16)

The separation between the European and Indian quarters expressed and perpetuated a spatial co-existence of two economies at work, the western capitalist and the indigenous bazaar economy. The southern Fort contained the central business district, in which were located the offices of the European agency houses, the growing number of banks, shipping and insurance companies, and warehouses. (Dossal 1996: 17)

The Indian quarter was the locale of domestic economy. The Indian bazaar merchants had settled in the quarter north of the Fort, outside the town halls. They lived in mohallas or localities consisting of four or five storied buildings, with the pedhi or shop usually situated on the ground floor of the same building. Often the lanes and roads of a mohalla ended in a cul de sac, making movement from one area to another difficult. No separate work place or distinct central business district developed here. What did exist were localities which were the centres of wholesale trade in specific commodities or residential areas of different castes and communities, many of whom were engaged in a particular occupation or in the manufacturing of a particular commodity. (Dossal 1996: 17)

Dossal (1996: 17) further says: 'Apart from the merchants, the Indian town was also the home of small manufacturers, retailers, peddlers, servants and a large number of temporary inhabitants in Bombay....' Also,

In the Indian town, residential patterns based on occupation and caste were common. The julahas or weavers, for instance, lived mainly on Duncan Road, at Byculla and near Babula Tank. Carpenters were to be found mainly in Khetwadi. Mandvi's southern section was the business quarter of the richest cloth merchants, while the northern portion contained sona chandi or the bullion bazaar. The granaries and major warehouses were grouped along the eastern foreshore. Wholesale trade in copper was concentrated in Paidhoni, in drugs at Ganeshwadi, and sugar and ghee in Mandvi. Bazaar Gate Street was the headquarters of the Hindu shroffs, indigenous financiers, crucial to the coastal and local trade of Bombay. Mandvi and Chakla were the most important commercial areas in the Indian quarter. Fronted by the docks, with warehouses and wholesale shops in close proximity, they constituted the heart of the Indian town. (Dossal 1996: 19, 20)

Meera Kosambi (1996: 7) gives a clear picture of the diversity of British Bombay. She writes: 'The Bombayites of the nineteenth century presented a large spectrum of racial, religious, regional and linguistic diversity, arranged within a broadly hierarchical and non competitive pyramid.'

Kosambi (1996: 7, 8) further goes on to says:

> Over the century, the city's population grew from an estimated 200,000 to almost a million. At the Census of 1881, the linguistic profile of Bombay's population (totalling 773,196) showed that 50 per cent spoke Marathi as their mother tongue, 28 per cent spoke Gujarati (including Kutchi), 12 per cent Urdu (the language of North India Muslims and only one per cent English.... Classified by religion, 66 per cent were Hindus and 20 per cent Muslims.

The multicultural aspect of the city is reinforced by the special relationship the Mumbai police has with the shrine of Sufi saint Makhdum Fakih Ali or Makhdoom Baba in Mahim. The chambers of the senior inspector of police at Mahim Police Station has an ante room which is filled with interesting items. 'A pride of place is reserved for a ritualistic ceremony and has a plaque bearing the inscription: "Makhdoom Baba Sandal Greater Bombay Police Committee, established in 1920"' (Rao 2007: 188). A green cupboard has silver ornaments and other valuables which are ceremoniously carried to the Dargah on the first day of the Urs (a festival) held every December. During the 10-day annual Urs, the zonal Deputy Commissioner of Police leads a procession, and out of the three bands accompanying the procession, the Greater Mumbai Police

Band has the honour of leading it, followed by the Band of the Nawab of Murud Janjira and the Makhdoom Baba Committee.

During the 10-day Urs festival celebrated every year around this time (beginning on the 13th day of Shaval, the Muslim calendar), lakhs of devotees visit the Mahim Dargah or the Dargah of Baba Makhdoom Ali in Mumbai. Like every year, in the 8,000-strong procession to the Dargah on Wednesday were two policemen from each of the 84 police stations across the city. And they were not there to maintain security. They were renewing the collective faith of the Mumbai police in the Sufi saint, a faith that dates back hundreds of years. In fact, each year, it is a representative of the Mumbai police which is the first to offer the 'chaddar' at the tomb on the first day of the festival. The procession begins from Mahim Police Station, which is believed to have been once the residence of the saint who lived between 1335 and 1360 AD during the reign of Mughal ruler Ferozeshah Tughlaq. A room adjacent to the office of the senior inspector of Mahim Police Station is a veritable museum with a steel cupboard inside it housing articles believed to have belonged to the saint. The cupboard, it is said, was purchased in 1920 by a British senior police inspector named Raymond Esquire as a tribute to the saint he worshipped. (Ali 2002)

Despite this continuing secular tradition, it is ironic that the Mumbai police earned a harsh reputation for its handling of the 1992–93 communal riots (Srikrishna 1998).

The Rise of Shiv Sena

In an interview for the research of this book, former Chief Minister Manohar Joshi says that the Shiv Sena started off as a social work organization. Mr Joshi, who joined the Sena six months after its formation in

June 1966, is one of its oldest and articulate members. When Balasaheb Thackeray, then an aspiring cartoonist, was working with the *Free Press Journal*, he found a lot of south Indians there—the Marathi presence was meagre. 'He must have thought that by organising the Marathi people he could get them some justice', says Joshi. In those days, *Marmik*, the weekly magazine, published lists of companies and their employees, revealing south Indian workers in great numbers. Thackeray used to appeal for jobs through *Marmik*, and spurred by his father, Thackeray launched the Shiv Sena. His father, Keshav Thackeray or Prabodhankar, named the organization Shiv Sena, which had a humble launch. Its first major rally was held on 30 June 1966 at Shivaji Park, a venue that is still popular with the Sena even today.

'It was a modest agenda—to get Marathi people jobs', says Joshi. He explains:

> Balasaheb also brought some other things to the party—no caste and class differences—and I believe in the last 43 years, he has not discriminated against anyone. This was also evident when he chose me as chief minister in 1995, even though I am Brahmin. He did not take this aspect into consideration.

However, there was much resentment in the party over this choice, which was to have far-reaching repercussions.

The party, when it was formed, did not believe in politics and was more focused on social work. Like Uddhav Thackeray, Executive President of the Sena now, who held a massive blood donation camp in 2010, the senior Thackeray too used to plant trees and conduct blood donation camps. In those days, civic amenities and clean roads were big issues. Joshi could see Balasaheb's popularity was growing steadily. He says he has attended hundreds of meetings and he never found a crowd of less than 1 lakh at any of them. 'There are two types of leaders, Balasaheb was an original leader and others like me, who hold a number of posts, to whom people come for help, etc.', grins Joshi. But he is amazed at his leader's crowd-pulling abilities which he says was tremendous. The

Sena fought its first election in the Thane Municipal Corporation and won it, and in 1968 it won 42 seats in the Bombay [later, Brihanmumbai (greater Mumbai)] Municipal Corporation (BMC) in alliance with the Praja Socialist Party (PSP).

Joshi was the third Sena mayor of Bombay. He says, 'People of Mumbai loved us and voted for our party. The roaring tiger was our symbol and our orange flag was the flag of Shivaji.'

The first time the party adopted Hindutva was in 1987, in the assembly election of Dr Ramesh Prabhoo from Vile Parle. Explaining the party's transition from a social work oriented, pro-Marathi party, Mr Joshi says 'that while working for the Marathi speaking people we were limited to Mumbai but once we adopted Hindutva we spread all over the state'. In 1990, the Sena contested assembly elections and Joshi was the party's first leader of the Opposition in the assembly. He sees clearly the connection between the party's rise to power in the state and Hindutva: 'Ours is a staunch Hindutva, it is the Hindutva of action.'

While Hindutva came at a later stage and the alliance with the Bharatiya Janata Party (BJP) in 1984, the Sena had brief dalliances with the PSP and the Muslim League in the Bombay civic corporation. The League leader, Ghulam Mohammed Banatwalla, and Thackeray once led a rally in 1979 and addressed a joint meeting in Mastan Talao in south Mumbai, recalls Joshi. Muslims shouted 'Jai Maharashtra', the rallying cry of the Sena. Thackeray promised them everything, provided they shouted the slogan. The issue was that of goat slaughter in Mumbai. Goats were first stunned and then killed and the League objected to that. Thackeray assured them that this would be stopped. 'It was a sight to see Mr Banatwalla and Mr Thackeray marching in a sea of saffron and green flags. Some other issues like amenities for slum dwellers and reduction in railway tickets were sorted out but the honeymoon was quickly over', says Joshi.

Before allying with the BJP, Thackeray also took up issues which he perceived were close to Hindus. The Durgadi Fort, where there was a mosque and a temple at the top, was in dispute, and Hindus were prohibited from going there. Thackeray defied this order and launched a struggle. The Mahikawati Temple too was on his list. The Muslims contended this was a mosque. Joshi explains that Mahikawati was like a precursor to the Babri Masjid issue in a small way. At that time, Thackeray emerged as a leader of Hindus and his standing was endorsed when the Sena won the assembly election in 1987 in Vile Parle.

On the connection between the Rashtriya Swayamsevak Sangh (RSS) and the Sena, Joshi says he was a member of the RSS for a year while studying in school, and even Mr Thackeray attended the *shakha* (or branch). 'He probably got the idea of Hindutva from there', he adds. However, he sees differences between the RSS *shakha* and the Shiv Sena *shakha*. The RSS *shakhas* are for imparting Hindutva and nationalism, but the purpose of the Sena *shakha* is social work.

Joshi feels the Sena is the strongest Hindutva party in India. However, if there is no injustice to Hindus, there is nothing to fight for. He says:

> Our main objection is pampering of people based on religion. The country belongs to all. We have not taken up the issue of Hindu Rashtra, it does not mean you push Muslims out but we are against anti nationalist Muslims. After the demolition of the Babri Masjid, there were riots all over the country and in Mumbai too. The stronger relationship of Muslims is not with Babar. But Muslims started rioting [and] beating up Hindus and we had to side [with] Hindus. So many lives were saved because of us. It was not action but reaction.

'Votes have spoiled this country. The Congress supports Muslims for votes which are guaranteed since Muslims vote en bloc, they are wooed', Joshi points out. The pampering policy of the Congress governments hampers progress. But now he feels things are better—Hindus and Muslims are living together.

As Chief Minister, he opposed the *Srikrishna Commission Report* and spoke for two days in the state assembly. He said concrete instances of mistakes in the Report were pointed out and Justice Srikrishna was misguided by officials. Joshi went to Ayodhya on 7 December 1992 as his flight was diverted the earlier day and even made speeches there. 'It was a historic event but we could not see it', he said. Joshi's speeches while campaigning for his assembly elections led to his election being set aside, but he won the case in the Supreme Court in December 1995. 'I am the first man to have won on Hindutva in the Supreme Court', he points out happily.

On 11 December 1995, a three-judge Bench of the Supreme Court in Joshi's case ruled that this was not an appeal on the ground of religion. It observed: 'In our opinion, a mere statement that the first Hindu State will be established in Maharashtra is by itself not an appeal for votes on the ground of religion, but the expression at best of such a hope' (Tarkunde 1996). Mr Joshi's election was set aside by the Bombay High Court mainly on the ground that they had committed a corrupt practice as defined by Section 123(3) of the Representation of the People Act, 1951. The corrupt practice defined in Section 123(3) consists of 'the appeal by a candidate or his agent or by any other person with the consent of a candidate or his election agent to vote or refrain from voting for any person on the ground of his religion....'

Joshi is said to have stated in one of his election speeches, 'the first Hindu State will be established in Maharashtra' (Tarkunde 1996).

While Joshi was saved, his leader was not so lucky. It was in Ramesh Prabhoo's election in Vile Parle that the party tested its Hindutva. It was also the election which earned Bal Thackeray a ban from voting for six years till 2006. In the 1987 Maharashtra assembly bye-election, Shiv Sena's candidate Ramesh Prabhoo won, defeating Prabhakar Kunte of the Congress party. Kunte filed an election petition in the Bombay High Court challenging Prabhoo's election and he also brought in Shiv Sena chief Bal Thackeray's election speeches. The court issued a notice to Thackeray under Section 99 of the Representation of the People Act. In April 1989, the Bombay high court upheld Kunte's contention and Prabhoo's election was set aside. Prabhoo and Thackeray moved the Supreme Court which on 11 December 1995 upheld the Bombay High

Court decision and also held Bal Thackeray guilty of corrupt election practices, of appealing to voters to vote for Prabhoo on the ground of his religion as a Hindu. In 1998, the Election Commission barred Thackeray from voting in state or national elections for six years.

Justices J. S. Verma, N. P. Singh, and Venkataswami made clear their hope that the judgement would serve a deterrent purpose. 'We cannot help recording our distress at these kind of speeches given by a top leader of a political party', they recorded. 'The lack of restraint in the language used and the derogatory terms used therein to refer to a group of people in an election speech is indeed to be condemned.' The judges concluded:

> This is essential not only for maintaining decency and propriety in the election campaign, but also for the preservation of the proper and time-honoured values forming part of our cultural heritage and for a free and fair poll in a secular democracy. The offending speeches in the present case discarded the cherished values of our rich cultural heritage and tended to erode the secular polity. We say this with the fervent hope that our observation has some chastening effect in the future election campaigns. (Swami and Venkatesan 1999)

There is little doubt about the Hindutva proclivities of the Sena and its attempt to polarize communities. In the Vile Parle campaign, Thackeray clearly appealed for people to vote for Hinduism and made derogatory references to the Muslims. While Thackeray was hardly muted by this order, the formation of the Shiv Sena on 19 June 1966 did not really give a premonition of things to follow. The Sena altered the course of politics in Maharashtra forever. Many studies, such as Mary Fainsod Katzenstein (1979) endorse the viewpoint that the local people did lose out on jobs and that was the root cause of their restlessness. The Sena grew out of this desire to give the Maharashtrians dignity and status and an economic push. People joining the party had to take an oath which clearly outlines the objectives and intent of the party:

> Maharashtrians should not sell property to a non-Maharashtrian, and if such a thing takes place it should be reported to the Shiv Sena kacheri (office), Maharashtrian shopkeepers should get their wares from Maharashtrian wholesale dealers and they should be more courteous to their customers, Maharashtrian employers should employ only Maharashtrians, they should boycott all Udipi hotels and should not purchase any article from non-Maharashtrian shopkeepers. (Gupta 1982: 128)

There are 11 points listed as part of the oath.

Gupta (1982: 39) further writes:

> Since 1964, Bal Thackeray, through *Marmik* (a cartoon weekly launched by Thackeray), steadily popularised an ideology which the Shiv Sena was to embrace explicitly in 1966. He made vivid the point that Maharashtrians were being deprived of jobs and economic opportunities in Bombay by non-Maharashtrian migrants to the city. In the early years of the Shiv Sena, the South Indians faced the brunt of its wrath, though of late the Shiv Sena has also attacked migrants from other states as well, such as from Uttar Pradesh and Punjab.

Initially the Sena agitations were directed against other communities, first the hoteliers from Udipi in Karnataka and later when it sharpened its Hindutva stand, against Muslims.

'He [Thackeray] advocated the concept of benevolent dictatorship as India, he believes, is burdened with a crippled democracy, where votes are meaningless' (Gupta 1982: 139). 'India needs a benevolent dictator', he declared, and 'the Shiv Sena is right to function in that direction'. In the issue dated 2 August 1972 of *Rajshree*, Bal Thackeray admitted that he admired Hitler and also respected him as an artist. Hitler, minus his anti-Semitism, he said elsewhere, was a good model (Gupta 1982: 139).

At the Durgadi Fort in Kalyan in 1968, for the first time Thackeray raised the issue of 'pro Pakistani Muslims' and how his party was going to throw them out of India (Purandare 1999: 102–04). After the riots over the Maharashtra–Karnataka border issue, which paralysed Mumbai, the Sena made its presence felt in the Bhiwandi riots of 1970. The Shiv Jayanti procession was the event that sparked off the riots which spread to Jalgaon and Mahad (Purandare 1999: 134, 135). Over 40 people were killed in May 1970 in Bhiwandi, a power loom town outside Mumbai, and in Jalgaon too, 39 people lost their lives. Justice D. P. Madon of the Bombay High Court was asked to probe the riots. That was when the Sena emerged as the self-appointed saviour of the Hindus in Bhiwandi, which has a dominant Muslim population. Justice Madon has indicted the Shiv Sena in his report for the communal situation in Bhiwandi and the use of anti-Muslim slogans during the Shiv Jayanti procession. The Bhiwandi episode was the first in which the Shiv Sena fought on the streets in the garb of 'saviour of the Hindus' (Purandare 1999: 138).

Thus, Bal Thackeray expanded his 'sons of the soil' approach and now elevated himself to a defender of the faith. In 1992–93, he would once again emerge as the man who saved Mumbai from the Muslim hordes. The role of the Sena in taking on the Communists and the murder of a prominent member of the party, Krishna Desai, also altered the working-class relations in Mumbai. In 1984, the year when communal riots broke out in Bhiwandi and Mumbai, the Sena clearly established its Hindutva identity. Over 100 people died in Bhiwandi and 87 in Mumbai, apart from those who died in the Thane and Kalyan riots (Purandare 1999: 241). This was how the Sena's policies of protecting Hindus and attacking 'anti-national' Muslims was clearly enunciated. From then on the Sena stepped in vociferously whenever it perceived an 'attack' on Hinduism and it reached its peak on the issue of the Babri Masjid when it tried to organize a Rath Yatra in 1986. For the first time, it fought elections with the banner 'Garv Se Kaho Ham Hindu Hain' in the by-elections to the Vile Parle assembly segment in Mumbai in 1987 (Purandare 1999: 312).

Jayant Lele points out:

> ... long lasting and gruesome riots occurred across India between 1980 and 1984. in Maharashtra, starting with 1978,

victims of such riots included not only Muslims but dalits and tribals as well. All these riots were part of an ideological movement aimed at creating a homogenous Hindu consciousness. (Vora and Palshikar quoted in Lele 1996: 201)

On 23 January 1989, the Sena launched *Saamna*, its mouthpiece, which was to play a definitive role later in the Mumbai riots of 1992–93. As a newspaper which advocated the militant cause of Hindutva, *Saamna* became a tool in the Sena's hands to spread its philosophy. After the demolition of the Babri Masjid, the Sena chief who had dispatched his men to take part in the mayhem took the credit for the assault and was proud of it. When riots broke out in Mumbai on 6 December, the party went headlong into supporting the *maha aarti*s (public religious gatherings) on the roads to counter the Muslims offering *namaz* on the streets. Through *Saamna*, Thackeray used the Gandhi (Radhabai) *chawl* incident in Jogeshwari, where six Hindus were killed, to launch a fresh phase of riots in January 1993. Between 9 and 12 January the city went wild; Shiv Sainiks had a free run and they went on a killing and burning spree. Thackeray called this a spontaneous reaction and referred to it as the Hindus opening their third eye. Mumbai was in shambles. Over 500 people lost their lives in January alone in the bloodbath. In the words of Justice B. N. Srikrishna:

> From 8 January 1993, at least there is no doubt that the Shiv Sena and Shiv Sainiks took the lead in organizing attacks on Muslims and their properties under the guidance of several leaders of the Shiv Sena from the level of the shakha pramukh to the Shiv Sena pramukh Bal Thackeray who like a veteran General, commanded his loyal Shiv Sainiks to retaliate by organised attacks against Muslims. (*Srikrishna* 1998: 22, Volume I)

From then on there was no stopping the Sena; it rode to power in the next assembly elections in 1995, and Thackeray's dream of flying the saffron flag on top of the state secretariat was fulfilled. Though clearly indicted in the *Srikrishna Commission Report*, the saffron alliance rejected the report when it was tabled in 1998 in the assembly saying it was one-sided:

> Bal Thackeray brands all non-Hindu gatherings as anti national. But his condemnation is fiercest when attacking the Muslims.... His views on Kashmir and Pakistan are similarly coloured by his anti Muslim feeling. He believes that Muslims are agents of Pakistan and that all Muslims, including Muslim ministers are creating riots in India at the behest of Pakistan. (Gupta 1982: 137)

The Sena's appeal to young men with its promise of macho power and violence was also irresistible. Thomas Blom Hansen in *Violence in Urban India, Identity, Politics and the Post Colonial City* (2005: 48) writes that the Shiv Sena's general ostracizing of alien-others believed to dominate Bombay, its appeals to an aggressive masculinity and the security and sense of self-esteem it provided to young, frustrated males in the metropolis was, and remains, undoubtedly more central to its success than its articulation of any specific class interests of certain upwardly mobile Marathi speakers. Hansen goes on to say that the movement's determination to use violence in most situations, its celebration of youth, masculinity, and the 'ordinary', and the cynicism of its leadership have, since the 1960s, created enormous de facto legal impunity for the public actions of Sainiks and their leaders and a concomitant fear of the movement among its adversaries and victims (Hansen 2005: 48, 49).

Vora and Palshikar (2003: 163) say that the:

> ... south Indian population constitutes only 6 per cent of the total population of Mumbai. South Indians had become the targets of anger of the Marathi youth when the Shiv Sena began its political career as an organization of the sons of the soil. Things have changed lately, with the Sena having changed its

stance. It no longer targets a particular linguistic community; indeed it has been deliberately befriending different linguistic communities on the Hindutva platform.

An article in *Mumbai Mirror* (Sadhwani 5 May 2010) perhaps exemplifies this:

> Three days after a Muslim businessman was not allowed to stay in the house he had recently rented, he got support from unexpected quarters—the Shiv Sena and the Maharashtra Navnirman Sena (MNS). Both parties stood by Chembur resident Majid Khan, and made it clear that he has every right to live in Venkatesh Sadan, where he had rented a flat and from where the society had bared him from moving in—just because he is a Muslim.

Yet this is an exceptional intervention.

However, over the years the party has weakened. Politically, the riots sowed the seeds of the disillusionment with the Shiv Sena. Many of its lumpen cadres were left stranded by the party with little or no legal support. Even victims like the Banes did not receive any help. Few are willing to speak up against their former party, but the fact remains that the Sena, after it came to power in 1995 and ruled the state, became the establishment. As Gerard Heuze (1996: 218) points out presciently:

> Today the Shiv Sena has become 'fat', as many cadres and activists observe. It is now ritualized, bureaucratized and structured. It has working machinery that does not depend upon people's initiative. It is difficult to say what is more characteristic, this trend, or the fact that Shiv Sainiks regret it. It seems that many expressions of violence, tension and provocation are related to the fear that the party is being institutionalized, ceasing to be a social movement, and the most dreaded fate, beginning to 'look like the Congress Party'.

Over the years it lost the fire of the anti–south-Indian movement and later the Muslim hatred that had forged so much unity among its workers from the *shakhas*. As a party it has survived on the issue of the 'Marathi *manoos*' and its upliftment. That was its unique selling proposition. Once the headiness of rioting and murder and looting diminished, there was little else to sustain the party. Raj Thackeray, nephew of Bal Thackeray, the founder of the Shiv Sena, has broken away and formed his own outfit—the Maharashtra Navnirman Sena (MNS) in 2006. Raj has found a new enemy—the north Indian migrant—to propel his party's aspirations and hate agenda forward. A series of attacks on north Indians and vicious campaigns against how they are depriving the locals of jobs and entitlements has struck a chord in the minds of the Maharashtrians who voted for him in large numbers in the 15th Lok Sabha elections held in May 2009. In the state assembly elections later that year, the MNS won 13 seats. The Marathi vote was divided and the Sena lost Mumbai and Thane unexpectedly in the general election. Clearly, the Sena has lost more than votes: it has lost its Konkani Marathi base and many of the young Sainiks have switched loyalties to a younger, more aggressive avatar of the party. The streetfighting or '*rada*' culture of the Sena has been taken up by the MNS. For the Sena then, aggression and hatred are necessary as fuel. Over the years it has toned down its approach, wooing migrants and trying to be more inclusive. For the party it is a moment of truth. MNS seems to have cut the ground from underneath it, leaving it a floundering, virtually leaderless unit, and Uddhav Thackeray the heir apparent with his soft-spoken, non-aggressive approach can only watch his more popular cousin moulded in the style of his father, emerge as the new challenge for the Marathi vote base.

It was after the impressive debut of the MNS in the Lok Sabha elections in 2009 that Uddhav Thackeray was plagued with the question of his party's future. Though shattered by the MNS show, in public, the executive president of the Shiv Sena was both unrealistic and optimistic. The MNS did not really dent the Sena vote, he maintained at his post-general election results press conference. That was the unrealistic part. Next came the optimistic portion, that in the assembly polls, voters would return to the Shiv Sena as they had realized that the MNS would not win any seats and voting for Raj Thackeray meant a vote for the Congress.

With the waning influence of the senior Mr Thackeray, over the years, Uddhav has managed to isolate himself with a small unimpressive coterie of leaders who cannot replace the party's stalwarts. As a result, first, Narayan Rane left in 2005—a major blow to the party after the exit of Chhagan Bhujbal in 1991—and later Raj Thackeray who went ahead and formed the MNS, a copycat party. Rane went public with his allegations of corruption and lack of democracy in the Sena, while Raj more specifically, targeted his cousin. The Maharashtra assembly election of 2009 has showed that the party is virtually shot to pieces, though it won 44 seats, lower than the 52 it won in 1990 in its first major election. After the Lok Sabha polls where it got only 17 per cent of the vote share and 11 seats, mostly in rural parts of the state, the Sena chose to bury its head in the sand. It discounted the power of the MNS to rock the boat, the charisma of Raj Thackeray and the fact that the 'Marathi *manoos*' was still so disillusioned after four decades of the Sena's existence. While toeing the Hindutva line, Uddhav tried to forge links with the north Indians and other communities in a bid to give his party a more broad-based approach. However, Raj Thackeray's blistering attack on migrants countered this and he went from strength to strength. The MNS knocked back over 100,000 votes in many of the 12 seats it contested in the Lok Sabha, but in the assembly polls, that promise transformed into 13 wins statewide. Though the Sena saved faced in Thane, in Mumbai it won four seats, two less than the MNS, and in its stronghold of Marathwada, it put up a pathetic performance, a far cry from the total 62 seats it had won in the 2004 polls.

The degeneration of the Sena has not come about suddenly. Mr Bal Thackeray had a coterie of advisers ranging from the first Sena Member of Legislative Assembly (MLA) Wamanrao Mahadik, Sharad Acharya, Dattaji Salvi, Datta Nalavade, Manohar Joshi, Leeladhar Dhake, and later a second rung of leadership, many of whom became ministers during the only time it was in power in the state. Now, Dhake and Nalavade are sidelined, as also Diwakar Raote who created a base for the Sena in

Marathwada. Senior Sena leader Madhukar Sarpotdar's son Atul is with the MNS and his daughter-in-law Shilpa contested the Lok Sabha and assembly polls on an MNS ticket. For the assembly polls, some of Raote's supporters were ignored in the ticket race and the results are there for all to see in Aurangabad and other places. Old timers like Ramesh Prabhoo who fought on a Hindutva plank for the first time for the Sena, have left the party, and Manohar Joshi, former Lok Sabha speaker and senior party leader, does not enjoy Uddhav's confidence.

The Shiv Sena looked weak already after the 2009 assembly elections, winning only 44 seats (the BJP won 46), but the death of its supreme leader and founder Bal Thackeray on 17 November 2012 seemed to spell doom. Raj Thackeray and his aggressive MNS looked set to offer a challenge to the Sena's politics but events in the future proved that was not to be. The anti-incumbency wave in the 2014 general elections and the larger than life prime ministerial candidate Narendra Modi gave a fillip to the BJP, which stormed to power at the centre and eventually in Maharashtra in 2014. The BJP won handsomely and rocked the Shiv Sena's aspirations with 23 seats of 48 in Lok Sabha, while the Sena won 18. The National Democratic Alliance trumped the Congress and Nationalist Congress Party (NCP) with an overall count of 42 seats. The three-term rule of the Congress–NCP alliance in Maharashtra was riddled with corruption and irrigation scams and caved into a populist wave in the Maharashtra assembly elections. The BJP outwitted its long-time ally bagging 122 seats against the Sena's 63 and the decision to contest separately and not in alliance for the state assembly elections proved to be more detrimental to the Shiv Sena. Though the Sena went on to hold its own in the elections to the prestigious and rich municipal corporation of Greater Mumbai in 2017, winning 84 of the 227 seats, two more than the BJP, where the Marathi vote and the old ruse of voting against the 'outsider' helped, the Sena is not the force it has once been. Its fortunes are tied to the BJP which is gaining more and more ground in the state, and treats it in a stepmotherly fashion. The Sena has to fall back on its old 'sons of the soil must get preference' vote bank, which is the foundation of its existence. One cannot write off the Shiv Sena which still has a base in a constituency where ethnic divisions hold sway in the minds of its followers.

2

COW PROTECTION, TEMPLE, AND MOSQUE DISPUTES GO WAY BACK:

A CHRONICLE OF COMMUNAL RIOTS IN BOMBAY CITY

The Riots of 1893 and the Cow Protection Movement

A century before the Babri Masjid demolition on 6 December 1992, Mumbai saw its first bloody Hindu–Muslim clashes. Unlike the desolate mosque, it was cow protection that was possibly at its root. Lokmanya Tilak writing in the *Kesari* on 29 August 1893 disagreed with this. 'To connect this riot with movements like the cow protection movement, as *The Times of India* has done, is to incite the Muslims indirectly', he says (Maharashtra State Archives Department, *Mahratta*, Poona, 4 July 1941, quotations from English translation of Tilak's original article). In the first part of the article, he writes,

Napoleon used to say that the French revolution would have been averted, if guns and bullets had been used at the proper moment. The same rule applies to the case of all riots. Had the police dealt properly with the mob that emerged from the Jumma Masjid at night with cries of Din Din (the faith), the riots could hardly have spread as it did afterwards.

Later on in his article he says it is perfectly obvious that the Hindus did not take the initiative in starting the riot and had police help reached in time they would have never joined the fight. He enunciates the principle of self-defence and the idea that Muslims are being favoured by the then rulers. Tilak added:

> If peace and goodwill are to be maintained amongst Hindus and Muslims, it is quite necessary that each should realise that the other is able to retaliate. It is an old saying amongst us that people of similar nature and in similar difficulty can live amicably. Tiger and tiger can live together as well as lamb and lamb. But if we attempt to keep the tiger and the lamb together, it is certain that as soon as the keeper's attention flags, they will attack each other. Hindus and Mussalmans come under the first and not the second category. This has been proved by the history of the Mahrattas and by the recent riots.

Decades later Manohar Joshi, the then Chief Minister of Maharashtra, in his testimony to the Srikrishna Commission in the context of the 1992–93 riots elaborated on the theory of 'retaliation' and self-defence. He says that this word has been used as a synonym for the Marathi word *pratikriya* (reaction). According to him, it has been used to denote a spontaneous and natural reaction to the incidents that were taking place. The use of the expression 'constructive retaliation' in Shiv Sena's statement of case denotes that 'the retaliation was not intended to be destructive but was for the purpose of self-defence and therefore, constructive'. He expounded it by saying that Muslims had tried to take revenge by terrorizing and frightening Hindu masses by using the demolition of Babri Masjid as an excuse 'merely because the Hindus had picked up the courage to retaliate' (*Srikrishna* 1998).

However, well before the 1893 riots there seemed to be enough provocation in the form of the cow protection movement. Tension was in the air even before that mob of Muslims came out of the mosque and started to riot. A 'strictly confidential' précis of the history of the movement against the slaughter of 'kine' (an archaic word for cows, cattle) in the Bombay Presidency up to the end of August 1893, just before the communal riots, is illustrative of how the movement aimed at creating discord (Maharashtra State Archives Department, File no. 1002, 1893, Home Department Special Branch). The Bombay Society for the Preservation of Cows and Buffaloes (or the Gaorakshak Sabha) was established on 28 July 1887 with Sir Dinshawji Manekji Petit as its president. The Society's patrons were Chaturbhuj Morarji, Bamanji Dinshawji Petit, Damodar Thackersey Mulji, Byramji Dinshawji Pandey, and Damodar Gokuldas. The Society's chief aims were to adopt measures to prevent the slaughter of kine and buffaloes and to memorialize the government for an enactment of a law to prohibit the slaughter of kine and buffaloes in India, among other things.

In February 1888 it was reported from Ahmedabad that the Mahajans (a powerful caste) and other Hindus of Dholera, disliking the slaughter of kine, were trying to make it uncomfortable for the butchers residing in that place. An essay contest on the evils of cow slaughter was organized in April 1889 and things gathered momentum. One Shriman Swami, Honorary Secretary, Central Committee, Cow Memorial Fund, Allahabad, held lectures at several places in Bombay calling for a ban on cow slaughter. On 29 June 1889, it was reported from Bombay that Shriram Swami had arrived there in the preceding month and had delivered three lectures against kine killing. Some of the non-Hindu supporters of the cow preservation society, apprehending that the government viewed its proceedings as an indirect political movement, were thinking of severing their connection with it.

COW PROTECTION, TEMPLE, AND MOSQUE DISPUTES GO WAY BACK

In February 1890, a notice was issued in Surat by one Tilakchand Tarachand that there would be a public discussion between Muhammedans and Hindus on the subject of killing cows. The discussion was not held as Moulvi Hafiz Gulam Muhammed of Rander, who had been speaking on the other side, would not be responsible for the Mussalmans keeping quiet. Meanwhile shelters for cows were being built and donations collected. On 25 April 1890, a meeting of the Society for the Protection of Cows was held at the Mulji Jaitha Market, Bombay, under President Damodar Thackersey Mulji. The Committee's report was read which showed that subscriptions collected from 2 August 1887 to 30 June 1888 amounted to ₹ 11,932. The firm of Morarji Gokuldas presented 83,000 suitable cattle sheds. Mr Damodar Gokuldas Manji, one of the honorary secretaries, promised to give 100,000 bundles of grass for the use of the cows.

While the report records several events related to the cow protection society's activities, it says that in August 1891 an Urdu pamphlet, published by one Abdul Rahman of Bombay, was distributed in Ahmedabad strongly attacking the Gaorakshak Sabha and stating that the agitation was only meant to incite the Muhammedans and to cause ill will throughout the country.

On 14 November 1891, the Commissioner of Police, Bombay, wrote as follows:

> On the 7th instant the secretary of the Gaorakshak Mandali applied to the Commissioner of Police for permission to take out a procession of cows in the Native town, on the termination of a general meeting to be held on the 8th instant. The Commissioner declined to comply with the request on the ground that the Police had not had sufficient time to make enquiries as to the character of the processions. The Society consequently have given it up for the present, but will probably again bring the question forward next year, when it will be for the Commissioner of Police to determine whether such a procession should be permitted, taking into consideration the fact that it will be

an innovation in Bombay and calculated to attract the attention of the cow eating population, more especially the ignorant and fanatic portion thereof.

A clear indication was that the police smelled trouble and also suspected the intentions of the Society. While activities across the Presidency continued unabated, on 18 March 1893, Anna Martand Joshi, employed at the Government Central Press and a preacher of the Arya Samaj at Bombay, delivered a sermon at the Samaj Hall, Girgaum, before a large audience and spoke at length on the subject of 'cow protection'. The sermon was to the effect that the protection of the cow was in reality the protection of the country and its inhabitants. Printed copies of a pamphlet entitled the *Aryabhiviniya Aur Govilap* (an appeal of the Aryans and a cry of the cow) were distributed on the occasion and in the town the next day.

On 3 July 1893, the Commissioner of Police, Bombay, wrote as follows on the growing tension in the city:

> The agents of the Gaorakshak Mandali and their friends took occasion on the night before the Bakri Id (the 25th of June) to go about the town and ascertain in what places the Muhammedans intended on the following morning to kill cows, heifers etc. They even went so far as to enlist the sympathies of several Hindu constables, and late at night asked the Commissioner of Police to forbid the kine killing in toto. The Commissioner took only such measures as tended to prevent annoyance to Hindus, and the Mussalmans most cheerfully did all they were asked to do.
>
> To put a stop to a custom which has obtained in this city for hundreds of years would have been a very dangerous measure, but the Hindus are evidently bent on provoking a row sooner or later. Only the day before yesterday, when a very restive cow, which was being taken to the cattle pound, died, in consequence of having (accidentally as far as the Mussalman sepoy who was

taking her to the pound was concerned) fallen into a deep gutter, there was every likelihood of a disturbance. The Hindus would not allow the carcass to be removed for 16 hours, and they accused the sepoy of having maliciously killed the cow by a blow or two on her back with an umbrella! Fortunately the Commissioner of Police succeeded in getting evidence from some Hindus, who saw all that happened, which proved that the sepoy did not maltreat the animal in anyway. As is usual, it was due to some Hindus who did NOT [*my emphasis*] see what had occurred, that the outcry of maltreating the animal was raised.

The Riots of 1893

On 11 August 1893, the *Bombay Gazetteer* records that a very serious Hindu–Muhammedan riot took place (Maharashtra State Gazetteers Department 2001: 192–94). Fears of an outbreak had been prevalent for a few previous weeks, and shortly after midday on the date mentioned above, a large concourse of Muhammedans issued from the Jama Masjid and with shouts of 'Din Din' commenced to attack a Hindu temple in Hanuman lane. Within a very short time, the whole of Parel, Kamathipura, Grant Road, Chinchpugli, Mazagaon, and Tank Bunder were given over to mob law. The tumult was enormous. Not only did the Muhammedans attack all the Hindus they met, but the latter also retaliated and both sides rounded on the police. Sticks and stones were the only weapons employed by the rioters but they were used in many instances with murderous effect. At about 4 pm, the police commissioner secured the help of the army. The troops were posted in different areas, but the fighting still continued, and the infantry was required to fire on the mob in the Grant Road area. The raging crowds, rioting from street to street, desecrated temples and idols and inflicted fatal assaults. The riots continued on 12 August in all parts of the city, and casual murders and assaults took place on 13 August also. But from the evening of 13 August, tranquillity was gradually established. About 80 persons died as a result of injuries received during the rioting, and 1,500 were arrested by the police. The damage to temples and mosques, exclusive of the value of property stolen, amounted to three quarters of a lakh. The riots had deep repercussions in the Salsette Island and even beyond. The butchers at Bandra observed a strike in consequence (Maharashtra State Gazetteers Department 2001: 194).

The actual number of deaths has been attributed to 80 in the *Gazetteer* while Edwardes (1923) makes it 100, and Shashi Bhushan Upadhyay (1989) says it was 81. What was the basis for the riots of 1893 and why did things reach such a pass? Sir Percival Griffiths in his book *To Guard My People: The History of Indian Police* (1971: 281) says:

> The first serious communal riot to which we need to refer occurred in Bombay in 1893. Tilak at that time was on the warpath. He had not yet revived the Ganpati festival which later did so much to inflame communal feelings, but his speeches had already taken on an anti-Muslim tone and the tension between the two communities was growing. In the middle of the year, in the course of the Muharram celebrations, a Muslim mob had indulged in an orgy of violence in Kathiawar, in the course of which Hindu temples were destroyed. The inevitable reaction to the news of this incident was unscrupulously exploited by Hindu fanatics in Bombay, who began to demand vociferously that the government should prohibit the killing of cows and even of sheep and goats. Muslim extremists stirred up the lower classes of their community by telling them that their religion was in danger.

Griffiths (1971: 282) goes on to say:

> Although the communal situation had been brought under control, the riots left behind them a bitter legacy of sectarian rancor which was exacerbated when Tilak, in 1894, organised the public celebration of the Ganpati festival. An unhappy new pattern was now established and the troubles which recurred

annually on the occasion of the Muharram and the Ganpati festivals, added greatly to the burden of the police.

S. M. Edwardes, the first member of the Indian Civil Service to head the Bombay city police force (also author of the *Bombay Gazetteer*), says:

> It was 1893, the year in which mill workers also struck work that grave Hindu Muslim riots broke out on August 11, which afforded startling evidence of the deep sectarian antagonism which underlies the apparently calm surface of Indian social life and may at any moment burst forth in fury.
>
> The predisposing cause of the disturbance must be sought in the rioting which had occurred earlier in the year at Prabhas Patan in Kathiawar during the celebration of the Muharram, when a Mohammedan mob had destroyed temples and murdered several Hindus. For a fortnight or more before the outbreak of violence in Bombay, agitators had been at work among the more fanatical elements of the population and were assisted by leading Hindus, who convened large mass meeting to denounce the author of the outrage at Prabhas Patan. This agitation aroused intense irritation, which was aggravated by the persistent demand of the Hindus that the killing of cows, and sheep and goats, should be prohibited by the government. The Moslem population became fairly persuaded that the Hindus had the sympathy of the authorities and that their religion was in danger. (Edwardes 1923: 99–100)

Edwardes records in some details the events of 11 and 12 August when the city was witness to the worst possible communal rioting of that century. Ordinary people were also targeted and the city was paralysed much as it was a hundred years later. Finally, the military had to be called, troops sent in from Poona, and armed police requisitioned from Thane and other areas. The mobs attacked the native infantry (Edwardes 1923: 102) and it had to open fire several times. Edwardes notes that the effects of the outbreak were for the time being serious (Edwardes 1923: 102):

> All business in the City was suspended for nearly ten days and fifty thousand people chiefly women and children fled from Bombay to their homes up country. About 100 persons were killed and nearly 800 wounded during the progress of the rioting, while the loss of property was enormous. The damage done to Hindu temples and Moslem mosques amounted respectively to ₹51,300 and ₹23,200 exclusive of the property stolen from them which was estimated to be nearly two lakhs of rupees.
>
> About 1,500 were arrested for rioting robbery and trespass.

This was followed by the plague riots of 9 March 1898 (Maharashtra State Gazetteers Department 2001: 195), which started off when plague searchers tried to remove an affected person from a Muslim settlement at Ripon cross road. The rioters attacked plague hospitals and spread to various parts of the city which was also celebrating Holi at that time. By next day though the riots were under control, 19 persons were killed and 42 wounded. Of the 247 arrested, 205 were convicted.

While there are many views as to why the riots in 1893 took place, the strictly confidential précis which is rather detailed in the original, clearly indicates some tensions brewing among the two communities. The cow protection movement may not have been the only factor but its role cannot be discounted. Whether it really led to polarizing communities is the question. Even if one trawls through the records of Bombay's past in the police files and in newspaper clippings, there is always an allusion to its history of communal peace. There are always attempts at dialogue by holding meetings, by having peace committees or joint meetings between communities especially in early 20th century.

Shashi Bhushan Upadhyay (1989) tries to argue,

> [A]lthough the intensity of the riot in 1893 in Bombay showed strong communal sentiments on both sides and the workers

majority of them being Marathas, participated on the Hindu side, it did not lead to the development of a long-term communal consciousness in them. Nor was it the most representative of their activities.

The riots were a result of the cow protection activities launched by the Gaurakshak Sabha which was established on 28 July 1887.

Upadhyay points out that the intent and purpose of this society apart from the protection of cows are not known. Most probably it did not have any other motives.

However, he also says:

> ... that though not much evidence is available, it is perhaps about this time (in 1890) that the cow protection agitation was undergoing an imperceptible change. Its meetings became more frequent. Cooperation from societies in the other parts of the presidency was sought and given. Money was collected from wealthy people. A change in the nature of the activity also came about. Earlier this society had satisfied itself with holding the meetings and distributing the pamphlets and handbills. But now it started a somewhat more active mass contact programme by collecting signatures and selling and distributing pictures which made more appeal to the illiterate masses. The religious movement now acquired a communal overtone. The cow was no longer an end in itself. It again became a means to an end. But now the end was different.

While the movement gathered intensity, with another cow protection society formed, Upadhyay says:

> Such activities and incidents were bound to have their impact sooner or later. In the minds of the middle class Muslims in Bombay, some sort of sectarian sentiment had already been injected during the late 1870s and 1880s by the Anjuman-I-Islam, 'a non religious yet communal' body. The issues centred

around Turkey and Khilafat had started to create Pan Islamic sentiments. But these things were limited to the middle class Muslims. The cow protection propaganda, however, reached down to the lower class Muslims that they would be deprived of their cheap and chief article of food. Some zealots of the Sabha also went into the Muslim dominated areas and preached their creed... All this was slowly preparing the ground for a conflagration by alienating the two communities from each other and creating tension between them.

The riots of Prabhas Pattan in the Muslim-ruled state of Junagarh had occurred end of July 1893, on the day of Muharram on which many Hindus were killed. This followed meetings by both communities and 'the atmosphere had become suddenly surcharged with passion'. On 11 August, the riots started and the rest is history. Upadhyay says the actual rioting had taken place only on three days, but its intensity was such that 81 persons were killed, 700 injured, and 1,550 arrested. In all, 60 temples and 33 mosques were damaged or destroyed. 'The aftermath of the riots saw another development and that was the shifting of quarters. Right from the beginning, people had started moving to the areas where their co religionists dominated.' Upadhyay (1989) concludes by saying:

> So the conclusion which presents itself is that though a variety of motives went into the making of the riots, the lines between we and they were drawn along communal lines. All the other motives and identities tended to get dissolved into communal identities at that point of time. Caste, class occupation and region were subordinated to the communal identity.

He further says that this was only for the time being. The relative proportion of Muslims in the Hindu-dominated areas or the Hindus in the Muslim-dominated areas did not show a major decline over the years, despite a few migrations. Similarly we find other loyalties taking over when the Sunnis attacked the Bohras in 1904 and the Julahas in

1908 during Muharram or when Muslims and Hindus fought together against the police in 1911 on Muharram day.

He explains earlier that as in any other riot, the people who participated in this riot had a variety of motives. Though the cow protection propaganda and the Prabhas Pattan riot might have started it, once the riot was on it had a logic of its own. The feeling of communal revenge, of personal defence, of group rivalry, and desire to loot kept it going. In fact, he argues that cow protection propaganda could not have made so much impact on the Hindu mind because many of the participants like Mahars and Telugu Chamars were not only cow-eating but cow-carrion eating. As for the mill workers even though they were Marathas, they had little time for this cow protection propaganda.

Older Riots in Bombay

There were a few significant instances of riots between Parsis and Muslims in Bombay in 1832 over the killing of pariah street dogs, in 1851 over a picture of Prophet Mohammed, and again in 1874 over an article on the Prophet written in a Parsi newspaper (Maharashtra State Gazetteers Department 2001: 146).

Writing about this episode, Edwardes (1923: 30, 31) says that the early 1830s were remarkable for a lot of crime and also for a serious public disturbance—the Parsi–Hindu riots which broke out in July 1832. These riots took place after a government order for the destruction of pariah dogs which were rampant on the island. Two European constables who wanted the reward of eight *annas* for every dog killed were killing one near a house when they were attacked by a Parsi and Hindu mob. Next day shops were closed and a mob assembled and the garrison had to be called in to control the situation.

Edwardes (1923: 36) says the period immediately preceding the year of the Mutiny was also remarkable for two serious breaches of public peace. The earlier occurred in Mahim in 1850 on the last day of the Muharram festival after a dispute between two factions of the Khoja community and resulted in the murder of three men and the wounding of several others. The latter riots broke out in October 1851, between the Parsis and the

Mohammedans after a 'very indiscreet' article on the Muslim religion which was published in *Gujarati*, a Parsi newspaper. On 17 October, Muslims attacked Parsi homes and destroyed property. The Parsi-owned public conveyance stables were wrecked and in Pydhonie liquor shops were attacked and private houses too. However, the riots could not be stopped despite 85 people being arrested and Bhendi Bazar under siege. Again the garrison troops were called in to stem the disturbances and the Muharram festival of that year, which took place 10 days later, passed off peacefully (Maharashtra State Gazetteers Department 2001: 156).

Once again in 1872, Edwardes (1923) records that disturbances occurred during Muharram. During the tenure of Sir Frank Souter, Commissioner of Police of Bombay, he said that public peace was disturbed thrice. Up to the year 1912 he describes the annual Muharram celebration as a menace to law and order. Writing about this festival in 1885, Sir Frank (Edwardes 1923: 67) said, it was always

> ... a laborious and anxious time for the police, as until recent years, it was almost certain to be ushered in by serious disturbances and often bloodshed, arising from the long standing and at one time bitter feud existing between the Sunni and Shia sects. For many years it was found necessary to place a strong detachment of troops in the city, where they remained during the last two or three days for Muharram and it is only within the last few years, that the usual requisition at the commencement of the Muharram to hold a party of military in readiness has been discontinued.

Apparently in 1872 the sectarian antagonism developed into open rioting, resulting in serious injury to about 60 people before Sir Frank Souter gained control of the situation (Edwardes 1923: 68). Edwardes writes that these disturbances were trivial compared to the Parsi–Muslim riots of February 1874, which was sparked off by another article on the Prophet Mohammed written by a Parsi in a daily paper. On 13 February, a huge mob attacked Parsi houses and two agiaries (Parsi temples) were broken open and desecrated by the Sidis, Arabs, and Pathans who also looted Parsi homes and attacked them on the street. The police charged 106 persons with rioting and convicted 74 who were sentenced to varying periods of imprisonment (Edwardes 1923: 69).

Muharram and Riots

Religious clashes in Mumbai go a long way back and one of the main causes of strife was the annual Muharram festival which invariably resulted in trouble. Rioting and unlawful assembly (Edwardes 1924: 11) frequently occurred in India during the last century and more. But until the last few years, most of the riots were due to agrarian disputes or to the fundamental sectarian hostility existing between Hindus and Muslims. Edwardes goes on to say that up to the year 1911, when the Commissioner of Police contrived by a twofold policy of force and persuasion to put an end permanently to the great Muharram processions through the city, the celebration of that festival in Bombay had earned an unenviable reputation for lawlessness and disorder. It may be noted that Edwardes says that the clashes took place because of the hostility of the Sunni sects to the Shia Bohras. The festival, he adds, had also degenerated into an occasion of blackmail on a large scale, levied by the lowest classes of Mohammedans upon Hindus chiefly of the trading and shopkeeping class. Bakri Id too with its goat slaughter to commemorate the sacrifice of Ishmael by Abraham is well calculated to arouse the hostility of the Hindu population, according to Edwardes (1924: 12).

After 1893, there were no communal riots for a while, but the Muharram festival was violent again in 1904. Again this time it was a sectarian riot between the Shias and the Sunnis. On 13 February 1908, Edwardes (1923: 139–40) records another clash between Shias and Sunnis. However, he notes that these Muharram disturbances though imposing a severe strain upon the Commissioner and the police force, caused less concern to the general public than the prolonged rioting in the industrial quarter in July 1908 when more than 400,000 mill hands indulged in open disorder after the conviction of Lokmanya Tilak, who was arrested in Bombay on 24 June. From 1911, when there was another disturbance during Muharram, Edwardes, who was then the city police commissioner, imposed restrictions on the festival and there were no processions or public collections of money till 1922. Muharram was celebrated peacefully after that and Edwardes also persuaded the leaders of various Muslim sects to cooperate with the new rules framed by him which led to a more peaceful form of celebration.

History of Clashes in 1900s

For a while, Muharram became an annual excuse for riots between the Shias and the Sunnis and later cow slaughter, which was the background of the 1893 riots, continued to be the bane of law and order not only in Bombay city but in other parts of the presidency. Riots broke out over seemingly trivial issues.

> Coming to the year 1927–28, the following facts stare us in the face. Between the beginning of April and the end of September 1927 no fewer than 25 riots were reported. Of these 10 occurred in the United Provinces, six in the Bombay Presidency, to 2 each in the Punjab, the central provinces, Bengal, Bihar and Orissa, and 1 in Delhi. The majority of these riots occurred during the celebration of a religious festival by one or other of the two communities, whilst some arose out of the playing of music by Hindus in the neighbourhood of mosques or out of the slaughter of cows by Muhammedans. The total casualties resulting from the above disorders were approximately 103 persons killed and 1084 wounded. (Ambedkar 1941: 164)

Again Ambedkar (1941: 167, 170) says:

> The number of riots during the 12 months ending with March 31st, 1929, was 22. But though the number of riots is comparatively small, unfortunately, the casualties which swelled heavily by the Bombay riots, were very serious, no

fewer than 204 persons having been killed and nearly a 1,000 injured. Of these, the fortnight's rioting in Bombay accounts for 149 killed and 739 injured. Seven of these riots or roughly one third of them occurred on the day of the celebration of the annual Muhammedan festival of Bakri Id at the end of May. The celebration of this festival is always a dangerous time in Hindu Muslim relations because part of the ceremony consists in animal sacrifice and when cows are the animals chosen, the slightest tension between Hindus and Muslims is apt to produce an explosion. Coming to the year 1930–31 there occurred innumerable communal disturbances mostly due to the Muslim Opposition to the Civil Disobedience movement started by the Congress that year. Bombay too was affected.

In addition, Dr Ambedkar (1941: 180) writes,

Leaving aside the Presidency and confining oneself to the City of Bombay there can be no doubt that the record of the city is the blackest. The first Hindu–Muslim riot took place in 1893. This was followed by a long period of communal peace which lasted up to 1929. But the years that have followed have an appalling story to tell. From February 1929 to April 1938, a period of nine years, there were no less than 10 communal riots. In 1929 there were two communal riots. In the first 149 were killed and 739 were injured and it lasted for 36 days. In the second riot 35 were killed 109 injured and it continued for 22 days. In 1930 there were two riots. In 1932 there were again two riots. First was a small one. In the second, 217 were killed, 2,713 were injured and it went on for 49 days. In 1933 there was one riot, details about which are not available. In 1936 there was one riot in which 94 were killed, 632 were injured and it continued to rage for 65 days. In the riot of 1937, 11 were killed, 85 were injured and it occupied 21 days. The riot of 1938 lasted for 2 and a half hours only but within that time 12 were killed and a little over 100 were injured. Taking the period of nine years and two months from February 1929 to April 1938 the Hindus and Muslims of the city of Bombay alone were engaged in a sanguinary warfare for 210 days during which period 550 were killed and 4,500 injured. This does not take into consideration the loss of property which took place through arson and loot.

In response to Dr Ambedkar's statistics which were published in a newspaper, the Bombay Police clarified to the Home Department that some of it was wrong. In a letter (SD 3884 A dated 3.5.1941 to J. M. Sladen, Secretary to government, Home Department), the police say that in 1930 there was only one riot and not two. Again in 1932 there was only one riot and not two, and in 1938,

> ... it will be seen that probably resulting from the misstatements in Dr Ambedkar's book, there is much misleading propaganda abroad about the wonderful steps taken by government in 1938 in stopping a riot in two and a half hours, when in fact it lasted much longer and the death toll was comparatively heavy. In 1933, there were two riots which only lasted one day.
>
> However, between 1918 to 1944 there were fifteen instances of riots in Bombay of which eleven were between Hindus and Muslims. (Maharashtra State Archives, Elphinstone College, Mumbai, File no 154/A, a statement of riots and disturbances which occurred in Bombay city between the years 1918 and 1944)

In eight of these riots, 498 people were killed and 4,684 injured. The city was shaken by constant communal upheaval and even the slightest thing could set off a riot. Just before 1947 and after riots engulfed the city and the polarization seemed to increase.

Each time there were riots in the early 1900s, citizen committees and the police sued for peace. Communal feelings did not entirely subside however, and they were quick to be raised by skilful hands. Every time there was a riot, the cause was trivial, but there were lengthy negotiations before the riots actually happened, as in the case of the Byculla temple–mosque dispute.

Since the Mutiny of 1857, when Hindus and Muslims fought together against the British, their unity splintered over the years. A look at some of the major riots preceding Independence gives some idea of how the city began to get polarized. Even if one looks at the 1929 communal riots, the tension was not deep enough for such prolonged clashes. But it was basically instigated by certain sections. This is reinforced in the Byculla temple–mosque riots in 1936 where there is evidence of hardliners from both Hindu and Muslim communities fuelling hatred. Much like in Mumbai, the Bombay Presidency was not really communal but each time it fell prey to propaganda spread by divisive elements in both Hindu and Muslim communities, rumour mongering, and political exigencies.

The existence of the Hindu Mahasabha and the Muslim League set the stage for communal tension with the backdrop of the demand for Pakistan. Temples and mosques seemed to be in the centre of conflict not only in the Bombay Presidency but all over the country. Leaflets calling for boycott of either Hindus or Muslims were not uncommon. People moving out of riot-affected areas and seeking safety in their own community was also not uncommon. In fact, polarization between the two communities got worse towards Independence and the years preceding that. Mumbai or Bombay was not a trouble-free city despite its seemingly cosmopolitan nature and the fact that it was a trading capital.

The Riots of 1929

The first Hindu–Muslim riots of the 20th century in Bombay took place in 1929. According to the Report of the Inquiry Commission, 1929 (Maharashtra State Archives Department, File no. 543[10] E[b]):

The troubles in Bombay began really in April 1928 when a general strike in the Bombay Textile Mills took place, which lasted till October 1928. During that strike inflammatory speeches were made by certain extremist leaders of what afterwards came to be known as the Girni Kamgar Union, later known as the Red Flag Union. On 7th December, 1928, a strike occurred in the Oil installations at Sewri. In order to carry on their work, and, among other things, to supply oil to the textile mills, many of which would otherwise have had to stop work, throwing between 70,000 and 1,00,000 mill operatives out of employment, the Oil companies engaged new men, particularly Pathans who could not be intimidated by the strikers. This led to serious clashes between the Pathans and the oil strikers, involving loss of life.

On the 17th of January, 1929, it was reported that the mill hands had agreed to support the strikers, and on the 18th January, four Pathan watchmen of the New China Mill were attacked by the workers in the Mill and three of them were killed. On the 25th of January, the police arrested 133 men in connection with these murders. After the 18th January there was quiet till early in February, which fact may have been due to the municipal elections, in which the leaders of the Red Flag Union were candidates for elections or to other causes. However, in the meantime, a rumour was spreading that children were being kidnapped from the streets. The rumour mainly connected Pathans with the kidnapping.

On the night of 2nd February the kidnapping scare may be said to have really commenced; and the first overt act of assault took place on that night, when an attack was made at 9.00 pm in Sleater Road, near Grant Road, on a Pathan motor driver and two Sindhi gentlemen, who were in the car. On the 3rd February at about 11.00 am a Greek engineer was assaulted at the junction of Bhendi Bazar and Sandhurst road, the attack being made on account of the scare. At 11.45 am a Hindu carpenter was killed in Maruti lane off Fergusson Road, within a short distance of the Branch office of the Girni Kamgar Union. On the same day there were attacks on Pathans and other persons and in various parts of the city. There was also a meeting of mill hands that afternoon, which was addressed by one of the Girni Kamgar Union leaders, in which the speaker indicated that Pathans are kidnappers.

On the 4th and 5th of February the disturbances developed into a regular Pathan hunt by the mill hands. Six Pathans were killed on the 4th and eleven on the 5th and many were injured. On the 5th two other Muslims and three Hindus were killed and Deputy Inspector Priestly who had advanced unaccompanied by his armed guard and had tried to intervene between mill hands and Pathans, was killed by the mill hands. A large body of Pathans went on the same day to the police head quarters to ask for protection and the military were called out at that time.

The Inquiry Commission Report (1929) notes,

> ... the attacks by the mill hands on the Pathans had been made in the North of the Island; and we are of the opinion that it was not a communal riot at that time, although it has been urged on us by some witnesses that the attacks were communal from the beginning. On the 5th however, it turned into a communal riot and the murders were committed in the South of the island. Attacks were made first by Pathans on Hindus generally and then by Moslems on Hindus and by Hindus on Moslems.

The report notes that in all 92 Hindus, 55 Muslims, of whom 26 were Pathans, one European Deputy Inspector of Police Priestly) and one Parsi were killed.

However, the inquiry report squarely blames the Red Flag Union for the riots. Clearly the Communist connections of the Union and its 'inflammatory speeches' which threatened those who would not obey the Union have been blamed for the riots. What is of interest in this report is the subsidiary causes of the riots in chapter four. While attributing some of the disturbances to 'an unduly large number of hooligans, specially of persons who are not residents of Bombay', we are of the opinion that, next to the communist menace, the hooligan menace is the most serious one in Bombay. In regard for the present riots, the evidence shows that though these disturbances were not begun by the hooligans, the riots would not have been continued but for them. The hooligans in particular committed many murders and looted shops in the latter part of the riots.

In respect of the Hindu–Moslem tension a considerable amount of evidence has been given on both sides. It may be hoped that this evidence has helped to 'clear the air' and to show both communities that there is a good deal to be said on the other side. In regard to the Hindu–Moslem tension in Bombay, the evidence goes to show that it does not normally exist here to any appreciable extent. A noticeable instance of this was the condition of the workers in the docks during the riots. The evidence given before us shows that although there were nearly 2,000 Pathans working in the docks together with Hindu labourers, there was not the slightest fracas between the two. We are informed that during the riots, even ordinary quarrels between the workmen did not take place. Communal tension, so far as there is any in Bombay, is a repercussion of tension outside Bombay. Further even the recent riots were not primarily communal they were in our opinion primarily communist versus Pathan and only developed later into communal riots.

The Inquiry Commission Report (1929) also says,

... in this connection it may be noted that Peace Committees and relief Committees were formed during the riots, and many Hindus and Muslims worked together in a most friendly way.

Some leading Hindus saved the lives of many Muslims while some leading Muslims saved the lives of many Hindus.

However, the Report gives some reasons for the tension between the two communities.

> Some of the witnesses who have appeared before us have ascribed the increase of the communal tension partly to scurrilous and inflammatory writings and speeches published and made in other parts of India and brought into Bombay. It is also stated that certain newspapers increase the communal tension by their articles and headlines. Some of the Moslem witnesses say that the Arya Samaj and (Hindu) Mahasabha movements also have this effect; but this is strenuously denied by witnesses on the other side. It is contended by the latter that though in other parts of India the Arya Samaj and Mahasabha movements may be ultra communal, this is not as in Bombay city, where the movements are under the control of moderate leaders. With this contention we are disposed to agree. In any case there seems to be nothing in common between these movements and the communist movement, and the suggested combination between them has not been proved before us and has no foundation in fact.... The tension is also attributed to the Shuddi, Sangathan, Tansim and Tabligh movements to music before mosques and to parading cows intended for sacrifice. The latter reason, however, has not arisen in Bombay. The other movements also have only an inappreciable effect in Bombay.

The second phase of the riots sparked off in April–May 1929, and according to same Inquiry Commission Report were not nearly as serious as the previous riots, the total mortality in these riots being 35.

The causes and origins of the second disturbances were the continued mistrust between the lower classes of the two communities and the fact that the Moslem workers did not join in the second general mill strike, which began towards the end of April 1929. The immediate causes were attacks by the Moslems on the 'palkhi' processions near the mosque on Sopari Baug road on 23rd April, and again on 27th April, and the retaliation by the Hindus. On the 2nd May the position suddenly grew worse, and serious disturbances began on that evening.

Again the Report notes that hooligans aggravated the situation. 'On the whole it appears the Moslems were the aggressors at the Palkhi procession incident on the 23rd April 1929.'

The riots took a turn in two respects which could not have been foreseen:

In the first place they were originally between labourers and Pathans, and only later took a communal turn. It is one of the very few cases in which a communal riot has arisen out of events which had nothing to do with religious differences.

In the second place not merely did the riots become communal, but they were a series of individual murders mainly in side streets; and this was the real reason why it took a comparatively long time to get the situation under control, even after the arrival of the military and the district police.

The Inquiry Commission Report (1929) finally comes to the remedies for the Hindu–Muslim tension.

The causes (of the riots) are all Indian, partly political and partly religious, the former dictated by the spirit of mistrust and fear felt by each community of the other. The removal of these causes can be accomplished only by the will to peace—a spirit of mutual tolerance and give and take—first of all among the leaders in the two communities themselves. As stated by the

Commissioner of Police (Sir Patrick Kelly), 'what is required is a complete change of heart. Moslems should learn to trust Hindus and Hindus should learn to trust Moslems, then the tension will disappear'.

The Inquiry Commission Report quotes from the Governor General Lord Irwin's speech delivered on 29 August 1927,

> I am not exaggerating when I say that during the 17 months that I have been in India, the whole landscape has been overshadowed by the lowering clouds of communal tension, which have repeatedly discharged their thunderbolts, spreading far throughout the land their devastating havoc. From April to July last year Calcutta seemed to be under the mastery of some evil spirit, which so gripped the minds of men that in their insanity they held themselves absolved from the most sacred restraints of human conduct. Since then we have been the same sinister influences at work in Pabna, Rawalpindi, Lahore and many other places, and have been forced to look upon that abyss of unchained human passions that lies too often beneath the surface of habit and of law. In less than 18 months, so far as numbers are available, the toll taken by this bloody strife has been between 250 to 300 killed, and over 2500 injured.

Since the date of that speech, the Inquiry Commission Report (1929) notes, at least 20 serious communal riots have occurred in various parts of India, the two Bombay riots alone accounting for the deaths of nearly 200 more persons. The problem has therefore become even more acute than it was in 1927.

> Another point we would urge is that, if the poorer classes are only left to themselves, they would rarely enter on communal strife. This can be seen from the instance given above, namely

that during these Bombay riots, there was no strife of any kind between Pathans and Hindus who were working together in the docs. When a communal disturbance occurs, it will generally be found that one party or the other, or both parties, have been stirred up by agitators.

The Inquiry Commission Report (1929) also discussed the communal vote, which many felt was the reason behind the riots. It concludes:

> That is a constitutional question, on which we can hardly give an opinion. We refer to it only because it has been pressed upon our attention by a number of Hindu witnesses, some of whom also suggest that it leads to government favouring Moslems at the expense of Hindus. We would merely observe that we do not think that the abolition of the communal vote would at all allay Hindu–Moslem tension, unless the question can be settled by the consent of both parties. In regard to measures for decreasing the tension we must look beyond the limits of this Presidency. It is a problem to be solved not by government but by the two communities concerned, and it has to be tackled in its storm centre, which is not Bombay but North of India.

Since this was the first major communal riot in Bombay in the 20th century, in many ways it was a precursor of the things to come. The communal vote was held out as a reason, another was that the British police and military were soft on Muslims, an echo of this is often heard today. The Report while slamming communists and their trade union for the riots also brings to light the fact that Pathans and Hindus worked peacefully in the docks at the same time, showing that there was no inherent animosity between the two religions. It also clearly points to instigation from either party as a cause which leads to riots. Many of these are true even today. I have quoted the Report to some extent to show the course of the riots. I have not independently corroborated the role of the Union. In later riots, the Union has played a role of bringing together people instead of dividing them.

As Upadhyay (1989) has noted in his article, there seems to be no inherent animosity between the two religions. However, a section of society did keep the communal sentiment going on both sides. After the 1929 riots, the next communal bloodbath in Bombay was in 1932 and later in the famous Byculla temple–mosque dispute in 1936.

The Riots of 1932

According to the *Indian Daily Mail*, an article of 18 March 1932, titled 'Riot averted by the police, Hindu Muslim clash', reports that a Gujarati boy who got into Hotel Sharad Vilas Hindu on Duncan Road wanted a glass of water to drink. After drinking the water the boy threw the glass on the ground and broke it and ran out of the shop. One of the servants ran after the boy and beat up two Muslims. The Muslims in turn thrashed the servant and the manager. A huge mob collected and stones, brickbats, and soda water bottles were freely thrown about and there was hand-to-hand fighting too. The trouble lasted for 25 minutes and the police dispersed the mob. Many people were injured and the Gujarati boy was taken into custody.

The owner said since the hotel was opened at Duncan Road, a few Muslims would allege that he had to pay them or they would create trouble as he had no right to open a Hindu hotel in a Muslim area. In 1932, a number of incidents contributed to tension: The Muslims did not support the Civil Disobedience movement and leaders like Maulana Shaukat Ali came to protest at a meeting of the peace committee, according to a report in the *Bombay Chronicle* dated 2 April 1932. Speaking at the annual general meeting of the Bombay Citizens Conciliation Committee, held at the Corporation Hall, the Maulana said in his tirade against the Congress,

> Today I feel that there is going to happen something which will ruin the peace of Bombay and the peace of whole India. You know that we are Muslims. We do not agree with the Congress or the Civil Disobedience movement. This programme has been made on our heads.

He also spoke on the boycott of Sardar Suleman Kassum Mitha, a leading citizen. 'The Congress was trying to bully Muslims and if this picketing is not withdrawn I am writing to Mrs (Sarojini) Naidu and we will start picketing the Congress.' He also said, 'I want peace between Hindus and Muslims. I am a man of peace but if a fight is forced it is unfortunate.'

The Beginning of the Riot

The prolonged 1932 riots began over the alleged Mohammedan tombs on the premises belonging to S. R. Khambatta at the junction of Cowasji Patel Tank (C. P. Tank) Road and Girgaum Back Road. The riot started at Barbhai Mohalla, near Nagdevi Street (Maharashtra State Archives Department, File no. 793 (5), Home Special). The tombs are located on a private compound belonging to a Parsi liquor shop owner and adjoining the extensive grounds of the Hindu temple of Madhav Baug at C. P. Tank. An extract of a letter from the commissioner of police dated 16 May 1932, (Maharashtra State Archives Department, File no. 2864/A/318, 16 May 1932) says, 'At about 2 pm information was received that the two newly found graves at C. P. Tank near Madhav Baug which the Mohammedans claim as theirs were razed to the ground and two Muslim custodians were severely beaten.'

It was on 22 May 1932, the Chief Presidency Magistrate H. P. Dastur issued ban orders (No. 3253 of 1932, Maharashtra State Archives Department, File no. 793, H. M. Riots in Bombay, May). A press note from the director of information dated 22 May 1932 says, 'the chief presidency magistrate issued an order yesterday closing the plot of land at the junction of C. P. Tank Road and Girgaum Back Road where the two tombs are situated which had been the subject of dispute before the riots'. It was found that during the disturbances both tombs had been demolished and that *sadhus* and other Hindus had taken possession of the place and set up images. They had taken over a small piece of municipal ground nearby and were making similar use of it. In view of the communal tension in the city and the dangerous situation that might have arisen if the plots of ground were ostentatiously used as places of worship, the chief presidency magistrate ordered all the Hindus and Muslims to abstain for a period of two months from entering the recreation ground as well as the vacant plot of ground where the tombs were.

The tombs were located on house number 62, land belonging to Shapoorji Rustomji Khambatta, which were demolished by unknown persons and some *sadhus* took possession of this vacant piece of land which was also a part of number 62 and a stone idol was placed there.

On 15 May 1932, troops were ordered on standby ready (Maharashtra State Archives Department, File no. 793 [2]). It is the considered opinion of the civil authorities that the number of murders and looting would have been much larger had no troops been scattered through the area.

On 25 May 1932, it transpired that the two Hindu idols placed in the municipal garden at Madhav Baug were removed by the police. The Hindu Relief Committee's Sir Purshottamdas Thakurdas, Vasantrao Dabholkar, and others called on the Commissioner of Police and were told the idols were removed in good faith as their presence was likely to cause breach of peace. In the Commissioner's report of 25 May (Maharashtra State Archives Department, File no. 3016/A/318, 25 May 1932), he notes a distinct want of confidence among the Hindus and few of them opened their shops. His report of 25 May says that a meeting of several representatives of commercial bazaars in Bombay was held a day earlier at Mahajanwadi to consider the question of opening Hindu shops in the city and also consider the removal of idols from the municipal garden at Madhav Baug. After a lot of discussion it was decided to open the commercial markets and Hindu shops on 25 May and to appoint a committee of six persons to represent Hindu grievances about the removal of the idols to the government.

Later a deputation met the Home Member of the Bombay government about the removal of the idols. Home Member G. A. Thomas said the government had not issued instructions to the Commissioner of Police on removal of the idols from the garden. However, the garden was a public place and it was not right that a section should seek to do things there which might not appeal to the general public. An inquiry

(Maharashtra State Archives Department, Section 147/CPC/in Presidency Town G. Davis, 26 May 1932) was also held regarding the idols and the authorities justified the removal of the idols from the garden by the police.

R. M. Maxwell, Secretary to the Government of Bombay Home Department, on 27 May 1932 wrote to the municipal commissioner (Maharashtra State Archives Department, File no. SD-3833, 27 May 1932) saying that one of the idols which was removed was standing on the municipal gardens for several years past, although apparently up to a very recent date it had not been an object of public worship. Mr Maxwell enquired whether the Corporation gave permission to place the idols on the garden and to erect a fence and also asked if the Corporation will give necessary permission to keep the idols back and the terms and conditions as the presence of the idols on this spot constituted a permanent menace to public peace in this locality.

The Home Member later agreed to have the idols restored to their original site on the expiry of the Chief Presidency Magistrate's order (Maharashtra State Archives Department, RI no. SD5083, Letter from Mathura Das Vissanji Khimji to Secretary Government of Bombay, 27 May). The government also assured the delegation that it had no objections to the restoration of the Hindu idols, particularly the idol of Maruti, to the original site under the *pipal* tree. However, the government clarified that the Home Member only agreed to the restoration of the idol of Maruti to its original place after expiry of the Chief Presidency Magistrate's order (Maharashtra State Archives Department, Government Clarification no. SD 3882, 29 May, from C. B. B. Clee to Mathuradas). The Commissioner of Police said the idols would be handed over if an application was made.

H. K. Kripalani, the municipal commissioner, on 31 May 1932 replied to the officiating secretary (Maharashtra State Archives Department, File no. G105, 31 May 1932–33, Home Department), saying that when the ground was taken over by the superintendent of municipal gardens on 31 March 1927; a Hindu idol existed under the *wad* (banyan) tree in the recreation ground. No regular worship was performed but a *sadhu* used to attend occasionally and collect offerings. Since the discovery of the tombs in the adjoining compound, the idol attracted greater attention and became an object of conspicuous worship. Formerly a tank at the recreation ground was filled due to the anti-malaria policy. The gardens superintendent who lived in this area states that a Hindu idol existed in a small recess in the wall surrounding the tank. The wall was demolished and the idol was shifted to the present position under the tree but it would not be possible to speak with certainty on this point. The commissioner also says that the additional idols were probably imported during the controversy and no permission of the corporation was obtained to placing these idols on municipal land and erecting a fence around it. He presumes no objection to the original idol being replaced subject to no fencing and no one posting himself on the garden nearby. He also said regarding the other idols the matter would be placed before the corporation for orders. He does not propose access to the recreation ground to the tombs even if the private owner agrees.

According to an official note on the tombs prepared by the Home Department (Maharashtra State Archives Department, File no. 793(5), Home Department Special), which traces the history of the plot from 1836, documents from that year, 1838, and 1842 did not make any mention of tombs in the area. It is therefore improbable that there could be any authentic tombs on this piece of land which has been in possession of Parsis since 1842 and which had no access except through the front part of the property. The issue was too hot even to be debated and the municipal commissioner wrote to the C.B.B. Clee, officiating secretary to the government Home Department, on 11 June, postponing a discussion on the issue because of the 'present state of public feeling in the city discussion in the corporation may lead to undesirable results'.

In a letter (Maharashtra State Archives Department, 21 June, RI no. SD 5831/23.6.32 Ref no 3, to G. A. Thomas, Member of Council), it was stated that the tombs had been on the land for over 100 years according to Shapurji, the landlord. No one worshipped them and it was not known if they were Hindu or Muslim. Shapurji's family members were tenants of the land for over 150 years and the liquor shop was 48 years old. Two years previously, Shapurji used to say when he was 90 years old, that the tombs were there as long as he could remember. The tombs faced north–south and not east–west, as preferred by Muslims, so the tomb was not Muslim. The note also said that the tombs cannot be Hindu as land was in Muslim occupation before the Parsi landlord bought it in 1936. Previous to this no one knew of the tombs. The Muslim dream story was invented for a reporter from the *Delhi Samachar*. (The media had reported that a Muslim had dreamt that the tombs belonged to two saints and they were in neglect. This caused an influx of Muslims to the area creating tension since there was a temple nearby.) A gang used to smoke *charas* at the C. P. Tank garden and two Hindu *sadhus* spoke of a hidden tomb behind C. P. tank garden. They confessed to publicity for the tombs for money. One member had a number of convictions and was in jail and another Muslim disappeared. An unknown Muslim was killed near the tomb on 15 May, according to Abdul Ghani Arab, who later vanished. As for the Maruti idol people believe it was placed there 10 to 12 years ago.

The entire matter ended with a portion of the municipal recreation ground being acquired for a police *chowky* to be built on it, as per an order of 12 August 1932. The repercussions of this riot later led to what was known as the Lalbaug Market dispute. The demand for a separate Hindu market came up after a fish worker of the Mohamedi Lalbaug market was molested. However, the Police Commissioner, Sir Patrick Kelly, on 19 January 1933 (Maharashtra State Archives Department, File no. 891/239, 19 January 1933, Commissioner of Police's Office to Mahmoud Suleman Mitha) said there was no report on record saying so, and though the police were told about the incident, no names were produced about the incident or her address and there is no record of this case on the police register though a woman was brought for treatment of injuries to her head. She said she was assaulted by Hindu *mavalis* (criminal elements) while going to the market to sell fish. At that time, leaflets were circulated in Marathi in the name of the Society for the Protection of the Vedic Hindu religion asking for a boycott of Muslims. Ten commandments of boycott were listed and it also urged Hindus to boycott members of their community who did adhere to this. An official translation of the Marathi leaflet issued by the Sanatan Hindu Dharma Pratipalak Sangh said:

1. No drums at marriage.
2. Not to purchase goods from Muslim hawkers articles like umbrellas, trunks, penknives, scissors, cutlery, stationery, boots, and bags.
3. Not to purchase milk from stables of Muslims.
4. Not to get plumbing, electric work from Muslims.
5. Not to give any help to non-Hindu beggars.
6. Not to serve Muslims working as menials.
7. Not to work as *hamals* (headload carriers, porters) and menials in the shops of Muslims.
8. Not to engage Muslim service.
9. Not to engage carts taxis of Muslims'.
10. To boycott those who do not boycott Muslims.

In response a call was issued to Muslims 'to awake arise and do away with your mutual differences and become a solid wall of protection for your rights'. Fears of a Hindu Raj were also expressed. A conciliation committee of three members was formed to resolve the differences but all the members later resigned. In February 1934, the municipal corporation decided to give a license to the new Hindu market. Since the Mohammedi market was Muslim owned there was tension, but despite earlier assurances, a licence for the new market was granted. The construction on the new place started on 15 February 1934 (Maharashtra State Archives Department, DO 20 Municipal Office, 13/14 February, H. K. Kripalani to R. B. Ewbank Secretary to the Government of Bombay, General Department Secretariat). The commissioner of police apprehended trouble (Maharashtra State Archives Department, File no. 845/H/3717, C. P. to R. M. Maxwell, 16 February 1934, Secretary to Government of Bombay) if the new market at Lalbaug was licensed and there were lots of protest letters. Muslims called off a mass meeting on the assurance that the dispute would be resolved but a sense of betrayal prevailed. About 500 Muslims signed a protest letter which was published in the *Bombay Sentinel* on 26 February 1934. Muslims were incensed at this demand for a new market and proposed a public meeting in protest.

Details of the 1932 Riots

The riots of that year began on 14 May when firing was reported on Nagdevi Street (Maharashtra State Archives Department, File no. 7931, 15 May to 28 May 1932, daily reports from the Commissioner of Police). On 15 May, riots broke out after rumours that a Muslim boy was assaulted by Hindus. Incidents snowballed into serious rioting all over the city. According to Sir Patrick Kelly, the Commissioner of Police, in his report on 16 May (Maharashtra State Archives Department, File no. 2864/A/318, 1932, from CP to Secretary Home Department), 5 persons were killed and 87 injured, while the next day the toll rose to 28 dead and 403 injured. Trouble was serious at Bhendi Bazar, Sandhurst Road, Two tanks (Do Tanki), and Girgaum Road. The Hindus opened a rescue camp at Bhatia Mahajan *wadi*, Kalbadevi Road, where huge crowds of Hindus took refuge while Muslims in different *mohallas* fed their community in distress. On 17 May, there were attempts to set fire to a mosque at Dongri Street (Maharashtra State Archives Department, File no. 2890/A/318, 17 May, CP to Secretary Home Department). Police went to the scene and found that the Hindus residing in the locality set fire to one of the gates of the mosque. Behind the mosque is Masjid railway station. Muslims threw stones at the trains and police fired on them to stop them. Meanwhile the Hindus began to throw stones at the mosque. Fighting broke out between *bhangis* (a derogatory terms for cleaners) and the Muslims after rumours of the Islampura mosque being demolished by Hindus. Mills too were shut and of the 71 only 37 were working at that point.

Curfew was imposed from 17 May and on that day the Jain temple near Pydhonie was set on fire. A total of 96 persons were killed between

14 May and 18 May and the toll climbed steadily (Maharashtra State Archives Department, File no. 2978/A/318, 23 May 1932, CP to Home Secretary). Finally a peace committee was decided to be formed and on 22 May a meeting was held at Dr P. H. Meisheri's home at New Chinchbunder Road. About 300 Hindus and Muslims were present and the meeting was presided over by N. V. Chandavarkar, mayor. A 15-member board for conciliation was appointed which decided to issue an appeal to both communities for peace.

However, the Commissioner of Police's report of 23 May (Maharashtra State Archives Department, File no. 2916/A/318, 18 May 1932, CP to Home Secretary) talks of continuing assaults. In the evening, writings in chalk in Gujarati were seen on the side lanes of Princess Street and Pydhonie announcing that Mohammedans should not enter Hindu localities and the Hindus should not enter Muslim localities. At 8 pm of 22 May 1932, information was received that two Pathans entered the compound of the private secretary to the governor and set fire to some matting in the corner of the compound and ran away.

Just as things were calming down, a cow was found bleeding at Sheikh Memon Street and the Hindus said the cow was running with the wound from Barbhai Mohalla, Nagdevi Street towards Khara Kuwa, according to the Commissioner of Police's report of 26 May (Maharashtra State Archives Department, File no. 3036/A/318, 26 May 1932). The cow was taken to the Hindu relief committee and *Bhoi Patrikas* (posters/pamphlets) appeared everywhere. On 25 May, Hindu workers of Ruby Mill told the management that Muslim jobbers and 25 Muslim mill hands should be dismissed or they would strike work. The management run by Sorabji Hormusji and Company, agreed.

Earlier at one of the meetings at Halai Bhatia Mahajanwadi at Kalbadevi on 22 May it was resolved that an organization called the Hindu Samrakshan Samiti be formed to safeguard the interests of all Hindus including untouchables living in the city, and a provisional committee for the purpose of framing a constitution was appointed. The committee had Mathuradas Vissanji, M. L. Dahanukar, Narayan Damodar Savarkar, brother of Vinayak Savarkar.

On 26 May, a dead body of a mill worker was found on Ripon Road and another worker from Bradbury Mills was stabbed. Shops of Hindus were looted and people were putting up false notices which encouraged the rioting. Even though 71 mills were working, a majority of Muslim workers were absent. About 270 workers from Western India Mill did not come at all and many mills were working with half the workers, according to Commissioner of Police's letter dated 27 May (Maharashtra State Archives Department, File no. 3054/A/318, 27 May 1932). Muslim workers were asked to leave when they reported for work. Hiralal Chotalal Gandhi, manager of Ruby Mill, was questioned by the police on 26 May. He said there were 25 Muslims prior to the riots but they were absent from work after the riots. He therefore engaged Hindus. On 24 May, 10 Muslim workers came but left after the Hindu substitutes objected to their rejoining. The Mill Owners Association has contradicted the rumours about the dismissal.

While all 71 mills started working after a gap and workshops too, Muslim shops were open after the Conciliation Committee's advice. However the Hindu relief committee was not for it as their shops were being targeted. All cloth markets, Swadeshi stalls, Javeri Bazar, and Dawa Bazar were closed. At Janjikar Street in Pydhonie, a *Bhoi Patrika* was issued which said that Mohammedan merchants should dismiss their Hindu servants and engage Muslims instead. Meanwhile, the killing continued, and till 22 May 152 people were killed and 1,676 injured (Maharashtra State Archives Department, File no. 3002/A/318, 24 May 1932, CP to Home Secretary). The Hindu traders were advised to keep their shops shut for eight more days (Maharashtra State Archives Department, File no. 2994/A/318/, 23 May 1932). The Bombay Citizens Conciliation Committee issued an appeal in Urdu, Marathi, and Gujarati requesting the shops to be open by 29 May and to forget the past. The Bombay Provincial Congress Committee too issued handbills appealing for peace (Maharashtra State Archives Department, File no. 2985/A/318, 1932, CP's letter to Home Secretary).

A confidential letter (Maharashtra State Archives Department, File no. 793 3, Express Letter no. SD 4018, 6 June 1932 to Home, Simla, Officiating Secretary to the Government of Bombay, Home Department), revealed that the government was not too keen on an inquiry and it would wait till the riots had passed. In an undated statement the Government of Bombay said that it intended to publish an official report on the riots when the communal tension subsided. A communiqué issued by the Government of Bombay on 20 May deals with the first phase of the riots (Maharashtra State Archives Department, File no. D5805/32/ Poll, 19 August 1932, Statement in response to Bombay riots in assembly). While a trivial incident in Nagdevi Street was the immediate cause of this communal outbreak, the fact was that feelings between the two communities had been strained for some time and were further embittered by the interference of Congress volunteers with Muslim traders.

The government asked the Commissioner of Police to justify the late imposition of curfew. Since 16 May was the last night of Muharram, the curfew order began the next day. A committee of Hindus and Muslims which came to meet the Commissioner of Police was not unanimous and so it was decided to postpone the curfew to 17 May.

The daily reports of the Commissioner of Police to the Home Secretary (RI no. 6588/18/7/1932) (Maharashtra State Archives Department, File no. 793 1, part 3, Hindu–Muslim riots, 1932) from 16 July 1932 to 18 August 1932 show minor incidents of stone throwing and soda water bottles were reported on 16 July 1932—four Muslims complained of assault. On 17 July, there was one case of assault and one more (Maharashtra State Archives Department, Letter No. 4016/ A/318, 18 July 1932). At 5 pm, two leading citizens Dr J. P. Meisheri and Jamnadas Virjibhai went to Maharbouri police station and reported that they received anonymous letters threatening them with murder and stating that cow's heads would be thrown in the Round Temple (Gol Deol) on Sandhurst Road.

There was also a group of Hindu–Muslim leaders like Mathuradas Vissanji, Goverdhandas Gokuldas Morarji, Rahmatullah M. Chinoy, and Sardar Suleman Cassum Mitha who had come together to settle a dispute on the ringing of bells at Mohammedan prayer time. All of them agreed that two Muslims and two Hindus would sit at the Round Temple every day between 6.30 to 8.30 pm to prevent mischief makers stirring up trouble. That night at 10.15 pm one Muslim was stoned by

Hindus. The Commissioner of Police in his report (Maharashtra State Archives Department, File no. 4016/A/318/1932) noted that feelings of nervousness and distrust existed. Curfew was imposed between 28 June 1932 and 16 July 1932.

In his letter of 19 July 1932 (Maharashtra State Archives Department, File No. 4036/A/318/1932), the Commissioner of Police recorded that at 8 am on 18 July, a postcard written in Gujarati was received at the Maharbouri police station addressed to the police issuing a warning that Muslims would attack the Round Temple and throw a cow's head on 17 July night. The Hindus at the Maruti temple at the junction of Sheikh Memon Street and Princess Street spilled on to the roads clapping and shouting Bajrang Bali and Shivaji Maharaj. After the prayers Muslims from Jumma Masjid cried '*Allah Ho Akbar*', but Sardar Cassum Mitha and others calmed down the crowd. The same thing happened at the night prayers. The Commissioner of Police reported that the crowd which collected outside the temple and the Jumma Masjid consisted mainly of riff-raff who do not collect at these places for worship but to create trouble. 'I am taking steps to see that no crowds collect outside these places of worship'.

He also attached to his letter the text of a cardboard written in Urdu put up on a lamp at Mohammed Ali Road, 'In the name of God Almighty wake up Mohammedans.' On 20 July, there were some minor incidents and explosions. On 21 July, the head of a pig was lying in the Karelwadi cemetery and the police had to remove it. There were incidents of stabbing, stoning, and potash bombs going off (Maharashtra State Archives Department, File No. 4088/A/318, 21 July 1932 and 4098/A/318 of 1932).

According to the Commissioner of Police (Maharashtra State Archives Department, Sir Patrick Kelly's Report, No. 4151/A/318, 25 July 1932, CP to Home Secretary), 132 Hindus were killed from 14 May 1932 to 25 July 1932, 83 Muslims and others 1—total 216. The number of injured for the same period were 986 Hindus, 995 Muslims, others 26, making a total of 2,006. This figure of injured went up to 2,706 by end of June, of which 1,345 were Hindus and 1,300 Muslims (Maharashtra State Archives Department, File no. 4200/A/318, 27 July 1932).

At 2 pm on 25 July, Shamji Jivraj, a Hindu, was assaulted near Sandhurst Road but the Muslims chased the assailant and handed him over to the police (Maharashtra State Archives Department, DO No. 4157/A/318, 25 July, Head Police Office to C. B. B. Clee, Secretary to Government Home). On 28 July, the Commissioner of Police said (Maharashtra State Archives Department, File no. 4216/A/318, to Secretary Home Department) that leaflets in Urdu and Gujarati were distributed a day earlier in Muslim localities appealing to Muslims to make their purchases from Muslim shops only because the Hindus were boycotting them. On 30 July, the Commissioner of Police's report (Maharashtra State Archives Department, File no. 4270/A/318, 30 July, CP to Home Secretary) says the honorary secretary of the Hindu Relief Committee informed Lamington Road police station in a letter dated 29 July that for the last two days bones were being thrown into Vithoba's temple at the junction of Falkland Road and Sandhurst Road. No such complaint was made to the police and nothing of the sort was found.

By 2 August, the Commissioner of Police said (Maharashtra State Archives Department, File no. 4322/A/318, Head Police Office to C. B. B. Clee) that things appear to be settling down now and no casualties were reported on 1 August. Finally on 10 August the Commissioner of Police (Maharashtra State Archives Department, File no. 4460/A/318, 1932, CP to Home Secretary) stopped his daily reports saying that he will not send a daily letter to the home secretary unless there is something special to report regarding the riot situation.

According to final figures by Kelly (Maharashtra State Archives Department, File no. 5410/A/318, 29 September 1932, Sir Patrick Kelly to Home Secretary), 3,757 were arrested and of the total 217 killed, 133 were Hindu, and 83 Muslims apart from one other. The number of those injured was 2,569. About 610 rounds were fired by police while military fired 33. It is recorded that 423 shops suffered losses, of which 173 belonged to Hindus and 250 to Muslims. In terms of monetary losses, Hindus suffered loss of ₹ 1,394,691 and Muslims ₹ 1,031,804, taking the total to ₹ 2,426,495.

It was only in September 1932 (Maharashtra State Archives Department, File no. 5410/A/318, 29 September 1932, Sir Patrick

Kelly CP to Home Secretary) that Sir Patrick submitted a report to the Secretary, Government of Bombay, Home Department. The riots started in May, but it was July before things quietened down, yet there were instances like dead pigs found in mosques, stone throwing on mosques, and on 6 July, three heads of calves in a gunny bag were found in a temple at Poibawdi. There was no trouble though and curfew orders were modified on 10 July and the military was pulled out on 6 July. The military was called in from 15 May and light motor patrols on the streets proved effective in maintaining order. While stray assaults took place till 2 August, Kelly in his report says that feelings of nervousness and distrust continued for a long time after the terrible ordeal through which the city had passed. Shopkeepers and businessmen were slow to resume normal working hours and many Hindus and Muslims shifted their shops and residences to what they considered safer localities.

Kelly dealt with the 'Hindu belief' that the real explanation of the disturbances was to be found in the Satanic policy of the government which aimed at promoting antagonism between two communities. He defended the police and said that no policemen would wish for communal riots. He dealt with the allegations of Muslims who asserted that Congress agents not only started the disturbances but fed the fire of communal frenzy whenever it showed signs of dying down. Muslims did not take part in the *hartals* (strikes) and the boycott of British goods. Kelly said no evidence was there on both counts that the Congress or the government and police had engineered the riots. However, he said that the actual outbreak of the trouble cannot therefore be attributed to a trivial incident like the slapping of a boy or to the wicked machinations of the government or of the police or the Congress. The explanation was to be found in the relationship between the two communities, he said. Coming from Kelly this was a rather significant observation which set the tone for the future.

> The mutual feeling and suspicion and distrust are more bitter today than at any time in my 30 years service. The fierce political struggle of the last few years has disclosed acute differences of opinion and with the prospect of constitutional

reform in the near future each community fears that the other will get too dominant a position. In particular the civil disobedience movement has served to estrange the two communities. The Mohammedans as a body have constantly refused to take part in it and as a result they have been subjected to pressure in the form of boycott and intimidation. When relations are so strained any trifling incident may lead to bloody warfare.

The Bombay government later took a decision not to publish Kelly's report in a letter of 19 December 1932, as it would not serve any useful purpose (Maharashtra State Archives Department, File no. SD 7657, 19 December 1932, Home Department (Poll) Bombay Castle to Home Secretary, Government of India). These riots and its aftermath led to the formulation of a scheme for riot control. The Home Department asked Sir Patrick (Maharashtra State Archives Department, File no. 793(15) H. D. Special, 1932) to formulate a scheme to implement when riots break out. He drafted a scheme on 20 June 1932, which created the Local Alarm Orders and a scheme to keep the peace and help the garrison deal with communal disturbances. The detailed riots scheme was approved by the government on 21 December 1932. The scheme was in force from 1933.

Warning to Editors

On 9 July 1932, the Director of Information, J. F. Gennings, warned newspapers against publishing exaggerated accounts of riots and that the government would take action against the papers which publish matters calculated unfavourably to affect the situation.

The Byculla Temple–Mosque Dispute, 1936

If the 1932 riots caused havoc in Bombay, worse was to come four years later. An express letter from head police office (Maharashtra State

Archives Department, File no. 5501/A-154, 28 October 1936, Head Police Office [Bombay]) from the Commissioner of Police (Bombay), states that 21 people were killed in firing in 37 occasions of firing. There were 47 whipping sentences between 15 October and 27 October 1936. Fourteen policemen were injured (Maharashtra State Archives Department, File no. 870 (6) H. D. Special Branch Byculla Temple–Mosque dispute, 1936).

On 9 November 1936 a question was asked in the British Parliament by the Duchess of Atholl (Maharashtra State Archives Department, RI no. SD 6025/2711/36) on the number of people killed and injured and material damage in these riots. The Undersecretary of State had nothing to say in reply. But the Duchess was persistent. She again asked him if he did not fear that there may be a serious increase in communal disturbances in Bombay if the police handed over the new constitution. In another answer to Sir Thomas William's question, dated 29 October 1936, the cause of the riot which broke out in Bombay (the reply is by the Additional Undersecretary Home Department), the nature of which is essentially communal, was the building of a Hindu assembly room (*sabha mandap*) next to a Muslim mosque. The disturbances continued for five days during the course of which the police had to open fire. A troublesome feature of the rioting was the continuance of isolated stabbing affrays between the members of the two communities.

By 22 October 1936 the Government of Bombay was able to report that the situation was fully under control and conditions had returned to normal. The total number of casualties was 60 dead and 500 wounded (Maharashtra State Archives Department, File no. 870, Home Department Special Report, 1936).

The military was called out to patrol the city and 2,601 people were arrested, of which 566 were for rioting and the rest as a preventive measure. In a letter of 20 February 1937, the Secretary to the Government of Bombay, Home Department, wrote that the city was on tenterhooks if reports in the newspapers are to be believed.

The dispute over a *sabha mandap* being constructed next to the Byculla mosque formed the cause of prolonged rioting in the city in 1936 (File no. 870, Byculla Temple–Mosque dispute, 1935–36). The Muslims launched an agitation against the construction of the *sabha mandap* at the Maruti temple at Byculla saying it was too close to the mosque. The Central Khilafat Committee India on 28 September 1935 held a public meeting of the Bombay Muslims which emphatically and strongly protested against the attitude of the Bombay municipal corporation in building a *sabha mandap*—a new construction for *bhajans* (religious songs and prayers) on the open land between the temple and the mosque at Guzri Bazar. The resolution it passed at the meeting feared that the *sabha mandap* will be a permanent source for creation of a friction and tension between the two communities and it warned the corporation to desist from their harmful actions. It also called on the government to intervene in the matter. The Jamiat ul Mussalmeen Guzri Bazar called a meeting of 200 Muslims on 25 September to protest the *sabha mandap* (Maharashtra State Archives Department, Bombay Special Branch Report, 28 September 1935).

The old *sabha mandap* was demolished by the City Improvement Trust when the Parel Road was widened. After that there was an agreement that a new *mandap* would be built away from the mosque. Special Branch reports agitation among the Muslims over the proposed construction (Maharashtra State Archives Department, Bombay Special Branch Report, 4 May 1936). Three protest meetings called by Muslims called for an amicable settlement to the issue. Meanwhile, Hindus too rallied support for the *sabha mandap*, and a public meeting of the Hindu Mahasabha was held on 16 May to condemn the action of the Muslims regarding the *mandap*. Earlier, a report by municipal commissioner I. H. Taunton on 13 December 1935 (Maharashtra State Archives Department, File no. 870, Byculla Temple–Mosque dispute, 1935–36) also says that all attempts to reach an amicable settlement was opposed by Muslims and he had no choice but to go ahead and enforce the original agreement with the temple *pujari* (priest) who gave up the land for the road.

The mosque and temple had coexisted for over 50 years without any trouble. There were repeated meetings by the Hindu Sabha and on 20 July 1936 it called on the corporation not to delay the construction of *sabha mandap* any further. The corporation which was to discuss the issue in July dithered till August (*Bombay Chronicle* 3 July 1936). On 20 August, the Majlis-e-ahrar met in protest against the municipal corporation's attitude of employing Muslims in municipal services and also the *sabha mandap* and congratulated Muslims who walked out of the corporation meeting on 17 August. A censure motion against the mayor of Bombay on the grounds of partiality on the Byculla temple–mosque issue was not carried by a vote of 66 to 15 (Maharashtra State Archives Department, 24 March 1936, Bombay City CP's weekly letter). A special meeting on 31 August to open negotiations with members of the two communities regarding the *sabha mandap* was adjourned without any result (CP's weekly letter dated 31 August 1936). No further action was taken on the dispute till 14 September (Maharashtra State Archives Department, CP's weekly letter dated 14 September 1936) when the Hindu Mahasabha distributed handbills asking people to sign a petition to expedite work on the *sabha mandap*. Muslims too sent a petition to the mayor opposing this. On 24 September Muslim corporators decided to refrain from attending a meeting of the corporation and resigned even as the corporation postponed the *mandap* construction till 13 October. Muslims sought legal opinion which said that there was no point in taking the case to court.

Riots broke out in the city on 12 October 1936 (Maharashtra State Archives Department, CP's weekly letter dated 5 October 1936). An official press note dated 14 October 1936 (Maharashtra State Archives Department, File no. 870 H. D. special), says,

> The Governor in Council desires to explain the attitude of the government in regard to the settlement reached by the municipal corporation of Bombay with the pujari of the Maruti temple at Byculla. On account of part of the temple site having been acquired for the widening of the road in front of the temple, the settlement provides for land adjoining the temple being given in exchange and also for the construction by the municipal corporation of certain buildings including a sabha mandap adjacent to the temple on its southern side. A mosque exists in

the rear of the temple and Muslims have objected to the settlement on two main grounds—they said the sabha mandap is a new feature in the temple adjuncts and secondly that the use of the mandap for purposes connected with Hindu worship including bhajans and kirtans will disturb worship at the mosque. They do not object to the maintenance of such arrangement for worship as previously existed.

The press note says that previously there was no friction in worship. So that there is no disturbance, a high wall is proposed to keep the quiet within the mosque precincts. There is on both sides a strong body of opinion which sees no reason why the consideration for each other's sentiments which prevailed in the neighbourhood in the past should not continue for the preservation of neighbourly relations in future also.

The origins of the dispute go back to 1928 when the City Improvement Trust agreed to rebuild a part of the structure called the *sabha mandap* as compensation for the removal of a portion of the temple buildings to facilitate a road (Maharashtra State Archives Department, File no. 870 (2), 15 October to 30 November 1936, reports by CP James Walter Rowland). Ever since the *sabha mandap* question has been raised, the Muslims protested and they attempted to postpone the construction (Maharashtra State Archives Department, File no. 52661 of A 154, 16 October 1935, CP's letter to Home Secretary). The Hindus were not silent; they asked the mayor to expedite the work. The corporation discussed the issue and decided to carry out the work and 12 corporators staged a walk out of that meeting.

There was an attempt at settlement on 12 October at the secretariat and leading citizens from both communities were invited including the municipal commissioner, N. D. Savarkar, S. K. Patil, Mathuradas Vissanji, Bai Seetabai, the *pujari*, and her son. The Home Member presided over this futile conference. Again there was some attempt at reconciliation but they did not succeed. In the meanwhile, a few incidents of stone throwing occurred on 12 October, at 10.30 pm. Stones were reported to have been thrown by some unknown persons towards a Moghul hotel situated on the ground floor of E. D. Sasoon building and at Northbrook gardens near Trimbak Parshuram Street and Durgadevi Road. One stone hit a *panwalla*, Dadamiya Bademiya, who was injured slightly. At the same time a cycle shop owner reported that some of the stones struck his shop next to Moghul hotel. On 13 October, 1.15 am, two Muslims reported being hit by stones at Trimbak Parshuram Street and sustained minor injuries. At 7.30 pm that day some commotion was reported at the junction of fifth lane Kamathipura and Duncan Road. Small incidents were reported and that evening a huge crowd gathered at the mosque in dispute at Byculla. The next day they gathered but dispersed on seeing no construction was going on. That evening Ali Bahadur Khan, a Muslim leader, went to the mosque and advised people not to create any trouble in view of the changed circumstances of the case. At 7 pm on 14 October, a Muslim crier of the Chatri Mohalla Masjid reported that the masjid was stoned and the police found some pieces of brick and plaster inside the masjid compound. On 15 October, a government communiqué was issued in the press and police arrangements were made in the vicinity of the Byculla masjid. Work began at 8.30 am that day. A series of minor incidents of stone throwing began and a crowd of 10 Muslims threw stones at the Khatau Makanji Mill injuring some workers. After that day the situation got worse and stabbing incidents were reported.

Meanwhile four Muslims—Haji Nurmohammed Ahmed, Haji Usman Poonawalla, Sulaiman Tar Mohammed and Mohammed Siddick Hashem—filed two petitions before the chief presidency magistrate asking for orders under Section 144 Criminal Procedure Code (CrPC) on the municipal commissioner and the corporation prohibiting them from carrying out the work of construction of the *sabha mandap* on the grounds of severe tension between Hindus and Muslims (Maharashtra State Archives Department, File no. 5289/A 154, 16 October 1936, CP to Home Secretary). The magistrate rejected the petition saying he could not interfere in civil rights of the subject or an authority since their action in exercising their right did not in itself give occasion for reasonable complaint. He also said how could a mere construction create annoyance to Muslims. Meanwhile, a private meeting of Hindu leaders on 15 October of L. R. Tairsee, G. M. Morarji, N. D. Savarkar, and Lilavati Munshi was held, presided over by Mathuradas Vissanji who decided to revive the old Hindu Samrakshak Mandal which was active during the riots of 1932 and to help stranded Hindu families in Muslim localities. The riots snowballed leading to firing and police being assaulted and prohibitory orders being issued banning the assembly of more than five persons. A number of stabbing and stone throwing cases were reported. Khatau Mills was stoned again and 100 Muslim workers of the Indian Manufacturing Mills at Ripon Road did not report for work on 16 October. Fourteen people died on 15 October and 119 were injured. There were reports of shops being broken into, tram cars being stoned, injuring conductors, and stabbing and firing (Maharashtra State Archives Department, File no. 5289/A 154, 16 October 1936, CP to Home Secretary). Every day crowds gathered at the temple and another petition was filed by two Memon merchants calling for a stop to the construction.

The Commissioner of Police's report (Maharashtra State Archives Department, no. 5306/A 154, 17 October 1936) says reinforcements were called for from district police to handle the situation. On 16 October too cases of stabbing, arson, and looting began to occur and the toll mounted. On 17 October, the *Bombay Chronicle* reported an appeal from both Hindu and Muslim leaders asking both communities to preserve the fair name of the city by maintaining peaceful and harmonious relations. However, on the same day, shops of Bohris in Hindu areas were looted and burnt in Chira Bazar and Girgaum and Muslims threatened Koli women at Crawford Market (Maharashtra State Archives Department, no. 5321 /a/154, 18 October). The fish market was closed for the day. A temple was set on fire at Babu Khote Street and people threw soda water bottles at Hindus. The *pujari* at Maruti temple at Dongri Bazar, Jail Road reported the temple was broken into and the images were smashed and ornaments worth ₹ 350 stolen. Later a crowd of 200 Muslims attempted to set fire to a building occupied by Hindu Kolis at Nislanpada cross lane.

There were attempts to set the Laxmi Narayan temple on fire at Sandhurst Road. Police found lots of kerosene oil everywhere. Later smoke was reported coming out of Nagoba temple and the door was set on fire at junction of Memonwada and Sandhurst Road. Pitched battles were fought and the police arrested 83 people that day which left 7 dead and 103 injured. On 18 October, a temple was broken into at Mastan tank cross road and idols were destroyed (Maharashtra State Archives Department, 19 October 1936, CP's letter 5336/A/154). Cases of stabbing and arson continued. A *dargah* was set on fire at Agar Bazar damaging the tomb. Section 2 of the Bombay (Emergency Powers) Whipping Act 1933 was enforced and on 20 October, the Commissioner of Police said the situation was improving but feelings between Hindus and Muslims are estranged.

By 20 October, the riots had left 60 dead and 500 injured (Maharashtra State Archives Department, File no. 5349/A/154/1936, 20 October). In the dead of the riots an individual, Bhupal Pandit of Dadar, printed a leaflet which was thrown in Bhendi Bazar on 31 October 1936 (Maharashtra State Archives Department, Appendix A 5399/A/154, 22 October 1936). He said,

> Unity of Hindu and Muslims brethren. My brother Shripal married Muslim sister Ashabi ... has brought about unity in Hindu–Muslim and Jain societies. Many such things have taken place and are taking place. What is the gain therefore in fighting over the question of mandir and mosque. There is no gain in it. The principle of Quran and Puran is the same. Signed your Jain sevak Bhupal B. Pandit.

While things slowed down a bit, a Muslim leader, Ali Bahadur Khan (Maharashtra State Archives Department, Appendix 5562/A/154, 31 October 1936), was restrained from speaking or writing for two months on this issue. By 30 October there was no incident worth reporting and no casualty, according to the Commissioner of Police (Maharashtra

State Archives Department, 5583/A/154, 2 November 1936). So far there were 1,603 arrests, of which 797 were Hindus and 786 Muslims; a total of 66 were dead, of which 33 were Hindus and 33 Muslim; and 522 were injured.

On 31 October, the members of the Muslim Peace and Relief Committee and some leading Muslims met Mohammed Ali Jinnah at his bungalow and consulted him on the question of the temple dispute (Maharashtra State Archives Department, 5583/A/154, 2 November 1936). Shaukat Ali, Cassum Mitha, and Currimbhoy Ebrahim met Jinnah who promised to guide them provided all the Muslims agreed to abide by his decision. It was decided to call a meeting of the representatives of various Islamic associations and pass a resolution appointing Jinnah as the sole representative of the Muslim community and authorizing him to do the needful towards the settlement of the dispute.

However, on 3 November, riots began again with minor incidents (Maharashtra State Archives Department, CP's report, 5608/A/154, 3 November 1936). On 4 November, leaflets were circulated in Marathi in north of the city, inviting people to attend a Satyanarayan *puja* on 5 December at the Byculla temple and to contribute two *annas* for the expenses (Maharashtra State Archives Department, Appendix A 5649/A-154, 5 November 1936). The Commissioner of Police ordered the arrest of such people saying this was an attempt by Hindu mischief mongers to dupe illiterate people in north of the city or to annoy Muslims. The Muslim Peace and Relief Committee executive body held a meeting presided over by Sir Currimbhoy Ibrahim to make Jinnah the sole representative.

However, incidents continued to disturb the city's peace and the toll rose to 74 dead. The police sought additional forces of 300 armed police in view of Diwali (Maharashtra State Archives Department, File no. 5771/A/154, 4 November 1936). Meanwhile, the *Daily Khilafat* said no to negotiations and riots resumed on 12 November. The final toll was 79 deaths and 574 injured.

At a meeting of the Muslim Peace and Relief Committee, 200 Muslims attended but could not take a decision on appointing Jinnah as the sole representative. Eight fatwas were issued at the meeting by *ulemas* from different schools of thought and the gist was they felt that what was not in existence before at the temple should not be allowed to go on now. They said though some compromise might be arrived at so as not to conflict with the hours of prayer at the masjid. The fatwas said no music should be allowed before the mosque at any time and no compromise must be made on this. The fatwas advised people to protest if the government allowed music but not to oppose forces of law at the same time. The eight fatwas were sent to the government for its opinion (Maharashtra State Archives Department, File no. 5807/A 154, 13 November 1936).

On 14 November, a crowd of Hindus read leaflets pasted on a tram pillar at Carpenter Street and Khetwadi main road inciting Hindus to attack Muslims. The leaflet read:

> Hit Kill Murder. So do not waste time, hit kill murder just follow me Die while killing Har Har Mahadeo The she goat and the tiger cannot live in one place. Prove that you are the sons of tigers. Do not applaud the names of Shivaji and Rana Pratap singhji but take into consideration what you have done. The government will not help you because you are cowards, impotent, weak. (Maharashtra State Archives Department, Appendix A of 5817/A/154 16 November 1936, Office of the CP to Home Secretary)

About 400 *bhaiyyas* (a derogatory term for north Indians) employed as servants in Haji Ali Mohammed at Jacob Circle struck work. They were given shelter by the Hindu Relief Committee. Their grievance was that wages were reduced and they did not want to deliver milk unless their safety was ensured. Haji Umerji Haji Moosa, secretary of the Bombay Milch Cattle Owners Association, issued leaflets in Gujarati stopping milk supply to 40 Hindu merchants from 15 November (Maharashtra State Archives Department, Appendix A of 5817/A/154, 16 November 1936, Office of the CP to Home Secretary). The Hindus closed shops in Muslim areas and opened 27 new centres for milk distribution in Hindu areas (Maharashtra State Archives Department, File no. 5844/A 154, 17 November 1936). A report of 17 November (Maharashtra State Archives Department, File no. 5844/A/154, 16 November 1936) said that the milk dispute was amicably settled with the Bombay Milch Cattle Owners Association issuing leaflets that milk would be supplied to all without distinction of caste or creed. On 16 November, Muslim weavers of the Indian Manufacturing and Hindustan Mills did not go to work. There were things written in chalk that no Muslim should go to work on that day (Maharashtra State Archives Department, File no. 5817/A/154, 16 November 1936).

The prolonged rioting till 29 November killed 90 people—46 Hindus and 44 Muslims—and injured 627—344 Hindus and 268 Muslims. Of the 2,135 arrests, 1,064 were Hindus and 1,036 Muslims, apart from 35 others (Maharashtra State Archives Department, File no. 6124/A/154, CP's report, 30 November 1936).

On 28 November, Urdu posters appealed to Muslims not to remain quiet while the *sabha mandap* was being built. The posters put up in Wazir Building, Bhendi Bazar, were removed by police. The next day Gujarati leaflets pasted on a wall at Panjrapole Lane asked Muslim dealers to boycott Hindus in all phases of business. Again posters asking people to assault 'kaffirs' (non-believers) cropped up, and the Hindu shopkeepers met the commissioner of police for protection to open shops on 27 November.

The opening ceremony of the *sabha mandap* was set for 3 December. The police issued orders saying that no music will be permitted after the evening prayers and necessary military and police precautions were taken. The *mandap* opening ceremony went off without incident and military precautions were discontinued after fourth afternoon.

Till 7 December, police recorded 93 deaths and 632 injured, apart from 2,477 arrests. The commissioner of police's report of 14 December finally said that no incidents were reported after 8 December 1936.

The government was worried that this dispute would have all-India repercussions and asked the CID to take special care. The invitation of the *ulemas* from other parts of the country worried the government and various letters indicate the government's anxiety on this front. But there is no indication from the Muslims that this was their intention.

Riots in 1937 and 1938

Hindu–Muslim Riots: Bombay City, May–June 1937

On Sunday, 30 May 1937 (Maharashtra State Archives Department, File no. 910 (1) 1937, No. 2947 of 1937/A/154, 24 June 1937, letter from Commissioner of Police to Secretary to the Government of Bombay), at about 11.30 am a marriage procession of some 60 Hindu Dhobis was passing along the Kamathipura Centre Road when between Kamathipura third and fourth lane the leaders were advised to cease playing music in view of the fact that there was a Masjid situated in the fifth lane at about 50 yards distance. But there was an argument by a young Mussalman (described a busybody in the letter). As care had been taken not to cause offence to Muhammedans by the playing of music in the vicinity of the mosque, the Hindus composing the party became quite naturally annoyed and assaulted the Muhammedan. This led to a free for all fight in which stones and other missiles were thrown.

The riots spread to other parts of the city—Kamathipura, Two Tanks, Round Temple, Null Bazar, and later Sandhurst Road. Curfew was imposed on 6 June and the riots were brought under control by promulgating prohibitory orders and the Bombay Whipping Act, 1933. Eleven persons died and eighty five injured on 31 May. In all, 2,273 people were arrested of which 976 were Hindu and 1,175 Muslims. While the riots subsided, wild rumours were floated, the Commissioner W. R. G. Smith (in the same report cited earlier) noted, calculated to maintain excitement at fever pitch in the city. By 10 June, rumour was rife in the city that the Bombay Municipal Corporation was contemplating demolition of certain *dargahs* on the ground that they were encroachments. The *dargahs* concerned were situated (*i*) at the junction of Jail Road East and Nowroji Hill Road no. 4 and (*ii*) Opposite Dr Meisheri's dispensary on

New Chinchbunder Road. As regards (i) the high court had ruled the previous year that the existing structure was in fact an encroachment. At the same time, the bench advised that efforts be made to arrive at a settlement between the municipality and the *mujawar* of the shrine and it was agreed to keep the existing *dargah* with some modifications. The visit by the BMC assistant engineer to carry out the modifications gave rise to the rumour and the *mujawar* was prevailed upon to publish a denial of the intention to demolish the structure and put the facts on record in the press. As far as the second one was concerned, Dr Meisheri had raised the question of this *dargah* 10 years ago being an encroachment on municipal land. At that time, a resolution was passed authorizing its removal. No action has been taken on this and the municipality has no intention of carrying out the demolition. The Commissioner says that the local police were able to persuade members of the public that this *dargah* too would not be touched. He also says that there was rapid restoration of order and no serious disturbances after 17 June. There was no organized communal agitation such as those which preceded the riots the previous year prior to 30 May. As the situation was brought under control there was no usual panic like shops being closed or arson.

After 1937, even in the rest of the Bombay Presidency, a number of communal incidents were reported from Sholapur, Ahmednagar, Thane, and Pune, ranging from tombs being desecrated to cow slaughter on Bakri Id. Small incidents continued to ruin communal peace (Maharashtra State Archives Department, File no. 844 Part 1, Home Department Special). There was constant fomenting of communal tension as well during this period leading up to Independence.

> At a meeting attended by about 250 Maharashtrians at Ahmedabad on 29.12.1937, Dr N D Savarkar (Maharashtra state archives department, 844 part two Extract from the Bombay Secret Abstract for the week ending 15.1.1938) said the Muslim policy of aggression and harassment was still rampant. The Congress and not the Hindu Mahasabha was a communal organisation as the Congress had silently accepted

the Communal award which gave Muslims double the number of seats they were entitled to. He exhorted Hindus to organise so as to win Swaraj by their own strength.

But tensions were often resolved as well (Maharashtra State Archives Department, Extract from the Bombay Province weekly letter no. 8, 26 February 1938).

In Jalgaon a partial hartal was observed owing to a cow being slaughtered by Muhammedans in a private place. The leaders of the community are to be congratulated on speedily coming to amicable terms when the hartal was called off.

But there was no respite from riots.

Rioting of a serious nature broke out on the night of 17 April 1938 as a sequel to a very trivial incident which occurred at North Brook Garden. At 4.30 pm on 17 April three Hindus and one Muslim the worse for liquor were gambling with cards in Northbrook Gardens (Maharashtra State Archives Department, File no. 965 1938, letter no. 1727/A/154, 18 April 1938, Office of the CP to the Secretary Government of Bombay Home Department). While gambling they quarrelled and the Hindu gamblers began to assault the Muslim by throwing stones and the fight started. The rumours about a Hindu–Muslim disturbance spread in the city and at about 9 pm things got worse. The riot spread to neighbouring areas and curfew was clamped as well as prohibitory orders. In the appendix of the same letter the death toll was 8 and injured 86. Six Hindus and two Muslims died.

Commissioner of Police, W. R. G. Smith, reported that as a result of the prompt measures the situation had improved and the entire previous afternoon and night passed off peacefully (Maharashtra State Archives Department, Letter no. 1734/A/154, CP to Secretary Government of Bombay, Home Department, 19 April 1938). The Chief Presidency Magistrate in consultation with the Home Minister issued orders under Section 144 CrPC, directing five newspapers to abstain from 18 April from publishing any news or comments related to the present riots which are calculated to promote hatred or enmity between two communities. Any news or comments published by these papers should have been previously approved by the director of information and certified by him to be fit for publication. The papers were *Roznama Al Hilal*, *Khilafat*, *Sadaqat*, *Insaf*, and *Prabhat*.

Sporadic incidents continued (Maharashtra State Archives Department, Letter no. 1756/A/154, 20 April 1938, CP to Secretary Government of Bombay, Home Department). There was a shop of a Muslim at Kamathipura 13th lane looted and two injured. Two shops were looted and one person was assaulted (Maharashtra State Archives Department, Letter no. 1782/A/154, 21 April 1938, CP to Home Secretary Bombay). The total toll was 9 dead and 92 injured. However (Maharashtra State Archives Department, Letter no. 1795/A/154 of 22 April, CP to Home Secretary Bombay), riots broke out again on 21 April with stone throwing and stabbing incidents killing three and injuring four, taking the toll to 12 dead and 99 injured.

Trivial incidents of panic were reported (Maharashtra State Archives Department, Letter no. 1844/A/154, 25 April 1938, CP to Home Department). Three Pathans playing carom in a room on the ground floor of Patel Mahal, Kings Circle, were disturbed by the throwing of a stone among them. A domestic upheaval, during which a husband beat his wife and her screams caused a mild disturbance in BDD *chawl* on Delisle Road at 12.45 am and police had to rush there and explain to residents the real cause of the alarm. Some Muslims in a *chawl* reported that stones were thrown at them.

In various incidents a total of 14 were dead and 98 injured (Maharashtra State Archives Department, Letter no. 1879/A/154, 27 April 1938) and 2,337 arrests were made of which 955 were Hindus and 1,247 Muslims.

The Riots of 1941

On Sunday, 20 April 1941, the Victoria drivers and Employees Union had organized a strike. At the same time, reports of the serious nature of rioting at Ahmedabad on 18 and 19 April were received in the city (Maharashtra State Archives Department, File no. 844 H, Letter no. 2305/A/154, 21 April 1941, Office of the CP to Secretary Home Department, Bombay). Special arrangements were made at Pydhonie, Maharbouri, and Nagpada, but riots broke out at 10.15 pm between Golpitha and Null Bazar over a minor quarrel and soon both communities began to assault each other with stones and soda water bottles, and three persons were stabbed. Tramcars were stoned and seven people were injured (Maharashtra State Archives Department, Letter no. 2331/A/154, 22 April 1941, CP to Secretary Government of Bombay Home Department).

On 21 April, a series of incidents took place including a case of stabbing and a total of 18 persons were injured. Curfew was imposed. From then on things took a serious turn. Every day some incident or the other took place, and by 26 April troops were called out. From 20 April 1941 four persons were killed and 96 injured. Sporadic incidents took place (Maharashtra State Archives Department, Letter no. 2468 of 1941/A 154, 28 April 1941, CP to Home Secretary), for instance, one Jamnadas Mulchand dressed up as a Muslim went to Ghoghari mohalla, Pydhonie, to see silk merchants on business. He was recognized and stabbed on 27 April 1941. A Muslim funeral procession was stoned at Chandanwadi by Hindus in the area. Muslims threw stones and five rounds were fired. Even a 14-year-old boy was stabbed at Lamington Road. In a telegram (Maharashtra State Archives Department, Letter no. SD 2938, 1 May 1941, Bombay Special Branch to Home Secretary), it was reported that the toll had increased to 15. There were 2,602 arrests. The riots in Ahmedabad, in which 76 died, added to the existing tension. Things quietened after 5 May 1941 (Maharashtra State Archives Department, telegram no. SD 3008, 5 May 1941). The peace was short-lived. Owing to the recrudescence of communal rioting in Ahmedabad there is some uneasiness in the city (Maharashtra State Archives Department, Letter no. 2953/A 154, 21 May 21 1941 from CP to Home). There were minor cases of stabbing and stone throwing that spiralled upwards (Maharashtra

State Archives Department, Letter no. 2991/A 154, 23 May 1941, CP to Home Secretary) and serious rioting was reported on 22 May night, which left 9 dead and 64 injured. Muslims were stoned at by Hindus and a taxi driver Sitaram Saduram was assaulted. There was firing and later violence occurred in various parts of the city and curfew orders were issued. The riots were concentrated in the island city. As things worsened the high priest of the Bohras issued a statement appealing to both communities to refrain from hooliganism (Maharashtra State Archives Department, Letter no. 3045/A 154/, 27 May 1941, CP to Home Secretary) and to remain peaceful and law abiding.

The Citizens Relief Committee which was formed by the municipal corporation in 1931 sprung into action as also the Bombay Pradesh Congress Committee, the Indian Merchants Chamber, were all discussing ways to bring peace. Even in June by which time 43 people were dead and 221 injured (Maharashtra State Archives Department, Letter no. 3241 of 1941, A 154), things were tense. Muslims shops were closed on Princess Street and Hindu shops in Pydhonie and Dongri areas till 10 June (Maharashtra State Archives Department, Letter no. 3309/A/154, 10 June 1941). All troops were withdrawn on 9 June 1941. However (Maharashtra State Archives Department, Letter no. 3319/A/154, 10 June 1941), the CP reports anonymous leaflets calling on Hindus to rise against Muslims in certain areas like Sheikh Memon Street. Rumours flew thick and fast and a Hindu was stabbed. The translation of a leaflet in Hindi, distributed on 10 June 1941, was as follows: 'O Hindus awake, arise open your eyes, Muslim goondas are taking undue advantage of your generosity and gentlemanliness, The Muslims regard your easy going nature as weakness and your love of non violence as cowardice ....' A little later, on 11 June 1941, an anonymous leaflet (Maharashtra State Archives Department, Letter no. 3339/A/154, 11 June 1941), posted outside the Lakhmidas Cloth Market, Vithalwadi, said: 'Timely warning to the Hindu brethren. In one month if you saw two riots ... The peaceful atmosphere which you now see was seen by you before the second riots commenced... It advises Hindus to be cautious, strong and alert.' The prolonged rioting ended only by 22 July 1941, taking a toll of 59 lives and injuring 255. A meeting called by merchants of the city regarding the riot situation on 25 June 1941 (Maharashtra State Archives Department, Letter no. 3668/A-154, 25 June 1941) condemned:

> ... unanimously and with all the emphasis it can command the riots in the city and expressed its deepest sympathy with the victims of the riots and their families. This meeting of Hindu and Muslim businessmen considers that the so called riots in the city have dislocated trade and commerce of the city by withdrawing that faith, confidence and security which are their backbone and apprehends that unless the meaningless and suicidal attacks and stabbing affrays are put down even the industries of the city may suffer, leading to the weakening of war efforts. Bombay's trade and industries afford a very good example of the work of cooperation of both the Hindus and Muslims and this meeting considers that this important cooperative working on which the prosperity of the city depends will be destroyed if the present situation continues.

Later in a final report by W. R. G. Smith, the then Commissioner of Police, Bombay, (Maharashtra State Archives Department, Letter no. 4458/A-154, 4 August 1941, to the Home Secretary), says some of the predisposing forces at work before the disturbances broke out were,

> ... political agitation—this was particularly the case in certain provinces including Bombay, where minority communities had come to feel that they were not receiving due consideration at the hands of the majority community. This feeling grew noticeably during the period when Congress ministries were functioning and became particularly marked when those ministries resigned. The agitation thereafter of such communal questions as that of 'Pakistan' tended to localize and accentuate the ill feeling that had previously existed between Hindus and Muslims.

That same year, on 23 October, communal riots broke out again in the Null Bazar area and by the time the night ended 11 persons were killed and 41 injured.

Riots of 1945

After 1941, the pre-Independence riots of 1945 were prolonged much in the manner of the Mumbai riots later in 1992–93, and took place in the backdrop of the stand-off between the All India Congress Committee (AICC), which just had a session in Bombay, and the Muslim League. In 1946 too bloody riots claimed at least 262 persons according to a press note of the government published in *Bombay Chronicle* ('Home Minister Tours City Riot Areas', 16 September 1946). In a fortnight, apart from 262 dead there were 791 injured.

Newspapers on 27 September 1945 reported that three persons were killed and 25 injured in clashes in Golpitha. The origin of the trouble was not clear according to the *Bombay Chronicle* dated 27 September 1945. Newspaper reports from 27 September 1945, say that riots broke out at Golpitha and spread to other areas of Null Bazar and Round temple. The *Free Press Journal* (FPJ) called it a communal riot between two rival groups of Hindus and Muslims and three persons were killed that night. This riot says FPJ disturbs communal peace that has been preserved for four years. Press clippings of that time show that there were two schools of opinion. One which refused to acknowledge the riots were communal in nature and in fact agencies like Reuters were criticized by the public for naming the two communities involved as Hindu and Muslim. Letters to the editor of that time reflected this division and newspapers which violated the rule of naming the people killed and the areas of the rioting were sent notices. Three Urdu papers, *Khilafat*, *Hindustan*, and *Iqbal* were served with notices under Section 144 CrPC in which they were warned to refrain from mentioning areas of assaults and nationality of victims. The Urdu newspaper *Inquilab e Jadid* was served with a similar notice, but the editor failed to comply and a complaint was filed against him (*Bombay Chronicle*, 8 October 1945). The *Bombay Sentinel* of 2 October says that instead of arresting communal rioters in Bombay, a number of newspaper editors (six according to the FPJ) were served with notices, which was easier and cheaper. Even Congress leaders like S. K. Patil objected to the disturbances being described as communal riots (*Bombay Sentinel*, 2 October 1945).

Again in *Bombay Sentinel* of 2 October 1945, a column titled 'Vesper Notes' stated, 'As Pundit Nehru has pointed out Muslim Leaguers and their public organs are openly inciting violence'.

An editorial in the *Blitz* of 6 October 1945, calls the prolonged disturbances a result of the Goonda Raj. It says that both Hindus and Muslims did not take part in these riots. It castigates the Anglo-Indian and British Press for damning the Congress 'and showing the world how utterly disunited we brutes are'. The *Bombay Chronicle* dated 5 October 1945 reported that Mr B. G. Kher, former prime minister of Bombay, contradicted Reuters reports that the Hindu–Muslim riots began after criticism of the Muslim League members by the AICC, thus suggesting the responsibility of the riots was on the Congress. Kher went on to say that the disturbances 'could not be strictly styled as communal riots; they were not a political but an administrative problem. Even Pandit Nehru said that the stabbings business is the job of an expert few and no a second should be lost in running them to earth' (quoted by P. V. Krishnan in *Bombay Sentinel*, 4 October 1945).

However, the riots broke out on 27 September 1945 and went on midway through October. On 12 October, the *Bombay Sentinel* continued to report riots which killed one person. On that day, the toll was 41 with injuries totalling 177 (*Bombay Sentinel*, 12 October 1945). The situation was so bad with daily reports of stabbing incidents and rioting that curfew was imposed in the city from 28 September to 10 October 1945. Police rounded up over 1,000 people in connection with the riots. Police had to fire on several days, killing people to control rioting mobs.

Also similar to the post-Babri Masjid demolition riots in the city, the military—both Indian and British—had to be called in to control the situation. It was withdrawn only on 9 October (*Free Press Journal*, 9 October 1945). The government even evoked the Emergency Whipping

Act of 1941 which enabled whipping to be inflicted on anybody convicted of rioting, voluntarily causing hurt, etc. (*Bombay Chronicle*, 4 October 1945).

Appeal for peace came from across parties including the Muslim League, the All India Hindu Mahasabha, the Communist Party of India, the Bombay Girni Kamgar Union (red flag), the Congress, and many peace committees were formed to promote communal harmony. The city witnessed empty trams and roads and a sense of insecurity prevailed specially among workers of the public transport services.

Conclusion

The events since 1893 raise more questions than I have answers for. Why did a city that welcomed people of every race and religion move from a culture of tolerance to enforcing bigotry? The riots starting off in 1893 show clear tension created in the first instance by the Cow Protection Movement which provoked the Muslim community with its focus on banning meat eating. Then came the riots in Prabhas Patan which resulted in the actual rioting. Lokmanya Tilak was of the firm view that those who came out of the mosque that day in August 1893 must have been dealt with firmly, a line that is echoed even today. Many myths prevailed in those days as well. The police were soft on Muslims, the ruling class was in favour of the Muslims, and Tilak's idea of tigers and lambs living together, albeit under a watchful ruler, has been often repeated. Who is the tiger and who is the lamb? Why did the unity between Hindus and Muslims splinter down to the level of murder and accusation? Clearly the Cow Protection Movement was a precursor into what would transform by the 1920s into a militant Hindu nationalism resulting in more violence over the years.

Why do temples and mosques which have coexisted together for years suddenly plunge a city into chaos? The Byculla temple–mosque dispute is a case in point. Why do prayer timings result in disharmony? The questions over a century have remained the same. In fact with each riot, history shows that people began to get more and more marginalized, moving into places dominated by their own community for safety and security. The country's division to create Pakistan was the cause of much rioting in the years leading up to the Independence and the few years after that also resulted in bloody riots. The strong right-wing movement from pre-Independence also contributed to much tension and a political line of thought which has continued over the years even after 1947. After the anti-Sikh riots in 1984, perhaps the worst communal bloodbath in the country, was in Mumbai after the Babri Masjid demolition on 6 December 1992. The Gujarat carnage topped that, the result of a well-planned pogrom ostensibly to 'avenge' the deaths of those killed in a train fire at Godhra.

Nothing is spontaneous about riots in this country or the events leading up to it. In Mumbai there seemed to be some planning and a definite method in the madness, as Justice B. N. Srikrishna has pointed out in his extensive inquiry report. Over the span of a century Mumbai too has been scarred along the way, but yet it is a city that has come together time and again, casting a veil over those scars. Hope and despair is evident in every story of a riot victim. It is a city that carries the weight of a century of bloody strife.

3

JOGESHWARI RIOTS

OLD WOUNDS, NEW GHETTOS

A special branch report (First Jogeshwari Riots, 7 November 1974, Special Branch 1 CID, Police Department) referring to the Jogeshwari riots says:

> The Jogeshwari police station area consist(s) of (a) shanty town, where Uttar Bharatiyas (North Indians) and Muslims who came there in large numbers started constructing unauthorized sheds and chawls. A major riot between Uttar Bharatiyas and Maharashtrians had taken place in 1964. After this the Muslims came into the area and started constructing unauthorized chawls, thereby causing influx of Muslims in the area. The low income Hindus occupied many of these chawls as tenants. The influx of both the communities naturally created problems, not only for the state but for the education of their children, worshipping of the respective religions, cremation/burial of the

dead. The Muslims created their own mosques, Idgah maidans, Madarsas and kabrastans. The Hindus had their cemetery and temples. None of these places was authorized, but the respective communities continued to live without any friction. However, the ever expanding unauthorized construction led to many clashes of interests. Chawl owners clashed with tenants over the latter's insistence of their rights and facilities. Chawl owners vied with each other in building unauthorized tenements. The tenants organized themselves as 'Bhadekaru Sangh' (tenants association), and often the landlords were Muslims while the tenants were Hindus. Tenants of Hindu and Muslim origin had different and conflicting interests in their places of worship, places of education and places of burial. Politics added a new dimension to this problem with the Congress trying to have a neutral role, with the Shiv Sena and the Muslim League playing the opposite role.

The Muslims around this time constructed a small hut and called it a 'madarsa'. This was in Meghwadi, in the middle of the Hindu locality. It was originally meant to serve as a school. But some time later, the Muslims started bringing dead bodies there and offering prayers, as if it was a mosque. This created misgivings in the minds of the Hindu population. The Muslims also claimed that this Madarsa was in existence for some years past (they put up a board there to indicate that it had been here since 1964, where as in fact it has been there since an year or so). The open space of this maidan was used by the Hindus for their sports activities and occasionally to hold a Satyanarayana pooja and other religious functions. It was also learnt that some Hindus from Meghwadi set fire to the roof of a darga known as Dadima's Darga [Dadima was a resident of Mahim but was buried in the Jogeshwari Kabarastan (unauthorized) over which a construction was made, known as 'Dadima's Darga']. To make matters further difficult the Muslims built a barbed wire compound fencing around the open ground, so that it could demonstrate their possessiveness over the ground. The ground did not belong either to the Muslims or to the Hindus. It belonged to a third party all together. In order, therefore, to counter this move on the part of the Muslims, the Hindus installed after holding Satyanarayana Pooja, idols of Ganpati and Maruti in that place. This created a tension between two communities in the area.

On 7 November 1974, at about 10.30 pm, one Mohamed Azada, son of Abbas Ansari, a Muslim of 28 years of age, was assaulted by six or seven persons, apparently Hindus, near Meghwadi. This incident of riot between the two communities resulted in arson, looting, and damage to property including assaults on police, and this riot spread to the adjoining area of the Jogeshwari Police Station and to the various colonies around. According to a table showing the loss of property and lives between 7 November 1974 and 14 November 1974, the total loss reported was ₹ 566,311 lakh—while the Hindus lost ₹ 63,275 worth of goods, the Muslims lost ₹ 503,036. Of the total 62 victims of arson, 35 were Muslims and 27 were Hindus. In addition, four timber depots, four bakeries, three shops, three factories, all belonging to Muslims, were burnt, apart from two mosques and one *dargah*. The Hindus too lost two shops to fire, two taxis, and two dispensaries, apart from a flour mill. Four people died in the riots, and four officers and 13 policemen were injured.

Jogeshwari grew as a far-flung suburb of Mumbai, with migrants settling down in large numbers, and who came into conflict with the local population. After the 1964 riots, that Jogeshwari would become a communal hotbed was only natural, given this history of early polarization. Every riot only served to widen the distance between the two communities and yet people did live together until 1992–93 when the final break happened. Today, Jogeshwari still has those old divisions: there are deep-seated prejudices, but there is talk of harmony, specially among the youth. There is no need now for communal riots. The polarization has already been achieved.

The Gandhi *Chawl* Incident

It was all in the eyes. Beneath the finely drawn brows, they were haunted and distant. For Naina Bane, the night of 8 January 1993 will remain a night of absolute terror. Her escape was miraculous as was her recovery. It took me several months and wrong leads before I met her finally at a family reunion in the suburbs. Dressed in a long mustard coloured 'maxi', her hair was drawn back tightly. I found it hard to recognize the same girl who was almost burnt alive on that fateful night in Gandhi *chawl*. Now 40, there is a faraway look about her and her eyes widen when I ask to speak to her. She got married in 1996 and lives outside Mumbai. Her 6-year-old son keeps her busy. Her husband worked for a mill which closed down, a typical story in Mumbai. He was a *badli* (temporary worker) and he lost his job. He now works as a watchman.

Naina's right hand is still swollen and scarred. The entire right side of her body was burnt, but corrective surgery helped restore it. For two or three months after she came out of the hospital, she could not do any work, and even now it is difficult for her to lift heavy things. Her brothers are jobless and insecure. She tells me to do something for them, for herself, she wants nothing. She pauses frequently and never wants to go back to that area. The fire of that night still haunts her. She still suffers from a lot of mental trauma and the sight of blood unsettles her. There is perplexity in her face and she seems dazed. She keeps repeating that none of them knew why it happened. Her parents, who lived there for a long time, had such good relations with everyone. Even after so many years, Naina starts trembling when she sees an accident or something untoward. She had to leave the flaming room from the roof. She suffered 50 per cent burns and had to fight for her survival. The family had to pay the hospital bills. Naina was the only one staying with her parents; everyone else was with her sister, Sujata Chavan.

In the end, she is bitter about the fact that the family was left to fend for itself. The youngest brother, Mangesh, has a temporary job as a telephone operator. She feels there is no hope now. Sujata had submitted an application for a low-cost house in the government's Maharashtra

Housing and Area Development Authority (MHADA) in 1995. Her husband, Kamlakar, says she is on the waiting list. He is indignant and says that the family at least deserved a house. He checked with the MHADA in June 2008, and they told him to wait some more.

She now feels what the rest of her family feels, to never live in a Muslim locality; there is disgust and discomfort with the idea. The Banes story is the story of many families in Jogeshwari who moved out and never want to live with Muslims ever again. The past relationships have been forgotten. That night the blaze in Gandhi *chawl* not only wrecked their lives and aspirations, but also created a permanent rift in their minds.

I met Naina and her family after a long search. I asked Ravindra Waikar, the Shiv Sena MLA and former chairperson of the standing committee of the BMC who promised to help. I was told to meet his secretary, Bala Nar, for information and whom I called many times. He said he had all the addresses of the 'Hindu' victims of Jogeshwari. But every time I called, there was some delay. Either he was travelling or was busy. I did not call Waikar again, but decided to rely on my own sources who finally tracked down the family for me. It was *Pitrupaksha Amawasya* in 2008 when I met them, the day you remember your ancestors and pray for them. It was a day when the entire Bane family gathered for lunch in the small one-room house of Sudarshan Bane in Gorai, and there was a certain poignancy about the event. When I called Sudarshan the day earlier, he invited me over. When I asked if I would be interfering in the ceremonies, he said no. He was most cordial in his invitation and asked me to come and meet his family. I was a little apprehensive if it was the right family as I had met many Banes earlier and they all turned out to be the wrong people. Walking into the bye lanes at Gorai, I met a man who turned out to be Sudarshan. It was almost a cinematic encounter. The area is a lower-middle class area with flat-roofed tenements and the day being Sunday, few people were on the road. Sudarshan was the one who spotted me as I was wandering around in the lanes searching for his house. Wearing a faded old shirt and shorts, his hands covered with white plaster of Paris, he was busy making a statue of Goddess Durga in a makeshift plastic tent. He later told me that he had hired a small bungalow plot on which he built a plastic tent, which functions as his workshop. We went to his house where his sister, Sujata, was sitting on the floor along with his wife cutting vegetables and making preparations for lunch. It is a small one-room house with a kitchen. His children run in and out playing around.

The first thing he tells me is that it was Gandhi *chawl* which was burnt and not Radhabai *chawl*. Radhabai *chawl* was on the main road and people mistakenly thought that was the scene of the riot. What he is bitter about is that residents of Radhabai *chawl* got a lot of support and benefits in their name, while they got nothing. When I met him, he was 37. He lives on rent and in his life few things are permanent. He has been through several temporary jobs since the riots. Emotions spill out as he talks about his life after the riots. During the festival season, he makes Ganpati idols and otherwise he gets temporary jobs as a driver. There is a look of dejection about him. The government had promised him and his family so much. He did the rounds with various political leaders including those of Ravindra Waikar, Sunil Dutt, the late MP, and former Maharashtra chief minister, Sudhakar Naik, and once he was even taken to meet the prime minister, Atal Bihari Vajpayee.

The Banes are a typical lower-middle class migrant family from the coastal Konkan region. Sudarshan's father, Rajaram, who lost his life in the riots used to work for Sigma paints. At that time, Sudarshan used to work for a company making tubes for Colgate and when the incident happened he was working on a night shift. Soon, that job was gone and he started driving an auto-rickshaw. Now, he has to keep moving from house to house as he stays on rent and it is difficult with his two school-going children. Youth for Unity and Voluntary Action (YUVA), a non-governmental organization (NGO), bought the *chawl* from the Banes and they were paid ₹ 40,000 for the rooms. It was their home, painstakingly built by their parents, who had lived there even before marriage.

Sujata was eight-months pregnant with her second child at the time of the riots and Sudarshan had come to stay with her in Charkop, not far from his present house. Her father had died on the spot and she was in a quandary as she could not leave home. The terror of those days still haunts her. The two boys, Sudarshan and Mangesh, stayed with her at that time because they could not go back to the house. Years later she cannot understand why that horrific incident took place. They were among the few Maharashtrians there surrounded by Muslims, but they never had any problems in those days. The two communities always protected each other. There was no reason to be attacked in this heinous fashion. She is silent as she tries to recall the events of that night. Suddenly she comes up with an answer: 'It was all to do with that Babri Masjid demolition.' She also remembers that the accused in the Gandhi *chawl* case, acquitted by the Supreme Court, were released later. And no one appealed against their release. I asked her if the family ever considered taking up the case and got a violent reaction: 'Why should we appeal? Who has the time to go court and waste time and money? We don't want to take revenge; their *karma karta* will take care of it.'

Sujata concentrates on cutting the huge mound of vegetables. Her thin face reflects her helplessness. At that time too, they were alone, despite much political support on the surface. The whole family kept saying how the big leaders promised them so many things, but nothing happened. Not even a simple job was given to Sudarshan, something he is very upset about. The place where they all live now is a Hindu locality. Everyone is Maharashtrian. They do not want to live anywhere else.

The old Gandhi *chawl* area is now completely a Muslim area. None of them venture back there. Sudarshan says they (the Muslims) used to threaten the Maharashtrians and many sold their houses and left. There was an atmosphere of fear and terror. However, even now Sudarshan and Sujata feel the two communities can live together. People in their locality were good. The riots occurred because someone instigated the attack. The words come out slowly now. They never thought of their Muslim neighbours as aliens. Sudarshan often played cricket together with the other boys in the slum. But both Sujata and Sudarshan are tired of the long wait for justice or social support. They have given up all hope now.

Once Ravindra Waikar had come and with a great sense of urgency had taken Sudarshan to meet Vajpayee. There was a momentary surge of hope and he thought something would happen. His face breaks into a sad grin. He ended up wasting two days running around and lost his two-day earnings as a rickshaw driver. Again more hope and promises. They had become a showpiece for the party and the face of the riots. They were paraded everywhere as the victims of a heinous crime, but their shattered lives were only theirs to deal with.

Sudarshan's children study in the sixth and seventh standards. His elder son is ticked off for putting a plastic helmet on a bronze-coloured bust of Shivaji Maharaj, which occupies pride of place in the small room. Sudarshan has been making Ganpati and Durga idols since the age of seven. Now, he often takes a loan for the capital. It is hardly a profit-making venture and he thinks of giving it up sometimes. Now it is the customers who insist that he makes the idols.

I spoke to Sudarshan in April 2010 to check if all was well. He works as a driver for a doctor now and has extended his rent lease by one more year in Gorai. Vinod Ghosalkar, the Shiv Sena MLA called him once and gave him an assurance that he would get a house. 'Once again I got an assurance', he remarked. The Banes story is no different from the other riot victims. They were victims of a heinous crime and they received no support from the government. The 11 accused of the crime were given life sentence by the designated Terrorist and Disruptive Activities (Prevention) Act (TADA) court, but later acquitted in 1998 by the Supreme Court which questioned the evidence in the case. This too was a highly publicized trial and the acquittal was criticized by the Right wing. However, that is a separate case of victimization, according to many activists. The political parties, who got so much mileage from the Banes' tragedy, have probably forgotten them altogether. Their story was used extensively to whip so much anti-Muslim hatred.

The *Srikrishna Commission Report* (Srikrishna 1998: 85, Volume II) has this to say on the Gandhi *chawl* incident:

> On 8th January, 1993, at about 00.30 hours a house in a chawl popularly known as Radhabai Chawl (though its actual name is Gandhi chawl) was attacked by miscreants who locked the door

of a Hindu house from outside and set it on fire. Although nine persons from the Hindu family of Bane had been confined inside the room, some of them managed to escape. Six of the family succumbed to burn injuries including a handicapped girl.

One male and five female members of a Hindu family (Bane) and their neighbours were charred to death and three other Hindus sustained serious burn injuries.

Revisiting Gandhi *Chawl*, Jogeshwari

It is a Sunday morning and I am going to attend the inaugural function of a youth group called Aagaz. Sitaram Shelar from YUVA, the NGO which has done extensive work in the area, is there to meet me and make sure I do not get lost. We climb the trademark narrow staircase into the loft above a medical clinic and a large group of young people had already gathered. The walls of the room are freshly painted and plastered with posters defining Aagaz. There is an expectant buzz before the formal inauguration and everyone looks justifiably proud.

Sitaram, who also grew up in Jogeshwari and is a field convenor with YUVA, says that its work with the affected communities in the area, and since 1998 with the youth, has made a big difference. The focus is on some core issues like gender justice, civic issues, and livelihoods. Many youth groups have sprung up in the area and are extremely active. Shaali Abdul Sheikh, one of the youngsters who has set up Aagaz, started it in 2006 with a handful of members. 'Aagaz' means beginning and they wanted to do something for the youth and started by organizing medical camps, and after the serial train blasts on 11 July 2006, held peace rallies. Shaali lives in Janata Colony, which is in Bandra plot, a predominantly Muslim settlement. Now 22, Shaali was a kid when the riots broke out. Growing up, he felt that Hindus and Muslims are separate entities. He lived in a ghetto surrounded by non-Muslims, and had very few interactions with other communities. His association with

YUVA helped him meet many people and dispel a lot of his misgivings. He was worried about religion. He lived near the 'border'—a road which separates the Hindu and Muslim communities in Jogeshwari—and had to shift inside for safety. After the riots his worried parents insisted they stayed at home, they rarely moved out.

His association with YUVA helped him look at people not as belonging to a particular religion, but as human beings. Aagaz has about 20 members from all communities and runs on private contributions. Shaali is hopeful and has the enthusiasm of youth. He is quite firm that they do not want any more riots here.

Jogeshwari East saw some of the worst rioting during 1992–93. But what happened in January 1993 changed the way people would live in that area forever. A lot of switching over happened which has been documented by YUVA in their report (1996 edition) titled 'Planned Segregation' by Miloon Kothari and Nasreen Contractor . Wounds are deep and time has been a healer in many ways. There is no political exigency now to kill and gain votes. Till that greed resurfaces, Jogeshwari enjoys its communal harmony, however fragile.

From Jogeshwari suburban station East you have to share an autorickshaw to Meghwadi. As you sit crushed in the back seat, the rickshaw carries through the narrow roads, past the large, stinking *nallah*, where some egrets search for food, and down the slope into Meghwadi. The centre of the storm during the riots of January 1993, today 'the border' as it is still called, is relatively peaceful. The bloody riots only intensified that separation, though bridges have been built over the years. As you get off the auto, the local Shiv Sena *shakha* greets you with giant posters of party executive president, Uddhav Thackeray, and saffron flags. Shops and vegetable vendors cram the 'border', which splits the Hindu- and Muslim-dominated localities of this western suburb.

It was in Gandhi *chawl* on Jogeshwari East that four persons were burnt alive; two of them died later. This led to the worst episode of rioting all over Mumbai. Today, Gandhi *chawl* has been rebuilt and is the office of YUVA, which bought it over since no one was willing to live here. Jogeshwari has witnessed repeated riots since 1964 in varying intensities, and for the people who live there it is an uneasy backdrop to their existence.

Another organization, which has been working for a while in Jogeshwari, is Society for Awareness, Harmony and Equal Rights (SAHER), run by Sheikh Masood Akhtar. The repeated riots in Jogeshwari already ensured the process of ghettoization. After 1992–93 that process was complete and Akhar says rather reluctantly that only about 5 per cent Hindus are left in this area. The riots left a deep impact on the children who had witnessed it and on those who had passed through that troubled time. Akhtar too was driven by the need to do something. They had street plays on communal harmony, and began helping students with their school books. SAHER was also part of the local *mohalla* committee. Meetings were initiated between police and people as there was a lot of distrust. SAHER held programmes like Diwali Milan to bring youth and police together. Another idea was to host sports meets so that children of Urdu- and English-medium schools would get a chance to compete with each and, later, even become friends. Now, lack of funds is hampering this event. SAHER has also held workshops to break down stereotypes with the help of International Association for Religious Freedom and also responds to various civic needs.

Walking down the road from Aagaz, you come to where the tenements end and a group of apartments have sprung up. Just before the end is a large square building with 'Akanksha Seva Sangh' painted across it. Set up by Shiv Sena's Ravindra Waikar in 1982, Akanksha functions as a *balwadi* (crèche) and has now branched out into working with women and helping them with credit and savings groups. Vasant Ambore of Akanksha tells me about the organization which also hosts *melas* and works with the handicapped in the western suburbs and with the youth. Though it worked mainly with Hindu communities in the area, for two years, as part of another venture, Samaj Sanshodhan Kendra, they interacted with other communities. This started an exchange between the youth and after that if there was a problem, they get in touch with each other and sort out problems. Initially, the police also had *mohalla* committees, but that did not work.

Ambore tells me that since the 1992–93 riots, many things have changed. He has also worked with Muslim youth in the area and mobilized them to form groups. There are some seven or eight groups now. People understand the politics behind the riots and both sides feel this should not happen. He was quite proud that Aagaz was set up with some of the youth he had worked with. It has members of different communities and the atmosphere is quite different now.

YUVA'S Community Resource Centre (CRC) worked in the area to bring together youth. Ambore used to stay on the border and, though his house was damaged, he did not move from there. He came across CRC and started attending their programmes. He confesses that he was attracted to the political meetings (called by the Sena), but he also went for meetings by YUVA and Salokha, which worked on communal harmony. He is happy he has, what he described as a 'realistic picture' of what happens. Like others, he too feels that the Sena is not as radical as it used to be. Youth groups try to keep a balance between all parties instead of adhering to any single ideology.

Both communities have found many common causes and the 26 July 2005 floods was a case in point. People come together on common issues and have good relations in that sense. Communal issues occupy very little time now, maybe about 25 per cent, estimates Ambore. There are some staunch 'Hindutva *wadis*', but the earlier fervour has gone down. Politically, people are divided and geographically too in many ways. Despite this there is an atmosphere of cooperation, at least for the moment.

Communities who live there know how fragile this peace can be. And the memories of those riots are very fresh for those who lost their loved ones. Rabia Apa or Rabiabi Ahmed Naik recalls the fear and terror of those times. She was among those actively involved in the peace efforts after the riots. Rabia came from a village in Deogad on the Konkan coast. After her marriage, she has been living in Pascal Colony since 1975. A housewife, Rabiabi was forced to come out of her house after her daughter's marriage broke up. During the riots, she was among those who tried to broker peace and help the affected.

The one thing that stands out in her memory is the eerie silence that fell over the slum after much of the violence had abated—a silence that many others remember too. I met her in the evening, interrupted with hectic activity as the water comes only once a day. She manages to make a cup of tea and talk to me while directing operations. Rabia's memory is sharp and she is a good narrator. Sitting in her house I begin to feel what must have happened in this area at that time. The close, congested houses, the narrow lanes, the need to be safe. Yet, the only Maharashtrian family living in her lane was not touched. However, many families left after the riots, making Pascal Colony more of a Muslim pocket. Many Muslim families moved into the area too. Rabia was among those who testified to police inaction and Sena's role in the riots before Justice Srikrishna. She tells me that both sides attacked each other and rioted, but the police sided with the Hindus. So many businesses were hit and it took so long for people to come back and get their lives on track. Now people can roam freely and there is no fear. Rabia is quite firm that the common person today understands that riots are not for them.

Like Rabia, Savita Khamkar has been living in Jogeshwari since 1975. From 1990, she worked with YUVA's Jogeshwari Rahiwasi Sangh. The suburb has clear divisions and few people venture into each other's areas. Recalling the riots, she says that all the Hindus left and, despite getting the police here, people died. For Savita, that was a terrible time, her worst memory was that little children were killed—her whole family used to huddle in one room. Her landlady is a Muslim and for three months they had to protect her, taking turns day and night. There were about 500 Hindu families here. Now about 100 are left. Savita is clear that they faced a lot of harassment from the Muslims. Many wanted them (the Hindus) to sell and leave, but people were offering a pittance. For three months after the riots there was tension.

It is only 15 years after the riots, that she feels peace has come back to the area. On 26 July 2005, during the floods, they (the Muslims) helped them a lot with food and other things—there was some unity for the first time. Now people will think 10 times before getting violent. Mohalla committees have been working here since 1994 and there are beat-wise meetings with the police. There are many new organizations of young people, both Hindus and Muslims, and they all work together. After the railway serial blasts in 2006 too, there was a lot of unity—people went to hospitals, contacted next of kin, and informed the police.

Worse than the riots was the behaviour of the police, she tells me. Savita's house was attacked and her roof tiles were all broken. The crude fire bombs fell inside and set fire to the clothes inside the house. No one could even repair those tiles for months. It was only after the riots that two police *chowky*s were set up there. Her house is right on the border, a short walk away from the Shiv Sena *shakha*, a trouble spot. After the Gandhi *chawl* incident, all the Hindu families there left and never came back. Savita stayed back, she had nowhere to go. But she did not stay quiet. She resolutely went about forming a housing society called Prem Nagar Gruh Nirman Sanstha; there are 126 families in it. The Muslims did not want to join the society, but there are no communal feelings. Housing is important, it means safety. She believes in *Sarva Dharma Samabhav*. She has a straight reason for housing; at least stones and bombs will not hit them and kill them.

Savita works with Muslims in the area. She feels slum rebuilding is important. For the first time after the riots, they organized a meeting in March 2007 to bring the two communities together. Many people came to visit the diverse stalls, 25 of them, and there was much camaraderie. This was a major event, unnoticed in the city. People who are usually suspicious of each other ventured into common terrain and enjoyed the experience. Muslims came out warily and so did the Hindus. Savita's aim is clear: riots must be prevented and only by communities trusting each other, can this happen. She does not see any reason to leave the border even though Hindus are in a minority. She cannot understand how people can kill on some political pretext. Savita's bitter rant against the police continues. She complained against some *goondas* in the area who were causing all the problems during the riots and the police gave her name away to them. For days she was under threat and she had a tough time keeping her children from going out and attacking the police who did this to them. For her, the only way to end all this rift is by educating people and developing the area.

Migration from Jogeshwari—The Hindu Ghetto

On the side of the Eastern Express Highway near Mulund is a huge Maharashtra State Housing Board colony. Single or one-storied tenements stand in organized rows on its dusty streets. It is a far cry from the congested slums in Jogeshwari as Subhash Kamtekar and his family, who moved here from Jogeshwari after the riots there in December–January 1992–93, discovered. Here, there is safety in numbers. It is one of the many Hindu ghettos that came up after the riots in an organized, government-supported manner. Kamtekar lived in Jogeshwari for 30 years before he decided to move out. He works for a private company and hails from the Konkan coast. Kamtekar moved here saying he was not willing to risk living in a Muslim area. He left in 1993, when the riots occurred. His old house was in his father's name and he sold it. Luckily, for him, the government provided for another house. His neighbours too left. Many Hindus were given houses in Mulund and they resettled here. Now his wife runs a shop in the small house.

Forty-seven-year-old Kamtekar, who hails from Kankavli in Sindhudurg district, lived in a locality in Jogeshwari, which had a Muslim majority. After the riots he was scared. He often stayed out for a week or so because of curfew. There were riots before this, but this was the worst, he recalls. However, Kamtekar affirms that he really had no problems in Jogeshwari. At that time his son was four months old. His children were very young and there was fire everywhere. For him, the Gandhi (Radhabai) *chawl* incident was the most frightening incident—he keeps imagining people in a room being burnt alive. His entire family was horrified, they kept thinking this would happen to them and wanted to leave after that.

Most people have moved out and of the 50 homes in Teli *chawl* in Jogeshwari, only two are left. Even while leaving he prevailed on his good neighbours to buy his house. Shubhangi, his wife, also had a trying time with two small children at the time of the riots. She cannot forget the fear and the threat to their lives after the Radhabai *chawl* incident. Earlier, there were riots, small incidents, but people sorted them out. Even their Muslim neighbours had told them not to worry; nothing would happen while the riots flared up. But after the Radhabai *chawl* incident people started leaving slowly. Shubhangi was afraid theirs would be the only Hindu family which remained.

Kamtekar, who dropped out of school after the fourth standard, was working in a company close by. He used to cycle to his office daily. On the day of the Radhabai *chawl* incident, he was coming back home late on his bicycle when the police stopped him from entering the area. It was so dangerous that the police had to escort him home. The question troubling him then was where could he go along with his family. The tension was unbearable in those days. Now he feels safe in a predominantly Hindu area with over 35 cooperative societies and over 5,000 families. Kamtekar, like the others who shifted here, did not suffer any loss of property or loss of loved ones. Politicians like Ravindra Waikar and others helped many Hindu families shift here. Kamtekar tells me that he and his family had no quarrels with anyone. He even preferred to live in a mixed locality; it was much more fun, especially during festivals. However, he travels outside very often and his family is left alone. He has no regrets about his earlier life in Jogeshwari, but now his preference is clear. It is safe and he feels it is better to stay with your own community. If he is not there, there are others to look after his family. He goes back to the 'good tradition' of coexistence, but now after the riots, it is a good trend to live separately. Kamtekar has not visited his old locality for two years. He also had to make a distress sale then in 1993. He did not have a loyalty to any party, but was grateful for the help received from political parties for resettling him here.

The Housing Board Colony has a maze of narrow, dusty lanes and most of the houses are single-storied tenements. Chandra Chabukswar and her husband Dayanand, now 75, used to live in Maruf Pathan *chawl* in Jogeshwari for 40 years. Dayanand, a fourth-standard drop out, used to work for the naval dockyard and retired in 1993. He hails from Ahmednagar district. He lived in Byculla in south Mumbai when he first came to the city. Peace took a backseat in Jogeshwari when during a Navratri festival, there was some trouble over the statue of the goddess. Shiv Sena's Ravindra Waikar, came and tried to sort things out. Like Kamtekar, Dayanand and his wife also reiterate that the Radhabai *chawl* incident was scary: 'We were confused and afraid and Waikar kept us in a *balwadi* (a crèche) for many days. He gave us food and clothing and we only had our photo passes which served as an identity.' They had all sealed their houses and from January to July land lived in the *balwadi*. Then Waikar made arrangements for them to shift here in 1995.

When they came to live here, there was no water or roads, but things have improved over the years. In Jogeshwari, there was no fear at all; in fact they (the Muslims) loved them and there was no problem. But still they felt it was better to move away from them. Nothing happened during the riots to the family, but the fear of the Radhabai *chawl* incident was the final deciding factor. They felt as if it was a personal threat. No Muslims moved out. Even in these new houses only Hindus are present. Both husband and wife say that it is better to live in a mixed community. They used to have a lot of give and take. It is a matter of surprise that even though they were Mohammedans, their neighbours loved them and they lived there together for 40 years. There was no personal enmity; instead, there was a lot of affection. But now they are happy here with what they describe as their 'own people'. In fact, Chandra, who has studied up to the seventh standard, used to teach the Muslim children Marathi in her spare time.

Forty-year-old Sunil Lanjekar was born in Jogeshwari, but the riots forced him to move to Mulund. He sold his house three to four months after the riots. While I sit in his relatively new house, with two rooms, he talks to me frankly. Till the Ram Janmabhoomi issue, things were normal in Jogeshwari despite the riots of the past. Even now, he thinks outsiders created the problem. There was no animosity and they lived together with Muslims. He cannot think of a reason why they would ever fight and yet when the government came up with a scheme for Hindus to shift out of Jogeshwari, Lanjekar promptly sold his house and moved out. At first, he and his family lived in a camp in Shyam Nagar along with 25 other families. People were scared of more attacks and sought refuge together. Later, they took a room on rent and lived there as his house was slightly damaged.

At that time, Lanjekar was very young, but he remembers the fear that prevailed. The Gandhi *chawl* incident made things much worse. Many people sold and left and he rarely goes back to the place where he grew up. An eighth-standard drop out, he works for a private company now and is married with two children. He complains that the maintenance for the house is too high at ₹ 500 a month. Lanjekar's memory of the old times is strong; he remembers that the atmosphere in his locality in Jogeshwari changed after the riots. There was a good relationship earlier, but it all ended. There was a lot of mistrust. He still believes that a mixed locality is better and he liked his old place. He thinks for a while and tells me that if you live in the same community your knowledge decreases. He is not going back though, his work keeps him busy and he is happy here. As I leave, Lanjekar takes great pains to tell me that he had good relations with everyone and there was no strife in his mixed locality.

Jogeshwari is a fast-developing suburb and one of the more lucrative options is to sell to a real estate developer. Umesh Kadam, a Congress loyalist and resident of Jogeshwari, recalls that 48 families were kept in two camps during the riots. He has studied upto the twelfth standard and is a draftsman. Now, he is into real estate development. One of the camps was in the New Shyam Nagar *balwadi*, where Lanjekar and the others lived for a while. For three months, the families were cared for by Kadam and his supporters. They were all residents of Bandra Plot, which was a Muslim area, and it was Waikar who brought them to the *balwadi*. People from various parties collected stuff for them and many NGOs also helped out. Their main role was instilling confidence in the Hindus who were scared after the Radhabai *chawl* incident. Even film producer

Ashok Pandit came here and appreciated their efforts. Radhabhai *chawl* was on Bandra plot and after it was burnt, residents of Shankar Wadi, Gandhi Nagar, Dias compound, Meghwadi and Pump House were at risk. Even Anand Dighe, the late Sena leader, came here to support relief work. Even though Kadam was in the Congress, he helped these people—there was a lot of spirit in those days. He feels if they had not helped the Hindus, they would have possibly turned to terrorism. They were given houses so they felt secure. About 20 families were re-housed in New Shyam Nagar and the late Sunil Dutt, MP, got approval for these *chawls* as they were not legal. He got the government to regularize the homes for those who had left the Bandra Plot.

Kadam says few Muslims were displaced from Jogeshwari during the riots. They stayed in their houses and may have left later, but not in significant numbers. He draws a line between Maharashtra and Gujarat. Had Radhabai *chawl* happened in Gujarat, the whole Bandra plot would have been burnt down. He testifies to the impartiality of the police; they even fired at Maharashtrians and many died in the riots and contrary to what people say, he avers that Muslims were well protected. Only the Shiv Sena was active then, but they did not have much support unlike in Gujarat. Kadam feels we cannot only protect Muslims; if Hindus are in minority then they too should be protected.

He also says that after 1993, people were so terrorized that they will never riot again. Now the youth which formed the cadre of the Sena are interested in jobs, not riots. Also, he feels the Sena leadership under Bal Thackeray has lost its charisma and Uddhav, his son, was not antiminorities. He has witnessed riots since 1984 and it is the politicians who literally cause a volatile situation. He also has a theory about riots. He has studied riots and according to him they happen mostly during winters. Even L. K. Advani chose winter to launch his *rath yatra* and it is significant that the Babri Masjid was destroyed in winter. That is the time people sit together and gossip and it is easy to spread rumours. When you have a community like Jogeshwari with Maharashtrians and north Indians living together, it is easy to manipulate them and cause tensions. After the riots, if people saw Muslims on the street, they made their hatred obvious. Jogeshwari had many riots; it is a fight of locals versus outsiders, but it did not affect the whole of Mumbai. After the Radhabai *chawl* incident, the whole of Mumbai was on fire. The Hindus came together and that single incident succeeded in uniting them like never before. Many Muslims were killed and the divisions deepened, he explains.

What has also contributed to the decline of the Sena is that many of the rank and file were not at all helped by the party. The present generation saw what had happened and they realized that the party loyalties did not help the earlier generation legally. There was a lot of disillusionment and this has led to the younger generation veering away from politics.

However, certain divisions in Jogeshwari are forever. The area near Meghwadi is still called the 'border' and even though there are efforts made by NGOs and people like Savita Khamkar, who try and bring together people from both communities, divisions exist. Kadam says now the whole country is like Jogeshwari. There are deep religious differences, but he also sees that incidents like Radhabai *chawl* are created to provoke the poor into hatred. He also does not believe that all Muslims are bad. Even Hindus have terrorists, as also Naxalites.

The Shiv Sena systematically made inroads into Jogeshwari and one of the young men who made it to the top is Ravindra Waikar. Waikar, 49, has not lost a corporation election since 1992 from a Muslim majority area in Jogeshwari. He was an elected MLA in the 2009 assembly elections from there. He claims that Muslims do not vote for him though. At the beginning of the border in Jogeshwari, which separates the Hindu areas of Meghwadi from Bandra plot and other Muslim areas, is the Shiv Sena *shakha*. People sit around reading newspapers, women comb each others' hair. It is the centre of activity. Huge pictures of Waikar, along with Sena leader Bal Thackeray and his son Uddhav, and the saffron flag mark the *shakha*. Waikar was much mentioned in the *Srikrishna Commission Report* and he is defiant about not being involved in any rioting and was acquitted much later in a riot case. He insists it is only for leading a *morcha* and handing over a memorandum to the police. He admits to the clear division in Jogeshwari where he comes from. He says:

> We felt the need to unite the Hindus after the Radhabai chawl incident. But we also tried to prevent riots and set up two committees. We tried to ensure the riots did not spread. We ran camps for Hindus who had to leave the Muslim areas they were living in. But the Radhabai chawl burning worsened the situation and the whole of Mumbai was affected. The Sena did not engineer the riots, it was spontaneous as the Hindus were brutally burnt.

I asked him about the inflammatory reports in *Saamna*—he said, 'yes the words of Balasaheb inspired us'. The culprits who burnt Radhabai *chawl* were let off. I asked if the Sena appealed, to which Waikar replied why only the Sena? Everyone should have appealed. Regarding the legal help for Sainiks accused in rioting, he said: 'We cannot help individuals, why should only we help out—society should also take responsibility for them. Yes we ran camps for Hindus only, there was no one to help them.'

> Radhabai chawl was an assault on the Hindus- a blot- even children were burnt. Are you saying that's okay? At that time there was no party affiliation—only Hindu and Muslim. The Hindus united against the injustice. Now after so many years the government has revived cases against us, this is harassment. Why only the Sena has been accused of rioting. Why not other parties?

However, Waikar agrees after all those years, now, Hindus and Muslims are living together. There is a lot of communal harmony. People are more literate now and worried about their jobs. Common people are not interested in rioting. Businessmen feel riots will hurt their business. People are more focused on their lives. He blamed the Congress for its communal politics and keeping its vote bank alive: 'We don't want divisions in the Sena but Congress is anti Hindu. We tried to include Muslims in the Sena but the Congress does not let us.'

Jogeshwari may have buried its past, but the people affected by the riots, even the Hindus, had to fend for themselves despite the efforts of Waikar and other Sainiks. New Shyam Nagar has a row of 20 houses, which have a special place. After the riots, a group of people living in Bandra plot got together and bought 5.5 gunthas of land from a private trust and built houses. Residents of Anusuya Nagar in Bandra plot, quite close to the Gandhi *chawl*, were terrorized by the incident and decided to leave. Rukmini, a former Shiv Sainik, who lives in New Shyam Nagar, says there was a lot of tension when riots took place earlier in 1974, 1984, and 1990, but nothing on the scale of the post-Babri Masjid demolition riots. They had come to live here in 1969. Though Rukmini did not suffer any personal loss, she wanted to leave. Her sons were young. One of them was a reluctant witness in a murder case during the riots and they were scared someone would attack him as he had to testify in court.

People got together all the money they had, some did not even have anything but they managed. Funnily, after they managed to build the *chawl* somehow, the chief minister sent a cheque of ₹ 20,000. No one there had a bank account then.

Rukmini's husband worked in the Bombay Port Trust then and she sent her children to live in a house the Port Trust rented for them during the riots. She was all alone at home. Her children, three boys and a girl commuted to school every day by train. In 1994, they moved to the house in New Shyam Nagar. The family was called out by the police soon after the Gandhi *chawl* incident. It was at 4 am one morning that they literally left with the clothes on their backs. That night a policeman was burnt and the situation was terrible. There is horror and disbelief about Gandhi *chawl*. Their house was close by—to reach Gandhi *chawl* you have to go past their *chawl* and it is right on the road.

Only her eldest son went back to the old house seven years later. Rukmini recalls that life in Anusuya *chawl* was happy—both the communities celebrated festivals together, but it all changed after the saffron wave. She enjoyed good relations with her Muslim neighbours and even now when they meet in the market, they exchange pleasantries. They even kept in touch earlier and exchanged sweets till some years ago during major festivals. Now all that has gone. Many of their Muslim neighbours have also moved out. After her husband died some years ago, they came to pay a condolence visit. At first, when they shifted to Anusuya *chawl*, there were many Hindus, but more and more Muslims came to live there. It was a safe area, but the riots caused a lot of tension. Earlier it was safe, people travelled at all hours and things were peaceful despite the occasional riot. Sometimes, when they go back now, some old neighbours ask why they left. Even their doctor was there and Rukmini used to visit him there till she found a new one nearby.

Rukmini and her son feel that for the communities to stay together now would be difficult. In New Shyam Nagar, which is completely a Hindu area, there is no 'tension', things are safe. They feel that human beings want peace—that is not possible when the two communities live together. Their Muslim neighbours were upset that they had moved away after the riots. Rukmini recalls that their old house was close to the police *chowky* and the police said that some of them should stay back and at least give them food. She had to cook for the police and stayed back alone for that reason. Rukmini is rather proud she met BJP leader L. K. Advani when he had come to visit Gandhi *chawl* after the incident. She was also interviewed by the British Broadcasting Corporation (BBC), being one of the Hindus left in that area.

For Rukmini that night of terror will remain in her mind for ever. There was such a huge outcry and the flames leapt up from the house. When she rushed there she saw pieces of burnt flesh lying here and there—the bodies were removed but everything was charred black. That moment of terror was decisive and she decided to leave her house. The only thought in her mind was to save her sons, and she was struck with the thought that something similar would happen to her and she would not be able to save her children. She knew the Banes well. Their children used to go to the other family, Salves', house for tuitions. They had close kinship ties since they all came from the Konkan region. They visited each others' homes often. Her voice drops suddenly and her face becomes still. The evening before this happened, she met Sulochana Bane—they were at the floor mill chatting at around 8 pm. Sulochana had no idea how her life would end just a few hours later.

Her son intervenes and says if they had just beaten up people and scared them the terror would not have spread. The way they were burnt was unimaginable and frightening. It really scared him. There was only one thought in his mind—their house was on the road and what if the same thing happened to them. So many people thought this way at that time—it was an incident designed to terrify people. Waikar inspired a lot of following after the riots and Rukmini too helped him for his first election. After the riots there were no issues for elections—it was all about Hindus versus Muslims. But people have slowly become disgusted with political parties. Every one voted for the Sena because of Hindutva. In the 1970s, Rukmini was also offered a ticket for the municipal elections, but her husband refused to let her contest. She has shared a platform with Bal Thackeray, Sena chief, something she is proud of even now. Like so many others, she too felt a lot of hope when she heard his speeches. After the riots the Hindus came together—it was one incident that changed things and that will remain forever a scar. Now people have put the riots past them and moved ahead.

Vijay More was a teenager when he came to live in Jogeshwari in 1993. Compared to the riots in 1992–93, the rest of the riots were like small gang wars, he remarks. After the Gandhi *chawl* massacre, More helped remove the bodies. There was a huge outcry and people were taking to the streets. He and the others brought all the Hindus to the Housing Board camp and kept them safe as there as it was a free-for-all camp. Now things have changed; there is lots of development. He believes the people arrested for the Gandhi *chawl* incident were not really the culprits. People also understand the politics behind riots—it is for personal and political gains, and communities are divided with that in mind. Many young men were jailed and no one helped them and that has caused a lot of disillusionment about political parties. The role of the Sena in those days is under the scanner by common people, and also the Babri Masjid demolition case in dividing communities. He is one of the few people who knows that the Muslims were not armed contrary to propaganda. After the riots every Hindu felt like a 'Shiv Sainik', he remarks, but that has changed.... There is little time for politics now.

4

EXTENDED GHETTOS

NAYA NAGAR

If the riots caused displacement within the city, it also led to people moving out in search of safety. This has formed closed communities in places like Naya Nagar on Mira Road. I want to begin with the story of Majid. I think it best exemplifies the feeling of alienation and desolation that came about after the riots. On the outskirts of Mumbai, Naya Nagar is infamous for the number of suspected 'terrorists' picked up from its spacious lanes. Its dismayed residents aver that it is hardly a hotbed of terror as it is made out to be.

Two stations after Borivali, outside the city limits, is Mira Road, once filled with paddy fields, swamps, and salt pans. Today, it is a fast-developing suburb, located in Thane district. Naya Nagar holds a special place in the middle-class dream. It offered an extension of Mumbai's dreams and, for Muslims seeking to escape from Mumbai's riots and its aftermath, it became a haven. After I met 75-year-old Majid, on a Friday just before he rushed off for *namaz*, I really wished I had not. The Chiliya Hotel was crowded, but it is a place where many writers and poets in Mira Road meet for a cup of *chai* and some literary discussion. Clad in a crisp *kurta* and *pyjama*, Majid's eyes took on a faraway look as he spoke. I sensed the reluctance, but we ended up chatting a lot. I realized how deep the hurt was and how much he wanted to keep it inside him. I met Abdul Majid Sheikh after many attempts, and after his initial reticence, he spoke at length about his life in Mumbai. Majid had a medical store in Bandra. He lived in a teacher's colony in Bandra East. On 6 December 1992, life went on as usual and he went to his shop like he did every morning after he had retired as a teacher.

But the next day things had changed. When he went to open his shop, he found it wrecked and looted. It was his wife who bore the brunt of that attack. She took one look at the broken shutters and the mess inside and fell unconscious. Majid had put all his money from his retirement fund into the shop. For years he worked as a school inspector in the BMC and this shop was his retirement plan. The shop remained like that for a week and there was curfew. He could do nothing. Majid lived with three sons and a daughter; one of his sons had bought a flat in Naya Nagar two months before the riots. He decided to go and live there as things were very unsafe here. He used to believe that this was a cosmopolitan area. In the teachers' colony, of the 80 flats, only six were occupied by Muslims and they never felt unsafe or unwanted. He lived in Nagpada, in south Mumbai, a predominantly Muslim area and then moved to Bandra because it had 'a good atmosphere'.

Majid and his wife moved to Mira Road and then came back because they thought things would blow over by 25 December. Then he heard someone had set his shop on fire and a woman had stopped him by pulling off the culprit's pants. Majid went searching for this brave woman, but never found her. He believes it was some sort of divine intervention. People told them the names of those who had stolen things from the shop. Still he thought he could restart the shop soon, though they lived in fear and kept the door locked from outside. The other families had left by then and Majid and his wife were isolated. In January again much frenzy was whipped up and Mumbai was burning like it never did in December. Majid once went to the terrace of his building and saw flames everywhere. That was when he thought it was time to leave. *'Jaan se pyara koi cheez nahin'* (there is nothing more precious than life), he whispers.

So, on one morning, his Punjabi neighbours took them by car to the Santa Cruz suburban railway station. It was not an easy trip though. It was early and they had to slink out in the darkness at 6 am. Such was the fear of helping Muslims that his neighbours told them to wait outside and they would drive up as if by accident and give them a lift. For two hours, Majid and his family sweated on the lane and finally, his neighbours came at 8 am. His neighbour was even more scared and pleaded with Majid not to leave as everything was on fire. Majid had hoped to escape with his help and here was his neighbour so terrified. He finally dropped them off to Santa Cruz where they caught a train to Mira Road.

Mira Road was a jungle then, it even had no phones. He had to seek police protection to go back to salvage his shop. He finally decided to sell out and leave. By March 1993, they had shifted and then his sons decided to rent another shop and sell medicines. After the serial bomb blasts occurred, Majid had no courage left. He felt it was better to sell the flat too. In 1993, they sold the flat and slowly his sons also got jobs; his daughter is a teacher now. The rest of the families are there in the teachers' colony, though he later heard some had left. He did not claim any compensation for the shop. He never wanted to come here—the house in Mira Road was bought for his son. If the riots had not taken place, they would never have shifted. For Majid, the move is a shock, something he has not come to terms with yet. He never intended to stay in a Muslim area, and like many people he came here for safety. His wife died 10 years ago and now he feels this is a good place. He cannot go to a cosmopolitan place and his children too do not want to leave.

Sometimes Majid goes to his new shop. His son who is a chemist, runs it. He finds communities are polarized in Naya Nagar too and attributes it all to politics. On a more analytical note, he feels politicians never want people to live together. Majid's memories of Bandra disturb him; he cared a lot for the people there. He used to give so many medicines for free. People touched his feet in gratitude. Even at midnight he opened the shop to give medicines and, in the process, saved so many lives. His flat was on the ground floor behind some hutments. The people there had no electricity. He used to allow them to use light from his shop—the Hindus never allowed that. They used to keep it on all night for functions. As he speaks, Majid's eyes become cloudy. *'Ekdam dil tut gaya* (My heart has broken), he says. Like many Muslims, he used to go for Ganpati festivals—he feels he was so broadminded and so involved with other Hindus. He felt a part of that society and he wanted to be together, that was his idea in living there. His medical shop was called Adarsh Medicals. There were only three shops owned by Muslims in the area—one was a salon and the other did repairs. It was his neighbour who gave him away. Everything was given out, where they lived, where the shop was. The Shiv Sena *shakha pramukh* used to tell people why nothing happened in their area—go and do something (an oft repeated phrase in those days).

His neighbours were of little help—they did not reassure them at all. But they bought him essentials like milk, sugar, tea, and some food. Majid sold his flat to a Hindu. What he misses the most is his small garden. He chose a ground floor flat because he loves plants. He was fond of sitting there—'*Maine apne dil se banaya*' (I made it with my heart). When he left they broke it and destroyed all the coconut trees and the flowers. They said this man had encroached and made this garden, he recalls.

Majid hails from Amravati. After Partition in 1952 he came to Mumbai. There was a shortage of teachers then and he got a job. He had a specific target to enrol children compulsorily. No playing around. In Bharat Nagar in Bandra, he worked to get every child to school. He even got an award for his work and his photo was published in *The Times of India* for being awarded the Best Teacher in 1986. He retired just a year before the riots in 1992. Majid is part of a literary group and he has a well-knit social circle in Naya Nagar, but regret and pain can be seen in his eyes and on the lines on his face. After the interview, he admonished me: 'You made me open my old wounds.' He looked distinctly unhappy and I really wished I had not caused him so much pain. As he hurries away for the afternoon *namaz*, I saw him for what he was—a man struggling with his dignity, but quite broken in a sense.

In contrast, Faiyaz Riffat, the chirpy former director of Doordarshan, comes every morning to have tea and read the paper at the Chiliya Hotel in Naya Nagar. He is a writer and poet too, and is part of the buzzing literary circle. In 1993, he was staying in Dindoshi, Malad, and his son was four years old. His wife is a Maharashtrian; she used to wear a sari, *mangalsutra*, and a *bindi*—she was not scared to do so. He too was not afraid, but kept thinking about his son. He had stayed in Malad for seven or eight years.

Riffat came to Mumbai in 1981. When the riots broke, there was a fear psychosis—every day they heard and read that Muslims were being killed and their property burnt. There was a feeling that Hindus were their enemies, they will kill them. The police paid no heed. He called so many police officers, but no one helped and no one was available. At that time, he was assistant station director of Doordarshan. The decision to leave was taken by his mother-in-law and wife—they thought it was proper to leave and to go to a place where Muslims lived. In November 1993, they took a decision to sell the flat and moved to Naya Nagar.

Naya Nagar was cheaper and it had an Islamic atmosphere (not *his* thinking, but the thinking of common Muslims) and it had cheap eating houses. He was compelled to move as his wife's sister was staying here. However, she has since moved to Millat Nagar. Riffat is all for communities living together. His neighbours were Hindus. They treated them like family and, during the riots, they took care of them. They bought them things and gave them food. Over 14 years later, Riffat rues the decision to move and longs to stay in a cosmopolitan place. He says he is unhappy with the facilities here. The water came 10 years ago, the roads are bad, and the gutters are open. More than that he feels the mentality is narrow-minded, lacking vision.

It's a ghetto. People are educated, not enlightened, they know nothing about etiquette, sobriety, a cultured attitude and cooperation is lacking. Young Muslim boys are least bothered about etiquette. There are no good educational institutions and we lack good schools and good teachers. I feel in a cosmopolitan place you will find a better set up. We are more interested in religious gatherings here.

Mr Riffat's feelings are shared by many who are used to living in a cosmopolitan area. It is a question of what one values more and it depends on the safety levels too. The other reason for his unhappiness is that though Naya Nagar has a strong cultural life and that there are many poets and writers here, it is labelled as a ghetto or a 'hotbed of terrorists'. Many boys were picked up from here after the bomb blasts and two of the main accused in the 11 July train blasts are from here.

Riffat is acutely aware that Naya Nagar is being dubbed as a criminal hotbed. He feels there is no platform to share feelings between communities. Even a simple demand for a passport can turn into a nightmare if you live in Naya Nagar. Riffat says after the riots people came here en masse. In Naya Nagar there is no tension; people are busy with business and small jobs. Real estate business is the mainstay here. Over the years, the Vishwa Hindu Parishad (VHP) and the Shiv Sena have formed some base here and there is some sort of segregation. 'People are poor, they don't really have a choice of being communal', he remarks. Other than Riffat and a few others, I notice a tendency not to speak about the riots. It was as if no one wanted to rake up the past. I even insisted that I did not want to hear about the riots, but people were very reluctant to even speak about what happened after that.

However, around Naya Nagar there are different ghettos springing up, aided by the builders who construct apartments for a particular community. So Naya Nagar is a Muslim area, Shanti Nagar is Hindu, and there are buildings for Khojas, Jains, or other communities. Mixed communities are no longer encouraged. Farhan Hanif, a journalist, has also moved here from south Mumbai. He says that earlier there was some attempt to create mixed communities. Slowly, Muslims were not allowed in places. He says in the building where he stays, Muslims are not allowed any more. Farhan used to live in Kamathipura near a huge Hindu colony. He grew up seeing riots. When Mumbai burned during the Bhiwandi riots he was there. They had no problems in 1992–93. But as a college student in 1984, the police arrested him for a murder case. He never slept at home and used to come only to meet his parents. Once someone tipped off the police and they picked him up. He was tortured for 15 days using a common practice called *nal bandi* where they tie up the person completely. Finally, he was released on bail.

He had marks on his hands due to the torture, but the police claimed it was due to rioting. The cops said he was a criminal known by the name Hanif Kaliya. Finally, he was discharged from the case as there was no evidence against him. After beating him, the police used to apply a popular pain balm everywhere so that the swelling subsided. Once they asked him to run. 'I was so scared they would shoot me I did not run', says Farhan. A postgraduate in Hindi and Urdu, he is now a journalist, a poet, and a writer, but the scars of those days remain with him. He moved to Naya Nagar because he thought it was a safer place. There were many Hindus living in Kamathipura, they were safe and nothing happened to them. However, many left the area due to the insecurity.

Naya Nagar, in a sense, was developed through the efforts of one man—Syed Nazar Hussain. His son, Muzaffar, a former Congress legislator [Member of the Legislative Council (MLC)] and an active member of the party, is trying to work for communal harmony in the area. His most significant contribution perhaps is a common burial ground where both Muslims can be buried and Hindus can be cremated. 'That has sent a good signal, both communities go to the same place after death', Muzaffar tells me. With a population of 1 lakh, Naya Nagar remains a secure ghetto. The only threat is from the police and anti-social elements. A broad road outside the Mira Road station separates Naya Nagar and Shanti Nagar and other areas. The road is often referred to as the border, much like in Jogeshwari. I meet Muzaffar's 73-year-old father, Syed Nazar Hussain, in his sprawling bungalow, which is a landmark of sorts in Naya Nagar. Hailing from a family of *subedars* in Amravati, Hussain first worked for an industrialist who was very fond of him. Everyone knows him and he is some sort of a patron of the area. The walls of his house are full of photographs and they take you through his life in stages. For a man who has studied till the eighth standard, Hussain has achieved a lot, much of it through his grit and hard work. It is largely due to him that Naya Nagar has become what it is today. He has built apartments, schools, and a hospital and is actively involved in the social set-up of the area. His story is complex and interesting. 'My life has four parts', he begins in the manner of a person used to narrating his story. He came to Mumbai in 1949 from Nandgaon, near Amravati, looking for work. He worked hard at odd jobs and is proud that no one could have done all the things he did then. Finally, he got a job in Goregaon and lived in a hut with ₹ 10 a month as rent. He spent a lot of time reading the papers. He even thought of going to Pakistan as he had relatives there. At that time, he worked for Ambalal Seth and did various jobs in Nalla Sopara (in Thane district, further from Mira Road). His first wife went away so he remarried and wanted to buy a flat in Jawahar Nagar. He asked the contractor of the building, but he refused to give him a flat since he was a Muslim. The flats were only for Brahmans, the contractors said. It was then that he decided to do something for his community. He was still working with Seth and with his experiences outside Mumbai he knew how cheap it was to buy land. He bought land in Nalla Sopara and some in Mira Road. Only one side of Mira Road has any habitation, the other side was all salt pans. At that time, at Mira Road, there was not even a railway platform. He met the Western Railway official who said that if he had to get trains to stop at Mira Road he would have to show there were commuters, at least 100 season tickets would have to be from there. There was only one shoe company in Mira Road and the owner supported Hussain. He spent ₹ 1.5 lakh buying passes every month to show that there was a demand for a station here. Slowly, the Railway agreed, and the narrow platform was doubled and they started making other plans for roads to the station. Soon a layout was prepared and he started selling plots. When people tried to resell the plots, Hussain got the court to allow him to buy it back from them. In fact, when he wanted to name the area, he called both Mr Bal Thackeray from the Shiv Sena and Mr G. M. Banatwalla from the Muslim League. In 1979 it was Mr Thackeray who named it Naya Nagar after Hussain refused to name it after himself. Thackeray spent a long time talking to him after that. Soon after many buildings came up, water connections were acquired, and people started living here. Now Muzaffar runs the Asmita Trust and it has a school and a hospital.

Nazar Hussain wants Mira Road to be modern and well equipped. Now there are 5,000-plus buildings here. There are three temples and he is keen on both communities living together. Muslims cannot afford the high cost of housing, but they should have a place which is neat and clean and that is what he strives for. Muslims are a poor community, but that does not mean they cannot have the best. They have contributed to the Jain temple here and also built many mosques. His relationship with Thackeray was good; he did meet him many times and he also helped him in difficult times. But it did not last.

Nazar Hussain relates a strange experience from his childhood in Amravati. Once he was fishing and there was a snake which wound itself around his neck. His neighbour saw him and rescued him. But all the Hindus said he was blessed by Shankar *bhagwan* and they started worshipping him. However, his own community called him a *shaitan* (a devil). He had no real family; his mother died when he was born and he came to Mumbai with his grandfather, after his father remarried. From then on, he has had close relationships with Hindus. Hindus have done a lot for him in his life, he says. There was a time when he was close to the RSS. He still visits many temples.

There were times when he could have left India, but he wanted to stay back. He wants Mira Road to look even better than Dubai. But his main aim is to spread communal harmony. From a young man who came to Mumbai, Nazar Hussain today is a well-known businessman, a man who seems to have fulfilled his dreams. As a youth, he was often assailed because he came from a poor communitywhile he grew up in Mumbai, he was determined to set that right. Mumbai is after all a place to fulfil one's dream. His son points out that though his father wanted to give homes to Muslims as a priority, he did not keep the Hindus or other communities away. 'That showed he was secular', says Muzaffar. He also showed he could develop a secular township; though the population of Naya Nagar is predominantly Muslim, there are 30 per cent Hindus here. He admits that after the 1992–93 riots, people felt highly insecure. Earlier, youngsters wanted to go and live in a cosmopolitan area, but riots changed all that. People wanted to seek security in ghettos once again. After 1996, it became a well-developed society and there is a lot of mobility within Naya Nagar. Muzaffar denies there is segregation, but there is a tendency to keep out non-vegetarians and refuse Christians too. It has nothing to do with any particular community, he feels. In the local Jain temple, he has donated the deity in his name. If people were communal then this would not have happened, he points out.

Muzaffar grew up here and he remembers it being largely an area of paddy fields and salt pans. The idea of involving Thackeray was to give this place a secular feel. However, over the years, builders took over and promoted it as a Muslim area. He adds:

> I am trying to change that image and create a secular township. I believe I have succeeded. We are working to eradicate stereotypes but it is a continuous process, it cannot happen in one day. The community has to be better educated and that is one of my aims. We are trying to push education and our trust pays the fees of nearly 2000 students a year. People come here to solve their problems regardless of their religion. You should not worry about creating a vote bank. People come because of the level of confidence I have created here.

However, what attracts people to Naya Nagar is not its secular image, but the fact that it offers cheap housing. Not all those who moved have come to Naya Nagar. Fifty-six-year-old Syed Sultan lives in Shanti Nagar in Mira Road. He moved here from Andheri where he was born. He worked in a transport goods company as a clerk. He studied up to first-year Arts. He lived in a housing board colony which had eight buildings. It was a cosmopolitan area. They had two flats there on the ground floor and the third floor. They closed the ground-floor flat when the riots started, and he and his family moved to the third floor. On 12 December 1992, a mob came and broke the houses and destroyed everything. Quickly, they moved in with relatives in the island city for a fortnight. They later sold off the two flats and moved to Mira Road. He knew Muzaffar and felt a sense of security here. He came here and like so many others started a real estate company. Where he lives now, there are more Hindus, mostly Gujarati businessmen. There are many civic problems like water shortage, but all that is okay. He too was keen on a mixed locality as he does not like to live in a Muslim area. 'Islam *mazhab accha hai, mannne wale achche nahin*' (Islam is a good religion, but its followers are not), he grins.

Sometimes, the riots were just a catalyst to move out of the city. Considerations of space also prevailed. Sheikh Bhakar Ali Mehboob Ali 49, and a graduate, had a shop selling hair oils and perfumes at Gokhale Road in Dadar, considered the stronghold of the Shiv Sena. His father started the shop in 1936. His family moved here because they could live in the manner they wanted to. When the riots broke out, he was in his village in Sultanpur and came back only in January. They had to leave again and this time returned only in April 1993. He came back and opened the shop. At that time he used to work for Videsh Sanchar Nigam Limited (VSNL) in the morning and run the shop in the evening. But living in Dadar was difficult, there were eight of them and not much space. He has five children. So he bought a place here in a nearby society. He does not believe people are biased really. There are some politically motivated people who think it is their business to mislead others. When he returned to Dadar, his old neighbours gave him so much support. He only moved to Mira Road in 2000. His brother still stays there and runs the shop.

Of all the people I met in Naya Nagar, the youngest of them, 33-year-old Mohammed Zaheer Yunus Khan, who hails from Gondia, in Maharashtra, was the most disturbed. As a real estate agent, he gets a close look at how his community is treated by people. His light brown eyes reflect his despair and frustration. He came here after the 1993 riots. His was a joint family and his father was abroad at that time. They lived in Dongri in south Mumbai after his father returned. It was a railway quarters and during the riots they shifted to his father's boss's house at Lokhandwala (in the suburbs) for a month and then went back. Almost immediately they came to Mira Road. It was a safe place and the rates of the houses were reasonable. They first lived on rent before buying a flat. The riots had another casualty, it was the main reason his family moved out.

In Dongri, he lived with his grandfather, who was the secretary of the society. People supported them a lot, but when they left, no one stopped them. He studied till first-year degree college and then dropped out. At first he sold mobile phones. He did various jobs and finally settled down to real estate business.

Zaheer can see huge differences between the area he grew up in and where he lives right now. They grew up in a cosmopolitan area, there was so much sharing between communities. They never thought of each other as Hindu or Muslim. But in his business he finds big problems. When he has to get a Hindu a flat, it is easy, but for Muslims, he finds it very difficult. Now not even Muslims want to come here to Naya Nagar. It is full of crime. Every time there is a blast, this area is targeted. Children develop all kinds of addictions here and it is an issue.

However, much as he dislikes this place, he has no choice. What worries him the most is the future and what will happen to the next generation. Muslims get homes only in Naya Nagar. The future is very dark for him, he thinks. Privately, there is sympathy for each other, but certain sections do not want this sharing. He is puzzled and says he does not know what is behind this. He loses customers because of these factors—because he is a Muslim, there is a '100 per cent loss' for him in business. Local politics also plays a part. He also blames his community. He says:

> We are divided—we have all sorts of tags that we are terrorists or SIMI [Students Islamic Movement of India] which

was banned. We cannot even organize and make collective demands as Muslim organizations are looked at with doubt. People are scared of coming together. Then the police deter people from organizing. They don't want us to organize, or fight but yet they want us to follow the Constitution. I also feel illiteracy is rampant and that has ruined our sense of humour. Muslim groups issue fatwas for Taslima Nasreen's blood, why don't they give us money for education. There is no option for the Muslims today.

I have met Zaheer a few times and once he took me to meet local builders in the area. While nothing is said openly, some spaces are out of bounds if you are a Muslim. The builders decide which community should not mix, who should live where.

Clearly, Naya Nagar, in many ways, is a better planned space than the congested localities in Mumbai. People found a refuge here after the riots. However, most of them moved from cosmopolitan areas to a ghetto and are not very happy. It is also a question of choices—few had a choice then and few seem to have a choice even now. But security considerations prevail though police now target it as a hotbed of crime. There are many writers, poets, filmmakers, and journalists in the area and there is a thriving cultural scene, but somehow the fact that it is predominantly Muslim obscures everything else. People like Farhan are working very hard to remove that stigma, but it refuses to go away. It is ironic that a refuge of people from the riots should be tagged like this, despite the best efforts of Nazar Hussain and his son and the other residents of the area. This, in a sense, also typifies the popular perceptions of 'Muslim' areas. It is a stigma that refuses to go away much to the sorrow of the people who live there.

5

DISPLACEMENT AND POLARIZATION

> I write to inform you with deep regret that during the course of investigation, it transpired that some of the rioters attacked your house and assaulted the following inmates who were then present in your house and killed them and threw their dead bodies in the huge fires on the roads and also ransacked your house and burnt the looted articles in the fire.

These lines are from a letter written by the senior inspector of police, Nirmal Nagar Police Station to Anisabi Yusuf Shaikh, resident of Shantilal Compound in Khar East to tell her about the fate of her mother-in-law, her husband, and his two brothers who were missing in the riots. The single white sheet of paper simply puts down what was an enormous tragedy for Anisa and the rest of her family. The police wrote to Anisa two months after the incident occurred on 12 January 1993. The letter closes with the line 'with all sympathy to you and to your little children'.

Anisa escaped with her life before her house was attacked. Her sister-in-law, Raisa Bano, who lives in Antop Hill got to know of the incident four days later. Since then, Anisa has left the city and Raisa is still grieving the loss of her mother and three brothers.

When the riots broke, many had to run away, often with just the clothes on their back, barefeet. They found refuge in relief camps or rushed to places where they had relatives. Often these people fled from their homes in mixed localities to ghettos, never to return. Like Suraiya who never even bothered to go back to the flat she and her husband left in Kandivali. When you see her mother, Razia Sheikh, sitting calmly, sorting out her clothes in their home in Naupada, you realize at one go what the riots have done to her. Her pale face mirrors the years of shock, of the trauma she has faced, yet she has managed to get back on her feet, raise and educate her children, and fight back in whatever way she can. Her husband is silent and traumatized by the events of the past. Razia has emerged the winner in many ways. The tears are there and so is the loss, but in that room, lit by one small window, Razia holds herself up. She is the epitome of a survivor who has imparted that strength to her daughters.

Like her there is Khatun Bi who lives in her old memories, or Salim who has fought back to regain a foothold in his old profession. The riots forced him to leave Tulsiwadi in south Mumbai and go to Mumbra in Thane district, out of the city, like many others. He spends most of his time in the city he has grown up in and goes home only for the night. Every day he travels with his equipment for work. It is a long commute, but at least he feels part of what his life once was even though it is not in the same style. Similarly, the others often go back to their old homes, meet their old friends and, in that sense, they keep in touch with their old lives, their place of birth, with communities where they are no longer wanted or can live. Their aspirations are shaped by their new circumstances. They are no longer free to choose what they want or where they live. It is not only the physical relocation but the mental adjustments they have had to make.

Living in a ghetto, often not out of choice, in that sense, has narrowed their focus, restricted their aspirations, and created a longing of the life they once knew. They have recast their lives in a new mould to suit their present status. The city for them exists as another image—it is part of their memory. They live with a split image of the city—one that existed in the past, which now only exists in their imagery and the reality of the present. In that sense the city too has taken on new forms: a city in the imagery of people affected by the riots and a city of the real, of the present, of what it means for these people to live here.

Naupada and Behrampada

Naupada and Behrampada are two sprawling settlements near Bandra suburban railway station in western Mumbai. The report of the Srikrishna Commission, appointed to inquire into the 1992–93 riots, after the demolition of the Babri Masjid, has extensively documented the events in Behrampada and surrounding areas. There were many riots sparked off by a temple being desecrated and the violent incidents continued well into January and February 1993.

From Bandra suburban station, as you cross the railway bridge, on your left is a mass of shanties. If you look down on the side of the disused railway tracks you can see that it is full of life—children playing, barbers shaving customers, people shopping. The homes are built on top of one another so much so that some are on the level with the bridge, and through the tiny windows you can see people sitting around or cooking.

Ayub Mohammed Sheikh, or Ayub *bhai*, a social worker who lives in Naupada, says that it was an old village or a *gaothan* with a 200-year-old history. Today, it is home to hundreds of Muslim families. The settlement of Naupada hugs the railway tracks and narrow dark lanes divide the houses. It was in the news in 2006, when many of its residents helped retrieve the bodies when a bomb exploded in a railway train as part of the serial blasts on 11 July 2006. One of them, a railway employee, was killed in the serial blasts.

The road outside Bandra station on the east side divides Naupada and Behrampada. Behrampada is surrounded by tall apartment blocks. Concrete walls separating the slum from the apartment blocks grew higher after the riots of December 1992–January 1993. Over a decade ago, children from both sides went to school together and played cricket. All that has changed now.

Behrampada

Both Naupada and Behrampada are settlements buzzing with activity and the narrow lanes are full of people at all hours. It is not easy to get people to go back to a time when for months, terror ruled. On the surface, things are forgotten and life seems to go on as usual. But underneath there is anguish and the memories of those days are fresh. In the riots of 1992–93, Behrampada was targeted by mobs and many houses were burnt. People were killed and injured in firing and riots and many of them lost their homes and livelihoods. Behrampada has always been portrayed as a hotbed of crime and many people at that time including filmmaker Madhusree Dutta in her film *I Live in Behrampada*, tried to dispel those myths. However, the Shiv Sena, led by the local MLA Madhukar Sarpotdar, campaigned against Behrampada saying it harboured illegal Pakistanis who were indulging in terror tactics. None of this was borne out with facts and while raids in Behrampada did yield crude bombs and some people were arrested, the police could find no evidence of organized criminal activity.

Sarpotdar himself was detained by the army with guns and other weapons while travelling in a vehicle along with his son, but he was let off. According to the *Srikrishna Commission Report*, he was not even chargesheeted for an offence as serious as this. One of the few people who tried to portray a different image of Behrampada was filmmaker Madhusree Dutta, whose documentary on the area later became a cult film. Dutta and a small group formed Majlis, an NGO, which just started before the riots of 1992 December. At first, Majlis did not have an office—it was a small room in a *chawl*. Dutta's first encounter in that area was when she and some others went there with a carpenter on 7 December 1992. She did not realize what a huge slum Behrampada was. For a long time, none of them knew what had happened inside

Behrampada. Once there was firing in Behrampada and when she went inside she found women crying and buses with shattered window panes. She had no idea of the gravity of the situation. However, there was no question of going there for a while as the situation was terrible. Then they heard that their office was burning. Of the 100 shops in the complex, only about 10 were burnt. How do you figure out shops owned by Muslims, which had Hindu names? 'No Muslim will call his shop Bismillah, I think that was the indication', she says grimly.

After the riots lots of relief requests came in. Dutta says she was distinctly uncomfortable with the idea of relief.

> You go with 60 buckets and it's your responsibility to see if everyone gets it. Who are you to decide who deserves it? The middle class is reduced to this. People fighting for buckets and relief. You reduce people to beggars. We had no choice but to help as we were the only NGO there. Still we did not venture inside. Some students were doing a study and one of them fainted after seeing a person wounded. Many of the injured had not gone to the doctor even. After that we went inside for the first time and found a full-fledged settlement. The rest is history. I realized people could not go out so their business was affected. We did a lot of work after that. What is needed is a little dignity—don't make them beggars. We also begged journalists to come to Behrampada. At that time the media was campaigning against Behrampada. Even the police refused to enter. We took journalists to the area after some 60 houses were burnt, but the stories the next day spoke of some *sadhu* being killed. We were defeated. We realized we can't do a media campaign. People were starving and crying and we were clear we did not want to cash in on this disaster. We decided to make a film and managed to shoot for five days. It was an act of complete desperation. After five days, the police were after us and I was called to the police station and asked for a copy of the footage.

They then asked me to be their informer. I was told to be a responsible citizen and report to them everyday.

After this, she thought it was better to stop shooting or else they would become the bone of contention. People would be victimized in their name. To some extent, the film helped in clearing doubts about the area. It even became part of police training for many years. The film became internationally famous and it was a campaign film—one of those success stories. Dutta feels that the film had a certain dignity which was important since people had reached a point where they were scared of saying they lived there. She points out:

> It was a major land issue too. It was the late Congress MP Sunil Dutt's vote bank and that was one area of contention. If you continue to marginalize people then they will become criminals. Conflict and marginalization is one thing, but in peace time marginalization is much worse. It happens quite normally and is not seen as an aberration. All marginalization is not physical violence. Polarization is much worse. We later found it so tough to get an office because of our name. It is all unspelt. We can't fight it then as there are no written rules. Ghettoization is not only for Muslims, it is everywhere—the Hindus too have ghettos.

Changes over the Years

Over the years, there have been changes and people seemed to have moved in and out of both Behrampada and Naupada. I met families in both Naupada and Behrampada to look at how they have coped with their lives after the riots. I find that people have moved to these places for reasons of security or because they had relatives already living there. Many of the Hindu families have moved out after the riots. Families have had to cope with loss of life, homes, and livelihoods, but the most disturbing finding is that there seems to be a lot of mental trauma which has not been addressed. There is no support structure in place for these affected families in terms of medical care or legal aid.

A bubbling teenager like Farhana, who studies in a college nearby, is about to give it all up. She was a child when the riots broke out and the family had gone to visit Jogeshwari, where riots were taking place. Her mother had to bring them back to Bandra. She was the youngest of four girls and two boys. Her father was abroad at that time. Her grandparents too lived in Behrampada. She is now 18 and few memories of those times remain with her. The only thing she remembers is that her mother took her and ran. The place where we are sitting now, a room next to Farhana's house, was destroyed by fire in January 1993. Over 60 homes were burnt down. It is rebuilt now and each house has a small room and a kitchen inside. Farhana can hear the loud noises, the sound of firing, then something like a blast, but she cannot recall anything she saw. She has heard of the blackouts at nights and that the military was everywhere.

When the whole *basti* burnt down, people moved to flats under construction nearby. Her father did not go back though he had a valid visa. They stayed in those half-built apartment blocks for many days. Farhana's experience at her college has also left her bitter. Even after the riots, she still feels there is some discrimination. Her father had to use some influence to get her admission in a college in the management quota. She says that she had more marks than any other girl, but was refused admission. She wept when she realized that it was probably because she was a Muslim. Then, in her college, students can answer their examinations in Marathi, but the Muslim girls did not know Marathi well. When they asked if they could answer in Urdu, it was refused. She and her neighbour Tabassum, both in the same class, were asked to leave once by the teacher who said that all non-Marathi-speaking students should leave class. There was no explanation; both Tabassum and she had to stand out. The teacher did not say why and neither did the other students tell them anything. She felt very bad about all this. She does not expect sympathy because she is a Muslim, but she senses somewhere there is a lot of 'partiality' to other communities.

The net result is that both Farhana and Tabassum have left college and have now taken up teaching courses in the hope that they will get a job. They feel that being Muslims, it may not be so easy. Both their families are spending a lot on their education, but the girls do not wish to pursue it for various reasons. Farhana's father, Sheikh Jilani Sheikh Yasin, was away in Saudi Arabia when the riots broke out. He finally came back in February end just before the bomb blasts. He had paid ₹ 80,000 in customs duty for so many things, but the riots took care of that. He went back 10 years in his life and apart from the clothes on his back, he had nothing.

Gilani now works for a builder and has rebuilt his life over the years. During the riots, his family moved from Behrampada to a building half constructed on the side and despite the situation, they managed to make a small committee, which would get basic food and clothing for everyone. They were also helped by the Bandra East Community Centre. Though many Hindus came to help, at first, Gilani and others were so angry that they almost refused help, but later they accepted everything. All Hindus are not bad, they decided; some were very good. It was all this politics which divided people. Gilani says they were true Indians at heart. He is touched that despite everything, Mumbai showed it had a heart. They managed to muster a lot of help and funds and rebuilt 68 houses which were destroyed, in two years time. It would have been tough to have done it alone.

Gilani after so many years has no grouse. He is not blaming Hindus for what happened. People who do these things have no religion. The police, though there were some good people, used to fine them for staying in the building. They tried to evict the Muslims. Of the 68 houses which were burnt, two were occupied by Hindus—they are still living there. No one left from here. A master tailor in Saudi Arabia, Gilani came back and had to start all over again. People were so mean they did not let the fire brigade come inside the congested slum. They threw bombs on the shanties from above and that is how the fire broke out. For two or three months, no one could move out. They stayed in the half-built building, with four walls and no real roof. At one point, he felt they could trust no one and no one would help them, so acute was the fear and tension. In that dark, half-built apartment, Gilani and the others waited for things to calm down. They huddled together for security and comfort and prayed no one would throw them out. There was so much tension; people had shaved their beards, they were scared to move out. It took some months for the fear to subside. He maintains there is no enmity with the Hindus—there are so many *pujaris* who live in a *chawl* nearby. They had to stay alert almost all night because that is when they (the attackers) come in trucks. Theirs was a *kutcha* hut, with *patra* (tin sheets) on top; the police watched them. There was a plan—the slums were surrounded by buildings; they wanted to trap and kill everyone inside, he recalls.

After the riots, Behrampada got many visitors and some NGOs too helped. Things have changed now. But justice is elusive. 'Big people don't get punished—it is the small ones who get caught. We are still fighting for justice. Who can stop Sarpotdar and Thackeray? Which leader has been punished? The judicial process takes too long', he feels. On the day I met him he was having a feast at his house. Lots of people and food. Puffing on his cigarette, Gilani seemed happy. He is waving to his other relatives who are leaving. I saw a man who has fought back, done things for his community and while people question his new found wealth, he rather seems to deserve it.

The Story of Khatun Bi

It is in the dirty bylanes of Naupada that I first met Khatun Bi. She is old, her eyes are rheumy, and her clothes faded. Khatun Bi is one of those who was forced to come to Naupada when the riots took place. She must be over 65, her legs are stiff and she has high blood pressure. She is unsure why I want to talk to her. Khatun Bi now lives with her daughter, Shakila, the only one who is as yet not married. Her strongest memory of the 1992–93 riots is that she had to hide almost neck-deep in a filthy gutter all night. '*Mahaul bahut kharab tha*' (the situation was very bad), she begins. The rest of her story comes out in a rush. A temple in the area was damaged. When the riots started, she sent her children away first while she stayed behind. She hid in the gutter and the police found her there—they called to her in Marathi and then they took her to the police station at Nirmal Nagar. Her clothes were dirty and then the police brought her to a relief camp in Naupada. She was only worried if her children were there. She was so glad to see her girls at the camp. Her children had given her up for dead. Her son Sajjid, was full of blood, he was unconscious.

She is full of praise for her Hindu neighbours who gave her a '*maxi*' to wear and helped her hide. Her younger son Ramzan had bought gold for her daughter's wedding. Like her he too was scared of leaving it behind. Ramzan was a master tailor; he was a specialist in *chaniya cholis* (long skirts and blouses, heavily embroidered). He lost so much in the riots, and all those expensive clothes he tailored were burnt.

After the riots Sajjid refused to work and he died a few years later of jaundice. Ramzan too became a silent, withdrawn person. Those who knew him a little in Naupada say he used to sit under a tree all day reading a newspaper. He contracted tuberculosis (TB), but could not get proper treatment and he died two or three years ago. His friend Taukeer Khan remembers that he spoke very little. Taukeer says, 'We did not ask him anything, he suffered on his own.' Both of them could not return to normal. Khatun Bi has no hesitation in saying that the riots killed her sons. She finds it difficult to sleep at night. The events of those days have left a deep mark on her and she often goes into a depression.

She kept repeating that no one helped her. Khatunbi's life changed after the riots. She used to live in Khar, a nearby location, for over 40 years. Theirs was the only Muslim family in the *chawl* and she did not fight with any one as she had four daughters. She still remembers the people who attacked her house—they were from Shantilal Compound. Her father-in-law owned six rooms in the *chawl*, but people occupied them without paying the rent even before the riots took place. She has rented her old house to a family for ₹ 2,000 per month. She never wants to go back and live there again. Now, apart from the rent, she and her daughter earn daily wages by fixing sequins on dupattas. She is also very upset that her daughter Shakila's marriage was called off after the riots. They had so many demands which as a bride's family she could never hope to fulfil. She had nothing to give her remaining daughter.

Khatun Bi is used to fending for herself. Her husband used to work for the Bombay Port Trust. He died many years ago and she was the one who raised her family by doing embroidery. Her daughters chipped in by making jewellery. However, despite the bad memories, Khatun Bi still goes back to her old home, though she admits to being scared as people drink and fight there. In Naupada, it is not like that. She only goes back to revisit old memories. Her account is a bit confused about the exact status of her property, but Shakila, her daughter, says her uncle usurped it. They have no one to turn for legal aid to help them sort out this mess.

Revisiting Old Memories

In Khatun Bi's story, one can see how the city has changed for her. In terms of physical space, security, and in terms of the bonds that had developed over the years, Khatunbi is still mentally where she used to live. For her, that old place is still her home, that is the place she has close associations with, which have not diminished even though she was forced to run away during the riots. Her idea of a home or living in a community is still deeply entrenched in her old place. She looks at Behrampada as a safe place, but all her memories reside in her old place. There is a mixture of nostalgia at the old comforts she had, her family, and her children. Now she is forced to live in a poky one-room tenement; she can barely make ends meet. Since her old home is close she visits the place often. Added to this is the anguish that she lost out on her rooms there and only has one left which she has given out on rent. But she cannot live there due to safety considerations. Khatun Bi then swings back and forth in her memory from what her life once was and her reality now.

Not everyone is like her though. People who moved away in the riots rarely go back to their old homes. The break is final in some cases. But the memories are haunting. Khatun Bi was keen that I visit her old place and she cordially invited me to accompany her. From Naupada it is a short ride by auto-rickshaw. On the way she points to the railway overbridge and said this is the bridge her son Sajjid took to escape from the mob. Her other son Ramzan swore he worked for an Udipi hotel in the vicinity and was spared. We go to Shantilal Compound from where she claims the mobs attacked her *chawl*. There is a man sitting near the Sai Baba temple. She whispers to me that all these people were involved. The shops are new and the place has changed a little after the riots.

Suddenly, we turn into a small opening next to a shop. Before us is a cluster of cemented rooms. We go into the house Khatun Bi had lived for 40 years. 'They destroyed all this', she says in the manner of an expert guide. 'My son rebuilt my house to some extent. Now the tenants are Marwaris—they run a catering business.' The tenants are away, but there are two cooks frying *puris* in the hot airless room. But the room is far more spacious than Khatunbi's present home. She looks around with pride at the grimy pink walls stacked with steel vessels. Like a good landlady, she goes up one floor to ask if her tenants there have paid the water bill. She asks the cooks for some *puris* and vegetable and finds a plastic bag to take it away. We leave and on the way back she offers me the *puris* for lunch.

Khatunbi's present home is a small one-room hole. It is not even painted and the walls are uneven—there is a single bare bulb which lights the room. She is desperate to get her property back but with few papers it looks difficult.

Nostalgia and Loss

I can see the same mixture of nostalgia and loss in Salim Jaffer Sheikh. The 10-storied building has a small terrace, a roundish one, connected by a spiral iron staircase to the larger one down below. Almost like an eyrie, with a view of south Mumbai. It is a charming nook lined with bonsai and other plants, and stone benches to sit. Above, a hoarding is being built, the iron railing already in place to take the huge panel that can be seen for miles. An unlikely place for an interview, but that is where I meet the 55-year-old Salim, who earns a living in the hoarding business.

As we speak, it starts raining and we scamper down and head for the nearest Irani hotel. From that height if Salim strained his eyes a bit he could probably see the place where he was born, a little beyond the mess of uneven buildings that stand in rain sodden disarray.

Tulsiwadi, the slum where Salim was born, was burnt partially in some of the worst rioting in Mumbai in 1992–93. He had a house there and ran his business of constructing hoardings of all kinds in the city. He and his family lived happily off that business till the riots happened. Putting up hoardings was not the only thing Salim did. He was an active member of the Congress party since 1975 and a part of its minorities cell. He was joint secretary of the Malabar Hill *taluka* Congress Committee and knew many senior politicians in the city and did a fair bit of social work. At one time, all you had to do to send a letter to him was write his name and the pin code. 'I would get it', he smiles. Tulsiwadi is located in Tardeo in central Mumbai.

Salim also helped his neighbours put up *pandals* during the annual Ganpati festival, and during Navratri as well, he was in great demand. Even during Janmashtami, he used to help in putting up ropes and hanging the pots of curd. Salim's family was one of the few Muslims who lived in this crowded settlement. He had a lot of things since his relatives were in Dubai. He owned a colour TV, a VCR, and expensive clothes. They could not burn his house fully because it was adjacent to Hindu homes. But all his things were taken out and destroyed or stolen.

When the riots broke out, Salim and his family went to live in a relief camp in Madanpura. He had to leave behind all his money too. He lived there for a month and then came back. But one thing was certain for him. He wanted to leave his home, the place where he was born.

Finally, through some contacts, he managed to buy a small plot of land in Mumbra (now an extended ghetto in Thane district), enough to build a room. For three to four years, his family lived without water and lights and the place was wild—there were snakes. He still remembers once a snake lived in his house for days. His house is located 3 km away from the railway station on a hillock which gets washed down in the rains. He used to walk all the way and it is only recently that he can afford a rickshaw for at least some of the distance.

His house in Tulsiwadi, which was worth ₹ 4.5 lakh at that time, was sold for ₹ 1.5 lakh. People were trying to cash in on his desperation. But help came from an unexpected quarter. A constable from Tardeo Police Station who knew him said his brother wanted a place and so they did not have to give it away cheap like many other riot victims did. He was grateful for that money. It gave him a roof over his head. He has four children and his wife is a heart patient. It was a difficult time and he found no work. But he had to run a family. He bought four cans of paint and some brushes and offered his services as a painter apart from small repairing jobs. For six years he struggled till 1999 when he landed a big contract from Midday publications for ₹ 1 lakh. Till then, he did small hoardings for shops which used to bring in ₹ 1,500 or less. Two years after the riots, once he did not even have ₹ 7 in his pocket for a train ticket.

The Midday contract changed his life somewhat. Now he works on three to four sites. His son runs a shop in partnership near Mumbra station selling mobile phones. He managed to educate his sons till the 12th standard and his daughter is still studying. They had no money for books and his children used to be fined often for not wearing proper uniforms. They borrowed money all the time.

The other major problem for Salim is commuting. Mumbra is in Thane district, adjoining Mumbai, and to come to central or south Mumbai where most of his work is, he has to travel for an hour with his implements and materials in packed trains. All his work is in Mumbai. He carries everything with him—heavy tools, ropes—and he did as much of the work himself as he could not afford to share his meagre profits.

DISPLACEMENT AND POLARIZATION

When he was living in Tulsiwadi, he had a store room to keep things, and he had many workers to help put up the hoardings. At that time, Tulsiwadi must have had 4,000 tenements. It was constantly under the threat of demolition. Still for Salim it was home. Why did he go away? He lived for others—he knew a lot of important people. He had helped them get ration cards, etc. In the riots, his things were stolen and he was afraid that his children would see others with their stolen goods. They would feel that these were old friends and neighbours and remark that 'they are wearing our clothes'. There was a lot of hatred which did not exist before. He called many people for help—friends in the Congress party, who are now ministers at the centre. No one helped. He called the fire brigade when they were surrounded and their homes were on fire. No one came. The local corporator, Shanta Baria, led a mob baying for Muslims, that is the time the police shot and killed her. After seeing that at night, Salim and others decided to leave. His neighbours did not reassure them or say that they should stay back. The slum is surrounded by tall buildings. They trained bright lamps on the cluster of houses. Those bright halogen lamps showed up every movement in detail and Salim felt they were being watched. He had excellent contacts with the police. Since he used to often take up issues like drug abuse (brown sugar), which was rampant in the area, some people were unhappy with him and they used to file false cases and put him in trouble. Despite those contacts the police did not help.

Some of Tulsiwadi's Muslim residents sold off their houses and left, but many still live there in this Hindu-dominated area. Even now when Salim goes back people remember him. When Tulsiwadi was on fire he saved so many people. He escorted many Hindu families to the relief camp in Madanpura. The flames were high—must have been 10 feet high at least. He felt the whole city could see their homes burning. Everyone fled, Hindu or Muslim, and while they stragraled along, the police, instead of helping them, pointed their guns at the refugees. Police said if they were unarmed, they should raise both hands over their heads. Some of the people had small bags with belongings—whatever they had managed to take out. How could they put up their hands? Salim had nothing; he offered to raise his hands for everyone else. When they reached the Madanpura camp, the Hindus were scared as the camp was filled with Muslims. They decided to give them a separate space and food was also served separately to them.

Sometimes he feels like moving out from Mumbra, but he believes that once you buy a house you must stay there always. He made an exception once, but the circumstances were different. It is uncomfortable for his wife though. She needs another operation. But he has this firm belief that those who keep moving homes are cheats and deceivers. He is not even in favour of changing his mobile number.

Even now he does some social work. He enjoys political activity. Often, Salim catches the last train home. It is empty; there is place for his stuff. Dinner time is early morning, at 3 am. His face reflects the suffering he has undergone and he has survived at great cost. His life was one of the hundreds which the riots turned around.

Moving to a Ghetto

Ahmed Ali Qureishi lives in a ghetto in Kasaiwada in Kurla (eastern Mumbai). Before the riots, Ahmed used to live in the Chunabhatti Masjid Compound. He was born there and lived with his family. His mother was famous as a person who sold eggs. He has four brothers and six sisters. The Masjid Compound had a mixed population—there were six Muslim families. He used to work for a small factory at that time. When the riots broke out, the police took all of them to Nehru Nagar Police Station. The next day they were sent to another building. Later, they took a room on rent nearby. The police were good to them and they allowed them to go back and collect their belongings. Finally, their room was sold for ₹ 60,000 though the actual price would have been much higher.

The family came to Kasaiwada which is a sprawling slum near Chunabhatti (eastern Mumbai) where the rooms were cheap. Ahmed worked for a brush company; they used to send the raw material home to him at Masjid Compound, but when he moved to Kasaiwada, they said they will not send the stuff to a Muslim area; so he lost his job. His whole family used to be involved in making brushes and that was their main income. The company was afraid that their materials would be looted. At that time, Ahmed was 28 years old. He studied up to the Secondary School Certificate (SSC). He worked nights as a watchman and during the day as a supervisor in a building. He ran the house on those earnings. For a year he worked like this. Then he got into selling cassettes. He used to buy them wholesale and roam around selling them. Later, he saved a little money and bought a shop in Kasaiwada. In 2001 he got married. Now his family is scattered over Mumbra, Andheri, and Kurla, and his brother also runs a cassette shop.

Ahmed hails from Aurangabad and never dreamt that one day he would be forced to leave Masjid Compound. It still breaks his heart that he had to leave after the riots because those people did not want them to stay there. When the riots took place, they were drinking tea together. He just kept his cup down and saw the mob—they were strangers and they broke everything. He thinks they were jobless *goondas*. He wanted to live there very much, but there was a worry that there would be problems. In 1984 too when there were riots, they had shut the house and gone somewhere else to live for three years. But they came back and their neighbours were so welcoming. They asked them where they had had gone and why they got so scared. This time things were different—they told Ahmed and the others not to return ever.

His old neighbours felt Muslims will cause problems. Ahmed is angry and his bitterness spills out.

> What have we got to do with who built the mosque [referring to Babri Masjid]? Was it made by Pakistan? In India the British made Railway lines; are you going to uproot them? Instead of building something that people need, you want a temple. The Masjid broke and along with it all our homes.

The riots affected him badly, he lost his income and had to move to a ghetto which he despises. Unfortunately, he cannot afford to stay anywhere else.

Ahmed echoes the feeling of many common people.

Is the Mandir and Masjid something to fight and kill for. No one fights for these things. I used to think of Holi as my festival all of us played it. We lost ₹ 3 to 4 lakh in property and they gave us ₹ 5,000. So many Hindus come to Kasaiwada for business; is anyone stopping them? Criminals looted us in the riots and now people want safety—our presence makes them unsafe.

Shifting from place to place has had an adverse impact, specially on business. Many small shop owners who were not even compensated for the damage find it difficult to start all over again. In addition, Ahmed is unhappy about living in a ghetto. His aspirations have been curbed and he really cannot do what he wants. He too lives in memories of his old place, the old camaraderie they had, and his frequent visits back there only serve to keep up his dignity. He still feels he has a right to live there and goes there to assert that sense of ownership.

The one thing that rankles Sheikh Haroon Ibrahim is that he had to put his children in schools run by the Jamaat (community) after pulling them out from an English-medium municipal school. After so many years, his children are educated; he still has not managed to do much in terms of restarting his livelihood. There is also the heavy burden of debt. Sheikh Haroon Ibrahim used to live in Asalfa, Ghatkopar, an eastern suburb, for more than 15 years. After the riots in 1993, he shifted to the edge of a swamp in Filterpada, near Powai. He is one of the 12 Muslim families living there. He sold his poultry shop which was burnt down in Asalfa. He restarted it here, but since five years he closed the shop because he could not afford the rent increase from ₹ 1,000 to ₹ 1,500 a month. He bought this house later and now his two daughters are married. His sons earn and he depends on them for his daily needs.

The earlier place he lived in was not far, maybe 5 km away, near Kurla in the hutment colony near the pipelines. There were lots of Hindus there. Most of them belonged to the Shiv Sena and they also

DISPLACEMENT AND POLARIZATION

burnt his house and all the belongings and clothes. The Hindu neighbours had already warned them to leave. A woman's ear was cut off, and this terrified them. They changed homes twice in three months. Once, they went home to salvage some belongings. By then all the Muslims had left from there and later moved to Mumbra. Haroon could not afford the flats there. No one was prepared to buy his house and he had to make a distress sale a year after the riots. His brother-in-law had a mutton shop—he still lives there. Though his shop was burnt he did not leave.

Haroon's wife Badrunissa can still feel the terror of those days. She saw people cutting up Muslims into pieces and putting them into the gutter. She has been living there since childhood and what she saw horrified her. She had young girls and did not want to stay there. Her brother also told them to leave from there. Here, in Pathanwadi, they feel much safer. Though there is a swamp and they live near the pipeline, it is a safe area for them. Nothing happened here during the riots. People are nice to them here. Filterpada has few Muslims, but the nearby Pathanwadi is mostly a Muslim *basti*.

Sheikh is still looking for a shop on rent, but the rates are too high. One of his daughters is a graduate and another, Shazia, is still studying and working. Haroon's house was flooded in the 26 July 2005 deluge and he has another small room where his daughter conducts classes. Their lives have changed after the riots in many ways. When they were at Asalfa they were much better off. The shop did well and his relatives were also close by. Earlier, they lived in harmony with all their neighbours, but after the riots, they made fun of Muslims. Every time they went back, they used laugh and say 'They've come back' and taunt them. Haroon did not feel like staying there. He knew the people who looted them. They are so well off now. Asalfa has changed a lot over the years, many Muslims have left and most of the houses have been sold to the Hindus. Their Hindu neighbours who warned them to leave, did not talk to them later.

Badrunissa, 45, hails from Miraj, and Sheikh, from Manmad (both in Maharashtra). Earlier they lived in south Mumbai at Do Tanki. They were compensated for the shop and house with ₹ 5,000 each.

Since then Haroon has found it difficult to work. The family is constantly taking loans and is heavily in debt. They had to pay for their children's education with heavy loans and also for their son's marriage a few months before I met them. His eldest son Shainur dropped out of school; he was in the 10th standard at the time of the riots. Now he sells cutlery. The children used to go to the municipal school earlier in English medium and they all had to drop out and join the Jamaat school. However, with the help of loans, he has managed to educate two children up to the graduate level and another two up to the 10th standard. His eldest daughter dropped out after the eighth class. Badrunissa says she often had to beg for money for her children's education. Now, they are hoping to pay off their loans for the marriage of their son and then think of renting a shop. Haroon, now 55, is in poor health and often has to take rest.

Areas with large Muslim populations like Naya Nagar, Behrampada, or Jogeshwari are suspect. The police and most ordinary people think these are criminal hotbeds. The fact that they are riddled with poverty and backwardness seems to bother only a few. Journalist and writer Firoz Ashraf had to move from the cosmopolitan Liberty Garden in Malad in north Mumbai, where he lived for 18 years, to a ghetto in Jogeshwari West. At that time he was working for Indian Oil and also was a freelance writer. He still remembers it was a Sunday when the riots started. The flames were visible from all around. People were hesitant to say that Muslims were being targeted. His was a Maharashtrian neighbourhood and the majority of the people told him not to leave. They advised him not to go out and they did everything to help. They could not sleep in their own house. For many days Ashraf and his family slept in different houses and they were not together. Only his old servant refused to leave. The whole night he used to smoke and his blood pressure shot up. The tension was unbearable at times. He felt a sense of hopelessness and despair and was taken aback by events which he had never imagined in his wildest dreams.

Once at 10 pm, a mob attacked his wife's parents' house. The people in the building reassured them and said nothing will happen. One night, people had put strobe lights and waited for the attack. The mob was chased by the police. Ashraf was alone at the gate and he suddenly realized how unsafe things had become. He felt no one would help them in the time of crisis. They were four of them apart from the servant. At that time, Dr Dharam Veer Bharati, a senior journalist and editor of *Dharmayug* magazine, and several Hindu friends stood by Ashraf and his family, giving them reassurance and mental strength.

Ashraf used to write in *Dharmayug* at that time and everyone supported him. He was active in cultural programmes and took part in the Ganpati collection too. He only read about the riots in the papers. His friends in Millat Nagar, Meher and Shafi Ansari, asked him to come and live in their house. There was a gentleman in Ashraf's society, a Mr Anand, a refugee from Peshawar. Anand told him to leave—his father was killed in a riot. There were two opinions in the building—all the boys asked them not to leave, but still they did, and later stayed with the Ansaris. He used to sneak back to his house like a thief. The sense of protection of a home was gone. But to his dismay, whenever he went back, the way people talked had changed. His wife's house was destroyed. His wife had four brothers, two still live there. His son was in college and they used to harass him calling him *landya*. He was like an untouchable; he was harassed and was attacked twice. They did file a complaint. Ashraf's family stayed for two weeks in Millat Nagar and then they started looking for a place in a Muslim area. Safety was the main issue. The riots had destroyed their feeling of safety forever.

Ashraf has left his old ideals behind. Now he tells others not to stay in a mixed area. There is no guarantee of safety. He sold the house in Malad. At first no one was willing to buy it. It was finally a distress sale. The new house was expensive. Jogeshwari is a ghetto, it had a bad name. Police refuse to give clearance for passports if you stay here. Police say it is full of *tadi par* (externed people) or Pakistani ISI agents. He took voluntary retirement from his job in 1993. The company's Union was taken over by the Shiv Sena and people like him were sidelined. He was under a lot of stress and in 1995 had a heart attack. He later had a bypass surgery.

The search for a new house was not easy. He thought it would be cheap in a Muslim area. The Muslim builders did not show any sympathy. The old house fetched him ₹ 5 lakh, and the new one cost ₹ 8.5 lakh. Ashraf put all his Provident Fund money into the house. Even where he worked people's attitude changed a lot. At the time of Partition, his father decided not to go to Pakistan. He was a government servant and they were all well educated. Ashraf belongs to a family of Syeds, descendants of the Prophet. His ancestor Jehangir Ashraf came to India from Iran and settled in UP in 1500s. They were part of the Sufi tradition and his family was liberal.

Now, Ashraf runs a school of sorts for poor children and spends his time teaching. He goes to the mosque to respect local tradition and feeling. His father never forced him to do *roza* (fast during Ramzan) and he still does not. He had no idea what it is like to stay in a Muslim area. Earlier, they were part of all festive celebrations. Now it is different. Diwali is not celebrated here nor is Holi. Slowly, he came to terms with the reality of the ghetto. The small cramped homes, the poverty, illiteracy, and unemployment was evident. They know very little about Islam and they are far from modernization. He found a lot of depression there among these people and women specially bore the brunt. Ashraf linked globalization and the poverty here and found that most of these people were cut off from any progress. Most Muslims had small shops and were self-employed. The unity among them is superficial and there is a strong caste system—the Ansari, Momins, Kasai, grave diggers. His anger is palpable against the middle class, which he thinks is most hypocritical: 'What have they done to change things? It's a feudal society. There is no revolutionary streak left.'

When Ashraf came here, he found few children going to school. In this community of 1 lakh, there about 30 Urdu-medium schools. Not even 1,000 copies of newspapers are sold. Many are dropouts. He collected money and runs a school of sorts, which costs ₹ 24,000 per month. He teaches them Psychology, Science, and organizes money to help girls study. There are no proper teachers in Urdu schools and textbooks. Boys run away, they do not study for long. He also took to vocational counselling. He points to a young girl who has come to visit him and hopes she will be a chartered accountant (CA)—her mother is a maid servant and her father has deserted them. For him, the riots are not over, they are still going on. People are hungry here, there is no food, and he keeps open house. He is scathing about the Sachar Committee Report.

> I don't need it to tell me how backward Muslims are. All before me the Muslim intelligentsia are not fulfilling their duties. It is the creamy layer issue again. After my shift here I have become more socially responsible. I was born in 1943, I had a dream of a new Hindustan. We grew up in Nehru's era, now that dream is shattered. Where did the Hindustan of our dreams go? When I came here I realized what the real India is like.

His daughter, Farhana, 32, a librarian, says she did not like it here at first, but she has grown to accept it. Now divorced, she lives with her father. Like the others, her sense of community is still her old home at Liberty Gardens. She still goes back there to meet her old friends. The atmosphere here is very different. She cannot relate to people and has no friends here. The conversation is limited, there is no intellectual discussion, and no one reads papers. It is difficult to move around or hang around like one can do in other places. It is the students who are a part of her life now. Now, young mothers want a good education for their children. Things are changing. She reconciles to the fact that her family is respected here and people look to them for guidance.

For 44-year-old Sabira Zahir Sheikh, who now lives in Kasaiwada, her life in a ghetto is something she never desired. She was Ahmed's neighbour in Masjid Compound and still yearns for that old place. She has made very clear demarcations between her world at present and what is outside. Her two-storied house is situated at the beginning of Kasaiwada. She spent her childhood in Masjid Compound; when the riots broke out they had to be taken away by the police and they stayed in the *chowky* for three days. She had to flee with her children—her daughter was only three-months-old then. She sold her old house and now she says she is quite happy here at one level. People dissuaded her from shifting and she got very little money for her old house. Her neighbours asked her not to leave, but when the police came, they realized it is not safe to stay back. But regret is written large on her face.

Her three daughters are studying and her husband runs a successful business. Her elder son dropped out of school, while one son died of a heart ailment. Sabira has grown up with this violence; there was always a lot of tension, even during the 1984 riots. She feels that her present home is surrounded by dirt and has a bad influence on her children. In a mixed locality, things are better, she mutters, trying to reconcile with her existence.

Like Ashraf, whose life changed to working for his impoverished community, Razia Rehman Sheikh too helps women in distress. When I met her, she was sitting in a well-lit room in Naupada, sorting out a bundle of clothes. President of the local Mahila Shakti Mandal, she has moved here since a few years. Her daughter Suraiya works with a voluntary organization, Women's Research and Action Group (WRAG). It was 22 November 1992 when Suraiya got married, and after that things changed a lot for the whole family. Her son Jabbar was very ill and she was taking him to Nair Hospital. It was 7 December 1992 and she woke early with the *azan*. That was the day when the riots broke out; she could not take him to the hospital. They waited at Kherwadi Gate Number One for a long time. They saw a lot of bodies being taken away in hand carts. Jabbar was there too watching all this.

Razia had six girls—two are yet to be married and are studying. She starts about her twin sons Gaffar and Jabbar and breaks-off to show me their pictures. She takes out an album and starts to turn the pages frantically, looking for Jabbar's picture. Bending into the album, looking for the right picture, she says distractedly that she does know what really went wrong with Jabbar. He used to sell nighties on Linking Road. He used to bring home ₹ 50 to 60 a day. After the riots, he kept muttering to himself. He used to say all of us will die. He was beside himself with grief. There was much fear at that time. Jabbar was eventually admitted to a mental hospital in Thane in 1999. He comes home once a year, but Razia says it is very difficult to keep him at home as he gets very violent. She is sure it is because of the riots that Jabbar could not be treated properly. It was a long time before she got him to a hospital and what he saw during those days left a deep impression on him. He never recovered.

In 1993, Razia's daughter Firoza, who is older than the twins was about to be engaged. She was to be married in six months. Firoza too was caught in a web of fear and terror after witnessing the riots. One day, she kept saying that people were coming to kill her and she suddenly collapsed and died. Everyone thought Firoza was getting fits. Razia shook her by the shoulders, but nothing happened. The doctor came, but it was too late by then. For Razia and the rest of the family, first, it was Jabbar's mental condition and, then, the sudden death of Firoza. She decided to sell her old house in Behrampada in Razzak *chawl* and move to Naupada. A change would do her good, she thought. She lives here with her husband and two daughters. She got involved in social work after one of her daughters had problems with her marriage and wanted a divorce.

The Mahila Mandal run by her has 32 members and handles a lot of cases involving marriage and violence. While social work keeps her busy, she cannot help thinking of the past. The situation was terrible; either there was firing or some mob violence. There was curfew all the time. It is a fervent wish that those days never come back. In the old place, there were five Hindu families who left after giving Razia the keys. They did not let anyone occupy those homes. Razia was scared too that the police would accuse them of taking over their homes—so they kept it locked. They later came back and sold the houses. As neighbours, they shared and cared for each other. They still keep in touch with them. In her album, there are pictures of a recent gathering at a birthday party with her old neighbours. Some of the families sold their houses in distress and went away. Now, just one family is left. Before the riots, everyone had such good relations. They lived like a large family. Razia had a black-and-white TV in those days and everyone from the *chawl* would come to her house to watch it.

After all that has happened, Razia still shares good relations with her old neighbours. There is an understanding that they are not responsible for what happened. The rioters were politically motivated. The loss of her daughter and her son's condition has left a deep impact on her. She was not so worried about the loss of property—it was human lives that concerned her. Married at 13, Razia's husband was a carpenter. He earned well and the family had a good life. She was born in Mumbai and she will never leave it, but the hurt is deep. She still cannot tolerate loud noises and little things make her tense.

A few days after I met Razia, I went to Behrampada to meet her daughter Suraiya, an assistant project officer with WRAG. We met in the office of the Mahila Mandal. When the riots broke out, she was 19 and had just got married. They used to live in Kandivali, a suburb in north-west Mumbai, in a large flat. Her husband was working in Saudi Arabia at that time. One day, a mob of 1,500 came to attack them. There was one man, Narayan, the chairman of the building committee, who helped Suraiya and her husband. He took them to a house and locked it from outside. The young couple sat in the dark, while the mob destroyed everything around. She was two-months pregnant then and very scared. The mob kept asking Narayan to open the house, but he called their bluff. He was so bold he said that it is locked from outside, so why would anyone be inside. He even offered to open it for the crowd.

For Suraiya, that night still holds terror. She was terrified Narayan would open the door, but he did not. In the morning, Narayan took them to the station so that they could catch a train and go to Jogeshwari. She saw a woman being burnt alive and that memory of hiding in the dark house and the riots will always stay with her. She later came to Bandra to stay with her mother. Her husband went abroad after that. They have never gone back to that place. 'It was such a nice flat.' Later, her husband developed diabetes and suffered a lot. They had left everything behind. Her husband worked as a driver for so many years and he was very well off. Now, he runs a shop and he has become irritable. He too is involved in some social group.

Suraiya has two children who study in a convent school. She has been with WRAG since six years and has done paraprofessional courses. She was preparing for her first-year BA exams when I met her. When she first went to WRAG with her sister's case, she cried a lot. This *jabani talaq* (*talaq* or divorce by word of mouth) is so common and so many people suffer because of this. She almost never wanted to get married. When she deals with cases of other women, she is happy she can be of help, and her worries ease somewhat.

When Suraiya talks of her brother Jabbar, it is with a lot of pain. She has never been to meet him at the hospital. She was standing next to her sister when she died. It was the constant fear that people would come and do something that got to her. Her father was so deeply shocked by all that happened. After all that, it was her mother, Razia, who became the strongest person in the family. She is the driving force behind making all of them study. Through her organization, Suraiya has attended courses which focus on communal harmony. Many people from the area also enrol for them. She feels some changes for the better have taken place after those courses. But she wonders if there is something that keeps the two communities at bay. 'Yeh dil kaise saaf ho sakta hai?' (how can the heart be pure?), she wonders.

Rising from the Ashes—Mahila Mandals

On a large terrace in Naupada, Khatun Bi (not the person interviewed earlier in this chapter) and Razia preside over a meeting of women. Most of them have come with problems related to harassment, divorce, or maintenance. Khatun Bi listens patiently, doles out advice as the meeting goes on, interrupted by children, by laughter and admonition. In the deepening mire of Hindu–Muslim relations, it is heartening to see how people have fought back to escape the marginalization. A case in point is the movement to set up Mahila Mandals in various Muslim areas. Women like Khatun Bi have emerged as strong leaders of the community and motivate other women to join their group. Meetings are held regularly and there is a lot of discussion on issues. It is a space for these women to meet. They also tackle cases of violence and dowry and have a full-time job.

Khatun Bi has emerged as a leader in Naupada and her story is inspiring.

> We were a mixed community here though Muslims were dominating. Now many have moved out, but our old neighbours still send us sweets for Diwali. They felt insecure here. Earlier the *basti* was almost equally split. In our society we had Hindus. They did not suffer at all. But I feel they moved out because they felt insecure. I live in Naupada for the last 27 years and my mother's home is in Bhendi Bazar. In the riots, my sister-in-law's house was destroyed—she used to live in Mahalaxmi. The Hindus did help her out though. After the riots, the bomb blast really scared us. Even now, when I hear crackers, I get scared. Many men were terrorized, women were manhandled after the blasts, and our community really suffered both times. We took out so many peace rallies. I am also a member of the *mohalla* committee. We tried to dispel the fears people had.
>
> The Mahila Shakti Mandal was formed in 1995. Even in 1993, I wanted to do something when the riots happened. I had only studied up to seventh class; now, through distance education I have passed 12th. I learnt Hindi to appear for my exams. I wanted to help women who had lost their families in the riots. I got my sister-in-law a sewing machine so she could earn some money. We also set up a cell for women suffering from violence and separation with the help of other activists. I worked with the help of Noor Jehan from WRAG, an NGO. When I met Noor, I was so impressed I wanted to be like her—a person who gets things done. Now, as part of the Mandal, I have 25 women who meet regularly and discuss so many things. Shama Dalwai from the Bharatiya Muslim Mahila Andolan helped us too. We

took up issues concerning rations and water. First, we were five women; they never came out much at first. We were so scared of the police—we remembered how they treated us during the riots. Now we are planning to take up civic issues in a big way. We also charge membership of ₹ 250 a year. Since 2001, I work as a field officer for WRAG. I feel driven to go out and see things and change them.

For Khatun Bi, the riots were a catalyst in making her leave her house and work in the community.

I built up courage to venture out and now I get calls from all over the state. The *mohalla* committee meets every month and we also train people to interact in public. I don't wear a *burqa*. I was very poor when I came here—my husband was a rickshaw driver. He died three years ago. Here many women don't wear a *burqa*, but people are keen that I wear one. Many husbands don't approve of the Mandal, but my husband Ghafar was good to me. I was married at 14 and the man kept me in a *burqa*—he doubted me a lot and beat me. I left him, I was 14 then. Later, I ran away and divorced him. I had to do all the leg work myself, but that taught me a lot. I later married Ghafar. First, everyone told me if I was in the Mandal, my daughters would never get married, but all four are married now.

Within the community too Khatun Bi has to battle forces, which tell her to dress in a particular way and behave as a woman ought to. She has resisted those attempts and inspired people to be like her.

As Sushobha Barve, who has worked extensively in Dharavi during the riots and documented the situation and the response of the community, says:

The women of both communities displayed enormous courage. They responded to the crisis and did what seemed to them right.

Mostly these were simple humanitarian gestures that assumed great importance in the existing situation. They acted without caring about the risks involved. They were not affected by the communal propaganda at the time. Responding to such crises together also bonded them further as friends. In their stories lies a glimmer of hope that in India the social bonds will not be destroyed so easily by the passing hurricanes. (Barve 2003: 87, 88)

Mukim's Survival

The shift in residence is often accompanied by a sense of helplessness. Yet, some find it important to keep those old ties. That gives them a sense of community. Like Ahmed, who still goes back to Masjid Compound, Mukim Mumtaz Sheikh (10th standard pass) too keeps in touch with his old *basti*. His is a story of survival in more ways than one. Now 37, Sheikh brings out his own magazine, *Hindustan ki Awaz*, and has vivid memories of the riots in which his father was killed and he barely escaped death. He has taken to photography recently and can be seen at all important political functions, a digital camera hanging around his neck. He was born in a *chawl* in Ghatkopar West. His family has been associated with the Congress party. He used to be the ward representative of Seva Dal. In December 1992, nothing happened in their area. He thought nothing will happen in January too. While they were conscious of their Muslim identity, living in the *chawl*, they had very close relations. They never felt insecure.

Slightly built, with wide eyes, Mukim unravels a long and rather complicated story. In January 1993, there were boards advertising *maha aartis*. (In response to the Muslims coming on the road for *namaz*, a common practice in the city, Hindu groups decided to have *maha aartis*, with large gatherings and much festivity. In the riots, often it was the *maha aartis* which sparked off violence everywhere.) He was going to attend some meeting. His father had come back early and by the time he returned, things had got tense, the shops had closed. People were playing cricket on the empty streets. He heard that some shops near the station were on fire and a lot of violence was reported from there. His aunt had a *pucca* house nearby and they rushed there for safety. He had already told his father to leave four days before the riots, but he did not go. His younger brother and mother hid in a Hindu family's house.

While they waited in fear, at around 7 pm, there were shouts of 'Har Har Mahadeo' and the mob knew where Mukim and his father were hiding. Someone had already told them. The mob broke the door and they found the two under the cot. He told his father to jump down from the window, which was on the first floor. Mukim was confident, he knew everyone and he was so sure they would help. They both jumped on top of the huts and started running—they saw some open space ahead, but below, people could see the two run for their lives. Mukim kept shouting, 'Don't kill me' and extended his hand for help. What he got instead was an arm broken in three places. They robbed his watch, stripped-off his shirt, and dragged him to the main road and beat him up. He thought it was the end and he remembered God. They said something about Radhabai *chawl*. He knew many of the people—he once sold cosmetics door-to-door. And then he lost consciousness, just before blacking out, he could hear them say 'Let's do a Holi' and that was his last memory. When he regained consciousness, he does not know after how long, he found himself in what must have been a septic tank. His father was below him.

Mukim could hear him calling out asking for help. It was dark and everything smelt awful. When he came to consciousness again, he heard people saying that he was alive. A relieved and dazed Mukim stammered in Marathi '*Deva Deva Mala Vachva*' (God save me)—by then he was sure he would be burnt alive. But he had a vision—he was in Ajmer, where he made a wish. His father, 40, was silent now. The third time he heard voices, it was the police. He was in the tank for over 30 hours and he still remembers the inspector, Charudutt Zende, who rescued him. He almost drank that shit water in the tank—he was so thirsty. It was the septic tank in the CSD Compound next to the hospital, he recalls. He told them not to leave him behind, his teeth were broken and he could not eat. But his desire to live was strong. He spent a fortnight in hospital; and his cousin found him there.

He went back to live near his old house—everything was sold off there, but he was not keen on selling out of fear. He gave all the names of the attackers to the police, but no one was arrested. He did not give evidence before the Srikrishna Commission because he was scared and he feared for his brothers. Later, he sold that room and bought a house in a new area not very far from his old place. People left for Mumbra and other places. He tried to sell cosmetics at his old home, but when people saw him, they acted as if they had seen a ghost. He tried to drive an auto-rickshaw, but it did not work. He has rods in his hand and it is difficult for him to drive. He was desperate for a press ID card, since he believed that would give him power. Mukim did not even know how to write, but he was determined and now brings out his own paper. Married with three children, he also runs a telephone booth.

He still has Hindu friends and he gets sweets from them on occasions. He is fond of his old home and believes that rioters have no religion. He wants to believe that the rioters died of various problems, he has left justice to Allah. He does not regret not testifying before the Srikrishna Commission. They too did not get any justice, he feels. The only thing that bothers him is the distrust among communities.

Thakurdwar—A Small Community Vanishes

The Badi (Home) and Its Residents

A combination of riots and real estate has caused more changes in Mumbai than can be imagined. This predominantly Hindu area in south Mumbai was considered relatively safe for the small number of Muslims who lived near the S. K. Patil Udyan since years. They lived together in a row of houses, built next to each other, often with a single storey on top, in Diamond Jubilee Compound as it was called then in Thakurdwar, very close to Charni Road Station. All was well till 1992–93. Huma Khan, daughter of journalist Haroon Rashid, who lived there for many years, has some bitter memories. Her grandfather shifted from UP 60 years ago and bought a house in Thakurdwar. Her father was born and brought up there. It was a predominantly Hindu area and she liked it. She finds that in Muslim areas, boys look at you and hoot. In her childhood, she used to wander around sometimes in Bhendi Bazar (a Muslim area, a ghetto) though it was taboo for girls to go there. She used to visualize what it would be like living in a Muslim area. She started going there because of a friend, but she hid this from her mother. During Ramzan, she used to go there—they used to call it the *mohalla*. It was a word which, for her, described Bhendi Bazar. She went there with a great sense of curiosity and she enjoyed the festive atmosphere and the crowds. She enjoyed all this, yet she could feel the difference. People there lacked education and were mainly businessmen. They did not see the world outside. She often argued that Hindu men are more civilized. The area where she lived was dominated by the Shiv Sena and lower-middle class. She used to find so many faults with Muslims.

But because her father was the editor of a newspaper, he knew everyone, and the then Joint Commissioner of Police (Crime), R. D. Tyagi, later indicted by the Srikrishna Commission, used to visit them regularly. The first phase of riots was quite tense. Tyagi used to visit them every alternate day. The day before her house was burnt, he told Mr Rashid nothing would happen. He used to sit in the house and reassure them. I went to Huma's old house at Thakurdwar (she first moved to Navi Mumbai and now lives in another suburb after her marriage). When we reached the entrance, she stopped and looked at me. 'This is where Tyagi stood and told us not to worry', she recalls, pointing to the exact spot. Huma's old house was a part of row of houses, single- or double-storied tenements, with a small frontage. Next to them was a building which is being demolished and rebuilt now. The builder has offered all the 18 houses money to shift out of there and most of them are in the process of leaving.

Even after all their houses were burnt in the riots, people came back here to live. Their houses collectively called '*Badi*', are surrounded by taller apartments on all sides. What the riots could not do, the builder succeeded in doing. Now, the area has almost lost that small colony of Muslims. Huma lived with her extended family and her cousins, all male, who kept seeing the warning signs at the time of the riots. They told her father Tyagi was making a fool of them. Everyone felt unsafe, but her father insisted it was all right to stay on. All the residents were looking to Mr Rashid for guidance. On the day of the attacks, her father was still in a denial mode. But they had to leave suddenly. Her father kept saying they were running away due to fear. About 5,000 people attacked them on 8 January 1993, and on 9 January, the houses were burnt. Huma called the police. Her sister fainted and her brother had fever. They were screaming. Their house was the last one and the most vulnerable to attack. When they called the police they said if you survive tonight then you are safe.

On 9 January, a 'killing' silence descended on the area, Huma says; it was as if she was on an island. She felt even if she screamed no one would come here. They were throwing small bombs on their houses. She saw her father out on the road begging the cops to help—he even touched their feet. Instead, the cops tried to shoot them. The houses had bullet marks earlier to prove that. Boys came in trucks and jumped over the wall of S. K. Patil Udyan and everyone in the *Badi* had to flee. There was one car. It was difficult to imagine how so many could cram inside that one vehicle. It could have been 14 of them or more. All the women and girls wore *tikka*s on their foreheads. The seat was full of glass and, yet, they sat on it. They were headed for a friend's place in tony Cuffe Parade. The biggest shock was when they reached Marine Drive—it was so normal. Life was going on. People did not even ask what happened. Huma was barefeet. They reached Mr Rashid's friend's place on the 22nd floor of a Cuffe Parade apartment. He was speechless looking at their condition. No one ate anything and everyone was scared. Only her father wanted to go back for his books. They kept calling the house to check if someone was there or someone had saved it. The phone stopped ringing at 2 am and they knew it was over. Yet, the next day her father went back to see the houses—a horrible sight was in store for him. The houses were completely gutted and Huma realized no one really had the courage to stand up for them. Some days before this happened, some of her Hindu neighbours did warn them and had asked them to leave.

On 10 January, they left for Mughalsarai, Mr Rashid's native place. At the Mughalsarai Station, there was a huge crowd to receive them. On the way, the train was attacked at Kalyan. They sat silently inside, holding their breath and hoping no one would enter the train. They were all in deep mourning. One of Huma's friends came to the station and cried so much. But those tears did not make a difference to her. It was beyond tolerance. 'That was the moment many became extremists I feel', she breaks off to tell me. But it was not her escape—her bare feet or the fact that others did not bother about her plight that pained her. When people gave her food it was fine, but when they gave her clothes, she could not get over it. It struck her forcefully that they had nothing. Nothing. Even their clothes were someone else's. Months later, she would search for clothes in her old house and for her hidden box of jewellery. Her mother used to stitch all her clothes. They had two fridges, a washing machine, three TV sets, many photographs, so many books, and her mother's wedding dress, which she loved. She wanted to wear it when she grew up. It was made of silver thread. The *dupatta* weighed a kilo.

Her father had kept meticulous diaries. Now there is nothing, all of it was burnt. After that sojourn, they came back for her exams. She was in first-year BA and her sister in the 10th. They came to live in another friend's flat in Santa Cruz. For the first time, she travelled in local trains. They had to wake up early to get to college. It hit her very badly. Things had changed so much. For her, like for everyone else, it was very important to have her own house. It haunted her and she was desperate to go back. By March-end 1993, they shifted back to their home. It was Bakri Id, there was a lot of tension as a BJP MLA was shot dead. Anything like this strikes fear in them. Now no one took chances, they stayed at home. All the families had returned by then, but every time there was tension they would leave their houses and seek shelter mostly with friends. The whole place used to empty out.

People look at Huma, an attractive young girl, and say you do not look like a riot victim. 'Is it written on my face?' she asks me. Some years later, in 2003, she moved to Navi Mumbai. Her father died in 2000. In Mumbai you cannot avoid the Sena. They are the only Muslim family in the building. She finds educated people are more communal and they are more poisonous. By and large people are not really communal. People are nice to her, they think she is Uma, a Hindu, but when she corrects it, the response is not always good. They moved to Navi Mumbai for a bigger place. It is not easy for everyone to move out. People warned them not to go to a mixed locality. But they never wanted to stay in a ghetto. Since childhood, her family was used to living in a mixed locality. They were never biased against any community. People told them to go to Pakistan. Huma says:

> But trust is shattered. I realized the power of mass thinking and how it can change in minutes. No one is there to help us. I feel I can't trust anyone—I felt I was on an island and each time a bomb went past our house I would die. It was a near-death experience for me. Congress has no moral right to rule and what about the policemen who did nothing—couldn't you stop their increments? I feel now everyone is becoming more religious and serials are poisoning people's minds. Earlier, religion was a private matter, but now people are obsessed by religion. I miss my old home so much.

Despite everything, she was clear she did want to fall into the trap of ghettoization. Her mother bought this house because of contacts. The broker tells them that people like them do not get flats. She tried to buy another house, but she had no luck. People do not want to sell Muslims houses. 'Isn't that also ghettoization when you are pushing people into a corner?'

DISPLACEMENT AND POLARIZATION

A few days later I visit Huma's old house in Thakurdwar. Her aunt Madina was still there at that time. She is known as Badi Ma. She came here in 1955 after her marriage. I met her before she moved to a new house in south Mumbai, a move that was painful but necessary. She had left this house only once earlier during the riots. She remembers Bal Thackeray as a young man. There was a lot of tension even then. Opposite was a building called *kali* or black building as it had a lot of tar on it. Many Maharashtrians used to live there. During the riots, people threw stones at them from there. The police ran away when they saw the mob. If they had done their job none of this would have happened, she says.

Though it was a Hindu majority area, people were so good to them. There was no problem at all. After the riots she felt like a stranger. They went back to UP for a while and came back to live in Santa Cruz. If there was any tension there would be a pin drop silence. People were so scared. No one had thought anything like this would happen in this area. Every time they called the police, they would ask if anything happened, if something happens then call us. The *Badi* was empty—stones were thrown at them. All that is behind them now. It is like a story, she says. It was their determination to come back: 'Why should we leave. We are as much Indian as anyone else. We really loved this place and now even to shift to a new flat nearby is breaking my heart.'

Badi Ma, like others, has a strong sense of being Indian. In fact this is a question many asked: 'Aren't we Indian, why should we leave this place and where will we go?' Her husband died of a heart attack. Opposite the *Badi* was Diamond Building, which was also Muslim-dominated. 'We were happy in our own world. Diamond Building was demolished some years ago and which is why the whole area is about to change with a new complex.' Badi Ma came here when she was 15 in 1955. 'I have lived here since then and when the question came of moving out of here—I refused to live in the suburbs. Mumbai is vulnerable and sometimes we get stuck. We need a place in the city.'

Buying a house in the affluent part of Mumbai was possible because of her sons.

I never dreamt I would have to shift. Even after the riots I came back. But with builders you can't do anything. I feel both communities can stay together. It was like an accident—the riots. My younger son had a Hindu friend. He cried for us when we were leaving. He kept wondering why it happened. We could not take anything with us.

Badi Ma is the picture of maternal comfort—surrounded by her grandchildren, she sits out in the open in the courtyard of her house. The building opposite is under construction. 'I will miss all this', she sighs. 'This open space, this airiness where else can you get all this in Mumbai. Many from the row of houses have moved to Mumbra. There was one non-Muslim family, Lalitbhai, he grew up with the boys from the *Badi* and he shifted out to Dahisar later.' When I met her, the most worrying thing for Badi Ma was Sanjay Dutt's fate—will he get punished, she asks me anxiously.

The Story of Salma Agha

Next door is Zaibunissa Gadkari's house. She is from Sangli in Maharashtra. She lost her husband early on and has two sons and a daughter. When the riots started, they were scared to go out. Her egg business was badly hit. People used to come looking to kill her sons. They used to abuse them and call them *landya*. They escaped to a building opposite and they were mostly old women. They did not take anything with them and after two days in the building they thought of going to Dadar. A mob caught them, but somehow they managed to escape. They sat in a closed train on their way to Sangli for three days without food or water. They wore *tikkas* so that no one would catch them and almost for a week they had nothing to eat. Finally, they had to leave because the people in the building felt unsafe. The police refused to help and a complete stranger gave them *tikkas* to wear. She stayed in Sangli for six months.

Here, Zaibunissa who used to keep hens in the compound, breaks off to talk about her famous hen Salma Agha (named after a singer and

DISPLACEMENT AND POLARIZATION

actor) at the time of the riots. The famous hen could not be found anywhere—she was burnt to death. It was her pet hen. Even her neighbour's poultry was finished. Her carefully hidden saving was robbed. It was her daughter's wedding and she had collected money and clothes apart from jewellery. Like everyone else she got ₹ 4,000 for the burnt house and lost business. It was her brother who rebuilt the house. Now faced with the shifting, she has no choices. She wants to be near a *dargah* and she prefers a mixed locality. She blames the owner of Diamond House for making a cheap deal and shortchanging them. Her daughter Sultana who stays in another suburb, Mulund, has problems living in a Muslim area as the girls get teased. Zaibunissa says she thinks of this small area as her ancestral land. Her mother-in-law's mother was born here. It goes back a long way.

Farida Ismail Gadkari, her daughter-in-law, who lives downstairs, is also resisting the move. Her husband works for the BEST [Bombay (later Brihanmumbai) Electric Supply and Transport Undertaking] company and her children go to the nearby St. Anne's Girls High School. At that time, they were looking for a place in Dadar or Colaba. She says in a Hindu area it is scary, but in mixed localities there is less tension. They know a lot of Maharashtrians and are happy to stay with them. She came here after marriage from Islampur. Even after the riots, they all came back and now it is difficult for her to accept that she has to leave. People were still nice to them when they came back and they sympathized with them. She does not want to leave and go to some ghetto— she does not want her son to become a *goonda*. She endorses the perception of a ghetto as breeding ground for anti-social elements. They have lots of friends in both communities and they hope they can live in a nice place. In a mixed locality, one learns about other cultures and how other people live. That is very important for her. She wants her children to have that experience and not stay closeted in one community.

For many this was their marital home and Dulhan Ma came to the *Badi* as a new bride and the name stuck. Everyone calls here by that name, though her real name is Asmat Banu. She came here when she got married from Junnar, her native place. She has two boys and a girl,

Heena, who now lives in Mira Road. She has been living here since 22 years. During the riots, she went back to Junnar in her brother's car and she was away for two months. She remembers how the front door was always open and how safe it was. The future is left to Allah. Heena, her daughter, says that Mira Road was a good choice as it was financially viable and they live in a mixed locality. Her mother is not keen, so they have been looking at places in Grant Road, but she finds find that Muslims are not allowed anywhere. They were told no Muslims are allowed in certain areas.

In Mira Road, the builder was their friend, and they bought the flat in 1999. Now, Dulhan Ma's son is searching for a flat. 'I want a ground floor flat as I can't climb stairs now and buildings don't have lifts', says Dulhan Ma. 'I want a home in south Mumbai, Inshallah', she says. For Heena, staying in a ghetto is okay, but her husband is not so keen. 'I want water, that's all', she smiles. Dulhan Ma's neighbour Salima Abdul Latif Sheikh came to the Badi in 1960 from Miraj. She has four children. After the riots, for three months, they went to Miraj, they left in a hail of stones. They stayed in the building nearby, but the police told them to leave. They spent a night in a senior BEST official's house as her husband worked for the company. That man bought them railway tickets. They thought they will not reach as the train kept stopping and stones were thrown at them. About 25 of them were together. Luckily, they did not suffer much loss, but they were scared of coming back.

Her sister-in-law, Saira, says that they thought of leaving and going after the riots, but they did not try so hard. 'We never felt discriminated here and we can't think of leaving. Now we are looking for a place in a mixed locality—if more Muslims are there something can happen and for our children too it's good to live with other people.'

Huma's cousin, Asif Khan, was 25 at the time of the riots. He used to work for a bank then. In 2003, he left and started an export company. The boys protected this area under Asif's father's leadership. There were 50 of them in the compound. On 7 January 1993, there was a lot of stone-throwing and the military was patrolling the nearby areas. His father was on the road and he saw shops being burnt. He came and told them be prepared for any eventuality. They also retaliated by stone-throwing and all night there were violent exchanges. They did not sleep—there was a lot of chaos. On the morning of 8 January, mobs attacked them from all sides and they called the local Sena leader, Vilas Awchat, who told them he was helpless. Though their family knew Awchat very well, he did not help at all. Police fired on them instead of those mobs, and one person was killed. In the night, the buildings nearby, Hemrajwadi, put up huge bright lights. Their homes were burnt and they had to leave. There is a small *dargah* near the *Badi* and the mob went inside it too with their slippers. Even after the riots, they could not go back immediately and every evening the boys used to sleep somewhere else.

Asif admits to being scared when the *maha aarti*s were held, it is not the same as *namaz*. He bought a house in Jogeshwari after the riots as he wanted to move out and he chose this area deliberately. He could not buy a house in areas like Vile Parle. His intention was not to go so far, but, in some ways, he really had little choice. The security issue is also important for him. He only wanted one secure place for his family in Mumbai. The rates in Jogeshwari also increased after the riots. It became a safe haven for Muslims, which is why people like Firoz Ashraf also moved there. Asif also says that even the municipal corporation and the Slum Rehabilitation Authority want to sanitize buildings and make sure that no Muslims are part of any re development. He also says that Muslims cannot buy houses in certain areas. Things have changed over the years.

Thakurdwar is now a stronghold of Hindus. Now, rich Marwaris live there, mostly even the middle-class Maharashtrians have shifted out. The four brothers recall those tense days. For nearly a month they stayed up all night. 'You did not expect these things to happen. Our Hindu friends used to feel bad for us. Perceptions of the Muslims have changed now—there is a lack of justice', they say.

Huma's mother, Rafat Jahan, in her late 50s, has warm memories of her home. She used to live in Lucknow and came here in 1968. It was only in 2003 that they moved out to Navi Mumbai. She loved her old house in the *Badi*, they had done up the loft so beautifully. After the riots she went back to stay there. Rafat is calm about the riots. She feels this can happen anywhere. Even in Lucknow they lived in a mixed locality.

When they left they could not stop crying all the way. Mr Rashid did not go with them. After the riots, when they returned, they lived in Santa Cruz. What really upset her was that they had their own place, but they had to make do with a rented house. She was not keen on leaving even at the height of the riots. She feels people can be good or bad everywhere. There is no bitterness even now.

When the riots broke out, Rafat was not in Mumbai. She was travelling in Lucknow and Ranchi. She called her children to reassure them. On 7 December, when she called Huma (it was her birthday), she said that petrol bombs were being thrown at them. Vilas Awchat, was a friend and he had told them he would help. Because of him they waited till the last minute and in the end he could do nothing. She is grateful that none of them had the thought of revenge.

Did she find anything different after the riots? When they were in Santa Cruz in the building no one spoke to them. They lived there for five months. They knew about riots, yet no one uttered a word in their support. One man, a photographer, whom they knew, asked if they were selling and leaving. That really angered her. She remembers the shopkeeper who changed her burnt money. She remembers the laundry man—he was even invited for a wedding in the family. She moved to Navi Mumbai as she thought the city was too crowded, specially the western suburbs. The broker was a Hindu—he was very nice to them. She has no problems with the neighbours too. To think one is safe in a Muslim area is wrong. Culturally and personally she feels better in a mixed locality. It is better to stay together in a sense.

When the riots broke out the second time, all the women were bundled to the top of the building opposite Diamond House. From the top, they could see S. K. Patil Garden and the boys in huge vehicles and matadors—boys and middle-aged men had gathered there to attack. It was a mob; it is not concerned with their sense of community. Some people did not help like Awchat, but they did no harm either, she says. They could see people were watching what was happening from their balconies. The balconies opposite were full of people. The last thing they thought of was that the mob would actually burn down the houses. Rafat says:

> Because of these riots there are divisions. I feel there are two kinds of people. Nice people and those who spoil things. Common people want to live together. In Uttar Pradesh, people live together; there is trust. Here I have *sukoon* [peace]. In the *Badi* we were all part of a community. Now the police are posted at the *Badi* to guard whom?

People would call Mr Rashid all day and night and consult him. He was the editor of a paper and he was accessible. He helped poor people. Huma says:

> We felt if we were nice to others they would help us. When we finally left, we could not take anything with us. The losses were irrecoverable. It set us back so much. We just took a few things in a briefcase. When we came back from Lucknow everything was in ruins—you can't forget it. It was the loss of our home. My father had a lot of watches, he loved collecting them. The clothes were kept in the cupboard—small things which you can't forget.

Her brother Adnan keeps going back to the *Badi*: every Sunday the boys meet there. Rafat was only worried about revenge, but nothing happened. 'For revenge, you need bitterness. *Jaan jab jati hai* you are bitter.'

When they came back to their old house, everything was burnt—all the books, the perfumes Mr Rashid was fond of. Rafat says she was reminded of Partition. 'We had no ATMs then. We broke an old piggy bank and found it had ₹ 2,500.'

For them, it was going back to history. They stayed at their native village, an hour from Mughalsarai. At that time, Huma was in second-year Arts. Her sister Darakshah topped in Marathi that year despite all the horror they had been through. After the riots, things changed in that area—societies put up big gates and increased the heights of their compound walls. The divisions were spelt out clearly now. The funny thing was that the Hindus were never attacked, yet they put up these walls. It was the non-Muslims who were scared, Huma says.

Choti Badi, Thakurdwar

Near the *Badi* on the opposite side is Syed Wadi, where again there are 22 houses all belonging to Muslims. No builder has staked a claim here, so the residents are still safe. Mohammed Shah was born here in 1932. For the first time after that they had to leave the house during the riots in 1993. The Wadi is also called Choti *Badi* and is surrounded by Kranti Nagar, which constructed a huge metal gate after the riots to secure itself.

Mohammed Shah used to clean the graves of the Syed community. There is also the graveyard of the Kutchi Memons and the Suleimani Bohras adjacent to it. This is a small sylvan locality in the heart of Thakurdwar. Mohammed says:

> In the old times, we were paid for cleaning the graves, but that has stopped now, so Nasreen my wife started selling vegetables. That's how we educated my six daughters and the youngest is a graduate now. The four are married and have moved to Ghatkopar or Mira Road.

'During the riots we went to the *dargah* at Mahim and lived there for 10 to 15 days. We had to run at the last minute wearing only our clothes.' Mohammed says he came back in a month and went to stay at Ghatkopar. They burnt all the houses in the Wadi except two, which had Ganpati motifs outside. 'We came back later and had to rebuild everything. It took me a year to redo everything and we got a lot of help from people.' Mohammed is a Syed is from a dervish lineage and has studied till the seventh class. Many people who left have come back and the settlement is pretty much as it was before.

Mohammed says:

> The police did not help at all they just sat and ate while everything around us burnt. Why should we leave this place? The same thing can happen anywhere. Death can come here or anywhere else. Staying next to the *kabrastan* is a convenient place; if we go too far that will become an issue. We were terrified during the riots, all night people threw stones at us and chased us away.

Syed Wadi is probably more than 100 years old. 'No builder will move us out', he adds confidently. Mohammed also feels the Sena must be regretting what it did in those days. He feels people are capable of staying together. 'There is no fear now. The people who burnt and looted say that it not us, but they will get justice. Many have died, one was killed in the firing. But what is happening now is even worse—why put bombs in a *masjid*?' he asks.

Earlier, his father used to work on the graves and before that, two generations did so.

> Now things are normal—we did not even a glass to drink water from when we came back, no clothes and no furniture. Slowly, we put together everything. We got ₹ 5,000 for the house. I still remember the local cable wallah tried to defend us and he tried his best to save us. He was beaten up so badly. My two daughters are still studying they don't have any problems.

Nasreen, his wife, has lived here for 40 years after her marriage. She is now too old to sell vegetables. She too remembers that things soon after the riots were very tense and people taunted her for selling in the bazaar, but she stayed on.

6

LOSS OF LIVELIHOOD

Local businesses were hit in a big way and Behrampada, which was once the hub of retail clothing, is no longer that. Many people have found it difficult to recover and regain their livelihoods after the riots. Also, the riots left a deep scar on the minds of those who were affected, an impact which has not been taken into account seriously.

People from Naupada were in the news in 2006 for their rescue of the victims of the 11 July serial bomb blasts in the local trains of Mumbai. One of the blasts took place on the tracks alongside Naupada. Mohammed Rizwan Asghar Ali Khan was one of those who helped retrieve the bodies from the wreckage. But no one helped him in 1993. He points to a scar running down his right leg, he still cannot walk normally. It was evening when he was shot in his leg and when he and the others were taken to a local municipal hospital, it refused to admit them. It was only after Sunil Dutt, the former MP, and his son, actor Sanjay Dutt, came there, that they took them in. He was later moved to a private hospital. Rizwan was one of those who was shot by the police

LOSS OF LIVELIHOOD

while running to help douse a fire in the neighbouring Behrampada. He used to sell ready-made *salwar kameez*es on the footpaths of Linking Road, a popular roadside shopping area in upmarket Bandra West, when the riots took place. Born in Naupada, Rizwan has five brothers and a sister. He has studied till the eight standard. He was a social worker of sorts too then. He recalls:

> I had spoken to the police and said that nothing will happen here in Naupada. But the fires burnt in Behrampada and the police did not want anyone to help. They did not even allow the fire brigade to go there. I also remembered that they used to go to the rooftops and fire from their guns.

There is a calmness about Rizwan—he is slow to speak but quick to act. It is not only the scar that rankles Rizwan. He said he became very disturbed. There were eight of them who were running to douse the fires and all were hit. There is bitterness too about his loss of livelihood. There were 313 shops on Linking Road on Bandra West, which sold ready-mades and today, none of them exist. The pavement has been taken over by other people. A lot of young men were jobless after the riots. Rizwan and others cannot go back there as the police manage the *haftas* (bribes) and even though they tried once, they asked them to pay a lot of money; it became difficult. In addition, because of his injury, he could no longer lift heavy things or run about like before. Selling ready-mades fetched about ₹ 100 to 150 a day, enough to keep a family afloat. Now, he has to support his wife and a daughter and he does odd jobs, which come by once in a while.

Despite all this, Rizwan can never think of leaving this place. He rues:

> Why should I leave? The riots killed so many people, people lost their lives, jobs, even children died. I don't know about the Srikrishna Commission, but I know no one has been punished. I keep thinking every day, where has my life led me?

No one paid me any compensation for my loss—no one came to help me.

Earlier, there were over 70 Hindu families living in Naupada, but now many of them have left. He even remembers Ganpati celebrations in the area. Rizwan does not think there is a communal divide. He feels there are many people who understand what was behind the riots of 1992–93 and there is a lot of camaraderie.

It is not only the small traders, but also big businesses which were hit. Mohammed Abdus Sattar, 58, who owns Suleiman Bakery on the busy Mohammed Ali Street, is not too keen on recalling those days. Sattar almost left the city after the riots. On 9 January 1993, nine persons were shot dead after the police, led by the then Joint Commissioner of Police, crime, R. D. Tyagi, stormed into the bakery to flush out suspected terrorists hiding on the terrace. 'My workers were killed in the firing, but many were also among the 78 arrested', Sattar says. 'It took two years for me to bring the business back. I lost my workers in the firing and yet the blame is on us.'

The bakery was established in 1936 and there is a date on the building. I met Sattar next to his bakery on Mohammed Ali street. Sattar says:

> About five of my employees were killed—they were shot dead by the police. Why should I file a complaint—there was curfew in any case. The Bombay police is responsible for what happened. When I went to collect the bodies of my workers, the police said they were firing all night with AK 47s. I said where are the bullets—the police said it was a terrorist attack and I said whose fault is that. Where are the bullet marks? Even *The Times of India* wrote a story saying terrorists were firing all night on the terrace of the bakery. The police came, broke open the door, and barged into the terrace. I wrote a letter to the *Times* editor saying this was not true. I met the editor and said let truth prevail in your paper. Now, we have an iron door after the riots, earlier it was wooden. [Sattar grins]

LOSS OF LIVELIHOOD

We never thought this would happen in Mumbai it usually happens in Uttar Pradesh. In a city like Mumbai, so cosmopolitan, how can this happen? Hindus and Muslims live together. After the riots the point of view has changed. People started thinking more about their safety—anything can happen. Those memories are very fresh. No one who seen has bodies in an ambulance or visited a morgue can forget. *Ajeeb waqt tha* [it was a strange time]. I could not find people or even pay to retrieve bodies from the morgue. I had to do it myself. The bodies were decomposed, there were no stretchers. There was no one to help because of curfew. My friend Suhail Lokhandwala came with me—I could not have done it without him. These memories kept turning inside my head. It took me more than two years to recover. I was under so much mental stress for so long. I wanted to leave Mumbai, that was my feeling at that time—everyone persuaded me to stay. I was so disturbed—I did not want to do anything, I became idle. It was very disturbing that our men died and we only got the blame. I had 30 to 40 workers and police arrested 79 people. I had to get them out on bail.

The bitterness and the injustice of all this has stayed with Sattar. Yet, he managed to get his bakery back on track. During the riots, bakeries run by Muslims were targeted and many of them were burnt down. Not all have managed to recover their business.

Like businessmen, women who lost their husbands in the riots were perhaps the worst affected. Many men went missing those days and still remain untraced. Those who did investigations at that time like Pappu Qureshi of the Citizens for Peace, have confirmed that many of the missing men were burnt to death. Rashida Kotawala's husband went missing in the riots along with his brother. Now she runs his shop on Vile Parle station road and has done wonders with her life. When you get down from Vile Parle station and walk on the west side, there is only one woman who sits on the side of the road with a makeshift shop, mending bags. Rashida is a cheerful bright young woman with two helpers. Since years she has been mending bags and is quite well known in the area for her work. The only insecurity she has is that anytime she can be evicted by the municipal vans. She is not a licenced hawker—she has the licence of a man, a Hindu she points out, but sometimes the municipal officials are attentive and when they see that her name does not match the one on the licence, her goods are confiscated. On the day I went to meet Rashida, she was sitting huddled in her makeshift shop with everything covered. She had plenty of time to chat, though she kept nervously looking around. It was the day the municipal van had chosen to come and evict unlicenced hawkers from that road.

Rashida, now 45 and a fifth-class pass, is from the Bohra community. She came to live in Malad after her marriage with Shabbir. Her maternal home was in Saki Naka. She had two sons. Two years after she moved there the riots broke out. 'My husband and brother-in-law went out. I remember it was a Sunday and they never came back', she says as a matter of fact. It was Shabbir and his father who ran the small shop which repaired bags. It is an old shop, about 35 years old. 'Even then I used to work here, helping doing small jobs', she says.

When Shabbir and her sister's husband went missing, they searched a lot.

> We still don't know what happened. It was only four or five years ago that we got compensation. One month we spent looking for them. My sister is young, Fiza; she has a son and a daughter. The police did not help us at all. We finally filed a case at the Dindoshi police station. We had no proof of his death. Shabbir was a few years older than me.

She sometimes thinks he may come back. What really upset her is that they lived in a Muslim-dominated area and there were no riots there. She keeps repeating that they really do not know what happened, as they did not see anything.

What happened after that can only due to Rashida's grit. She has managed to educate her two sons and one of them is now a medical student.

The younger one studies in the 12th standard. The community did support her and give her interest-free loans so that she could educate the children. Eight years ago, she has moved to a flat under the Slum Rehabilitation Scheme. Her sister Fiza makes jewellery at home and has married again.

> Many people told me to get married. I had just got out of the mental mess I was in. But I decided to work and earn money instead of depending on my family. I can't remember how time went by. If I did not work, my children would have to stop studying and work.

Now she works from 10 am to 8 pm, and Sundays are off. She goes to buy some materials for the shop on that day. She says:

> I like staying here, everyone knows me and the people are nice. In Saki Naka where I grew up, it was a mixed locality. I came to a Muslim area which had a mosque nearby as it had a madrassa where I wanted my sons to study. I prefer a mixed area though.

Going back to her husband's case she says: 'It was my fate, why blame anyone for what happened? They left on Sunday morning and never came back.' Suddenly, she looks around; the grey vans are coming closer. 'It costs a lot of money to get a licence. So we make do with this borrowed one. I hide all the bags and stuff—I pay them some *hafta*.' Rashida waves as I leave and invites me to meet her again.

Not everyone, though, has the support Rashida had, specially from her community. In the case of Ayesha Nadaf, her husband was a stove repairer and she had never worked before. Her life was destroyed in the riots. Yet, she continues with a calmness that is quite frightening at times. It is almost dark and one has to go up a hill at Pimpri Pada in Malad West, where there is a market of sorts in the evening. Ayesha sits on a stone behind a small makeshift tray of fish and prawns. There is a single candle burning beside her and in the dark one can just about see her face. She is 35 now and she used to live in Kranti Nagar where her husband, Ismail, worked as a stove repairer. He went missing in the riots. He is suspected to have been burnt to death. Now, since 10 years, she sells fish at this place from 5.30 pm to 10.30 pm. On a good day, she earns ₹ 100.

Her two daughters are married and her son works in a clothes factory in Kolhapur. She stays on rent and her life is insecure. Every day she is harassed by the municipality as she is not a licenced hawker. Sometimes she gets no money from her sales. She vows never to return to Kranti Nagar even though she lived there for seven years. Pappu Qureshi, who was with the Citizens for Peace at the time of the riots, has kept track of her life. He says that Ayesha's husband Ismail was killed between 7 and 9 January when he went to check on his brother at Ban Dongri, a small hillock nearby. Ismail was hidden by a Hindu couple, but their grandson, a small boy, spotted him hiding in their house and he called the mob. Three people were burnt alive in Ban Dongri. 'On that day, I went to the place where the killings occurred and all the evidence was not destroyed. I got testimonies of people who saw the murders. In fact I was assaulted for gathering this evidence but I did not press charges', says Qureshi. Ayesha complained to the police that her husband was missing. What followed after that was terrible. She and her children were kicked out of the house and she went to stay with her mother in Kurar village. Till 1997 she had not got compensation and the police kept telling her Ismail must have run away with a second woman. Qureshi made his own report and tracked down the place where the incident occurred and also got witnesses to prove that Ismail was killed. No case of murder was filed despite this evidence.

Ayesha went to live with her brother and mother and she only got her compensation in 1998—Rs 2 lakh. She bought a house next to the highway, but later it was demolished as it came under the highway expansion—they were not compensated. In the midst of this, her daughter was assaulted and was missing for days. Hers is a tragic story and the tragedy has not ended. When you see her calmly sitting near the dim candle-lit tray full of plastic bags of fish and prawns, in a single moment, her tragic life unfolds before you.

LOSS OF LIVELIHOOD

The riots are not something that Sadiqa Sheikh will ever forget. She stays in a small tenement in Jogeshwari East. When I met her, it was evening and she was cutting vegetables on the floor. She earns a living by selling lunches and dinners to a few people. Her son Mohammed has appeared for the 10th standard examinations and is waiting for his results. He stares at the TV set.

Mohammed was six-months-old when the riots broke. She says:

> I managed to educate him ... sometimes I don't know how. At times some others paid my fees and once his school teachers saw me on TV and then they did not take any fees from me. For a few years I did get money for school fees. Once, I got ₹ 2,600 and then ₹ 3,500, but after that nothing. I had to run around so much making affidavits after my husband died.

She was married in 1991 and her husband was a tailor who used to work in a factory. 'I can never forgive the police, they shot my husband deliberately—he was just standing outside.' Behind where she lives is Shankarwadi—the police aimed their guns through broken toilet windows. 'I don't want to spoil my son's life by making him work. I want to educate him and make something out of him', she tells me.

Her husband was among the four men shot dead in that area. Sadiqa has spent her life after the riots working from home to make ends meet. She used to deliver milk early morning, do odd jobs, and now she makes tiffins which her son delivers. She stays with her husband's brothers who want to throw her out of the house. Her mother-in-law was good to her and she kept pleading to be allowed to stay on till her son did his schooling. Now that has come to an end. 'They say I got ₹ 2 lakh as compensation and now I should get out of this house and live somewhere else. Where will I go?' she asks.

Looking at Sadiqa in her early 30s, and the way she has managed to put her life back on track, well almost, I think, she will come up with a new survival strategy.

Changing Relations

The riots affected people in so many ways. Relations between the two communities too have changed definitely. Youngsters like Taukeer Khan, a civil contractor, say that it was his generation that was really affected. Taukeer was in the 10th standard when the riots broke out: 'We could not get over it. People lost their jobs and there was so much unhappiness.' He feels, as a result, Muslims are more determined to educate their children. In Behrampada, now about 25 per cent of young people have jobs in offices or call centres. 'People are also going in for smaller families. The Muslim community forgets easily, things on the surface are normal', he maintains. There is deep disillusionment with vote banks too created by the Congress, for instance. 'Now we just want basic amenities, jobs and our constitutional rights', says Taukeer.

Sheikh Yunus Sheikh Musa, 37, runs a small grocery shop in Behrampada. He studied in the school in nearby Kherwadi till the seventh standard. His house was burnt down in 1993. He says, 'People used to attack us often. In January 1993, the New Nirman *chawl* was totally burnt. There were 60 houses there. People threw fire bombs from the buildings around us and the police fired on those who tried to put out the fires.' His house was among those gutted and all the families sought refuge in a building under construction. Many families lived there for a year and some local NGOs helped them. Relief agencies and *The Times of India* Relief Fund rebuilt many of the houses, and now Yunus lives in a room there. At that time, Yunus was part of a 12-member family. There was a shoe factory and he used to work there at first. His father ran a store and used to make glass shades for gas lamps. Now, the shop is the sole means of a livelihood. His father now helps him. The riots changed many things for Yunus. He said earlier there was nothing between the two communities, but the riots changed all that.

There was a *dhobi* [washerman], Ramkiran [who was Yunus's neighbor], who was also affected. His family too was given shelter here. I had Hindu friends too, but after the riots their contact with me became lesser and lesser. In fact the people from buildings around us came and apologized to us—they did not throw the bombs or set Behrampada on fire. I remember that Madhukar Sarpotdar, a leader of the Shiv Sena, was arrested with weapons but he was let off. The government should punish all those responsible. It should be done as a lesson. I see that punishment is being meted out in other cases.

'I did get compensation of ₹ 5,000, but many others did not get. The collector came and gave us the cheques', he says. What did Yunus do after the riots? 'I managed to get some loans and set up the shop. When I think about those days, I am scared. I am scared will it happen again', he fears. For a while, Yunus kept clippings of the newspaper stories. He still has some in his possession, mostly depicting Behrampada as a hellhole of troublemakers. 'They wrote all bad things about us', he remembers. He made a list of all those injured and killed in Behrampada, but has misplaced it.

At the end of the conversation, he tells me that his father suffered a severe shock after the riots. What he saw during those days left him upset. He never went back to his normal self: 'When our house burnt down, it really hit my father very badly. It was a huge setback and he never recovered from that. He suffered a lot and later contracted TB.' I see Yunus's father in the small shop that he runs. He sits very still, his eyes are fixed in steady stare and yet he is kind and gracious.

Impact of the Riots

Like Yunus' father, many people, specially children, who grew up in those times have effects which are not really understood. Along with the loss of livelihoods, there is also a feeling of despair and hopelessness. Many did not recover from the loss of lives like Aamir Khan's mother. In Behrampada alone, I met families where at least one member is affected this way. I meet Aamir Khan and his friends at a corner of Behrampada. A high concrete wall separates the slum from a set of apartments on the other side. 'I used to live here at that time. We were surrounded by the police and there were shoot-at-sight orders. That wall was much lower in those days', says Aamir as a prelude to explaining his father's death.

> It was 15 January 1993; my father was coming back from *namaz*, and entering the house when he was shot. There was some commotion in the morning as a result of which shoot at sight orders were issued. He was 60 at that time and worked as a tailor in Dadar.

Khuda Yaar Khan, his father, got a bullet in his back. When Aamir heard the shots and went to help him, he too was under fire. After that the riots continued for another month. Two years later, he went to Kuwait and worked there for five to six years. Now, Aamir has moved to Latur, where he deals in ready-made garments. But the worst affected was his mother, Hazra Bi: 'My mother had a mental illness after my father's death. She died two or three years later. She could not sleep. For two months, she saw a lot of the riots, the firing, the petrol bombs and she had a psychological problem.'

'She really changed after the riots and we moved to Hyderabad for a while but despite taking her for treatment she did not improve. She died in Hyderabad never having recovered from her problems.' Amir said he had to be strong for the family. He has a brother and a sister. A fifth-standard dropout, he has now moved to Latur and sells clothes. He comes often to Behrampada, but he feels the business has changed a lot. A lot of people moved out and there have been a lot of changes.

Shahid Ali lost his elder brother who had left for work on 7 December. He used to work as a tailor and had four children. His sister-in-law moved to Delhi after two years; 'she could not live here anymore', says Shahid. At that time, Shahid was in school; he has studied up to the eighth standard. It was very tense then, he remembers.

Behrampada was famous as a wholesale cloth market. It no longer enjoys that pride of place. Many shops were looted and none were compensated. Shahid says:

This was a good area. We were surrounded by the MIG [Middle Income Group] housing colony, they did try to help us, but it was of no use. Earlier, we used to go and play with these people. We had friends, now many have joined the Shiv Sena. They even tried to take us to political meetings, but one of the meetings was being addressed by Narendra Modi and it was too provoking and we left. Our friends are far from us now.

Living in Ghettos

While the riots polarized the city, and people left to live with their own community, there are places where things have not changed. That goes on to prove that, inherently, there were few reasons for enmity between people, and the bonds of trust developed over the years continue to exist. In fact in places like Behrampada, people fear builders, who are trying to evict them, more than communal riots. In Kasaiwada, Hindus and Muslims continue to live together in small pockets, while in places like Mazgaon increasingly Muslims are moving in. Many of the Christian and Hindu families have moved out after the riots. In Farid Vora's case, in Mazgaon, south Mumbai, people took a decision in his building not to allow Muslims to buy flats there. That has changed over the years though the rule still persists. In the case of Samar Khadas of *Divya Marathi* (a Marathi Daily) his family still lives in a Hindu-dominated area. There is only one other Muslim family there in the complex of 90 flats. The families which moved out of Thakurdwar do not ideally want to stay in a ghetto, but they seem to have little choice. Huma Khan and her mother too moved to Navi Mumbai, and she is the only Muslim in her building. Many Muslims still prefer to live in a mixed area and are not happy with staying in ghettos. Some like Alifiya are determined never to return to a mixed locality for safety reasons. But existing ghettos like Behrampada have seen an influx after the riots and people flocked there for the safety. Even places like Naya Nagar and Mumbra outside Mumbai offered a safe refuge for the riot-affected families who wished to move to an affordable safe place.

In the gullies of Behrampada many Hindus still live. In Kamathi *gully* there is a temple of Ganesh. Ashamma, who migrated from Andhra Pradesh many years ago, still lives in there. 'We are not scared of riots, we are scared of builders', she says. 'We did not even think of leaving when the riots broke out.' In Behrampada, 75 per cent are Muslims and the Hindus now form a small minority. Her neighbour, Shehzadi Begum, says: 'Our relations have remained the same over the years. One of my relatives was killed, my sister-in-law's son, he was killed in firing saving the temple. It's a very old temple down the lane.'

Ashamma's husband used to work in the textile mills and she hails from Mehboobnagar. She feels there is a lot of goodwill left between the two communities. She adds:

> When I came here it was a swamp, I used to get very scared. We built the temple and we celebrate the Ganesh festival every year. The 30 to 40 families living here contribute money irrespective of their religion. What is the reason we should leave? The riots did not cause any displacement, but now we are under threat from builders who want us to vacate. Many who left during the riots came back—we had no insecurity here.

Down the road in another small cramped lane called ninth *gully*, Ashappa Jamappa says: 'We came here 50 years ago and even during the riots no one attacked us. We used to stay awake all night and guard the place—we all used to have tea together', he recalls. 'We were protected by the Muslims who said we will die together—we did not leave and run away. There was no need for us to leave. About 60 families live here—only during the riots the children were sent away.' Ashappa sells vegetables for a living. In the adjoining lane, there were a lot of attacks; many people were running to escape but the families in this *gully* stayed put.

Gulzar Sheikh, a former corporator of the Congress and now with Samajwadi Party, also testifies to the communal amity. In Razzak *chawl*, where he lives, there are many Hindu families. Many have, however, moved out over the years. The earliest settlers in Behrampada were Gujaratis and Kamathis. The people who lived here thought they were safe, but everyone outside thought it was a hotbed of criminals.

However, Madhukar Sarpotdar of the Shiv Sena targeted us because we never voted for him and during the riots, Behrampada was a sitting duck in that sense. People were shot inside the *basti*, houses were burnt, yet we rebuilt everything. Crude bombs were thrown at us from the surrounding buildings, even the Ganesh Mandir was attacked. We showed the police the bombs. About 15 to 20 persons were killed in Behrampada. It was made a target thanks to Sarpotdar who wanted to defame us and get us out of here. He wanted to consolidate his position and get new votes.

Sheikh had three cases against him, but he was acquitted later. 'There was never any tension in Behrampada and there is no record of people from here going out and killing anyone. Now the only threat we have is from builders', he adds.

A little walk from Chunabhatti leads to you the crowded hilly settlement of Kasaiwada, where Ahmed and Sabira now live. Razia Akhtar, 46, a school teacher, says the whole area was completely affected during the riots. There were about 100 Hindu families living here, but many have moved out. Despite assurances they left. Some homes were destroyed. Razia lives in the middle of a Hindu *basti* in Kasaiwada.

We were surrounded from all sides by people of other communities and for three to four days we had no milk and no food. My daughter was a year old at that time. I went to the Teen Nal *basti* to get supplies and there was no light and no water. We had nothing to eat. Then some time later people from Chunabhatti came and helped us. Two people were shot dead in the riots. After that many left from here.

Razia teaches English in the nearby C. T. School. Police used to come and search for Muslim men in this *basti*. Razia hails from Sangli and it was here that her mother settled after marriage. Her husband is a principal in an Urdu-medium school.

Her brother Dilawar had seven to eight shops, which were burnt. He managed to start them later. 'We are not scared', says Razia. *'Ham abhi bhi azad hain'* (we are still free), she adds. However, there is a fear that anything can happen anytime. People are worried. Razia explains:

> While Hindus are scared of coming to live here—we are also scared of moving out. We did think of leaving even before the riots. My son studies in Bangalore—we sent him there for a good future. Here, the surroundings are poor and people don't believe in education. They prefer to do business. You know earlier this place was a slaughter house. But I feel it's all fate, even in Bangalore something can happen to him.

Her brother Dilawar feels that after the 12 March 1993 bomb blasts, many things changed.

> I am a civil engineer, earlier they used to speak rudely to me and they called me a *bhai* [a *goonda*]. I felt that living in Mumbai would not suit me anymore. After the blasts I felt there would be more riots. I felt some outsider had done it. Common people had nothing to do with this. It is not so easy to take a life. People hesitate to even hit their children. I don't think people realized the impact of the blasts.

He feels that the good thing is that people have realized you cannot fight—you also realize you cannot do without each other.

> It is still a cosmopolitan city, people have relations for economic reasons too. My tenant was a Hindu—many people came here when the riots broke out, they all were from Hindu-dominated

areas. We used to stand outside and not let Hindu mobs inside. My employee came and stayed with me. He was a Hindu and he was later escorted out by the police. After the riots so many protection rackets began—so many young men were taken away by the police.

He warns:

> Now I feel things have changed. We can stay here safely but if we leave, it's a risk. I have three shops near the *masjid*. Eighty per cent is Muslim here and it is ghettoized now. Only the neo-Buddhists come here to live, but of late, they too prefer Hindu-dominated areas. This is a dangerous trend; it could lead to a civil war. Earlier riots were milder now there is no quarter given. Even bodies are not found. It is becoming more vicious.

Kasaiwada has a population of about 50,000. Around it there are many new buildings, but only Muslims come here to live. It is a sad place, congested, with many dropouts. It lacks basic amenities too.

Unlike Kasaiwada, Mazgaon in south Mumbai is an old locality, once populated by Christians and few Muslims. Thirty-five-year-old Farid Vora was born in Mazgaon. He was very young at the time of riots. It was known as a 'mixed locality'. Later, more Muslims have come to live there. And now the locality has become predominantly Muslim. Farid studied till the 10th and his father used to run a shop (a small grocery). He says:

> I was involved in a fake case of arson at Reay Road. Me and my brother were arrested. My brother Firoz was in the Congress at that time. He was in jail for five days. Six months later he was discharged. People are not communal here. Very few riots happened here. I did not go out much during the riots and nothing really happened here. Now since five years we have formed an organization called Rightway to foster communal harmony. We

don't want communal discord. We formed it mainly to focus on education. In Nagpada, we work with runaway kids and try and send them back to their homes. We organize programmes for communal harmony.

However, many Christians and Hindus are leaving from here. The building Farid lives in is called Durga Bhavan and has three Muslim families here. After the riots, the building committee said it will not allow Muslims to buy flats here. However, two people wanted to sell and leave and the buyers were Muslims. The property rates are high because the Bohra community is buying up flats. When one Hindu sold to a Muslim, people took out a *morcha*, Farid recalls. Santosh Gaokar, now a committee member, confirmed that after the riots, the building committee made the rule that no Muslim should buy houses here. 'We are still enforcing that rule. However, the person who made that rule has left. I feel it should not be there. Such a rule should not be there but it has not been changed.' He adds that he is not a very important person and cannot take decisions. In some buildings in Mazgaon, no Muslims are allowed, Farid points out.

Like Jogeshwari, people here too are working to build bridges. Asif Sheikh also works for communal harmony in the area. Asif, a businessman, was barely 12 when the riots broke.

> We wanted good relations between the two communities. We celebrate festivals together and we call all the *maulanas* and *maulvis* and solve small issues and don't allow them to escalate. Earlier we used to request people to be peaceful—Navratri and Baadi Raat come together sometimes and we make sure it's peaceful. Very few Hindus remain here now. The Christians are moving out and going to the suburbs. Even Muslims have moved out due to harassment. However, we don't want to leave from here, its centrally located. I feel we are not against Hindus, but they should not harm us either. I feel there is little scope for our community, but awareness is increasing. More Muslims

move here as they feel safe. However, we want to come into the mainstream. But what is the message we are getting: 'Mainstream means say Vande Mataram, wear a *tikka*'.

We did have strong feelings after the riots. There was a lot of tension. The police used to tell us we have showed you once, is it not enough? However, when people were arrested, it was the local corporator, a Hindu, who bailed us out. Many Hindus felt she was supporting communal elements. We also organize cricket matches for peace. We have a totally anti-Congress stand now. We need jobs—you continue with being Hindus, just let us be. We should join parties like the Nationalist Congress Party [NCP] or regional parties. We want our community to do well.

Sanjay Todankar who lives in Durga Bhavan agrees that there are less Hindus here now. Due to economic reasons they are moving out. Though the rule not to sell to Muslims was there, he says: 'We don't enforce it now. More and more Muslims are coming here now they have the money to buy flats. Earlier the rule was strictly enforced, not any longer.'

Moving to a ghetto for safety reasons has also led to the community being further marginalized. Perceptions about Muslims have changed and often those in jobs face some kind of discrimination. Those who move to ghettos often feel this more than the others. Salim Khan (name changed), 23, a software programmer, says:

> I studied in a Muslim area and the outside world was totally alien to me. I never felt any discrimination though. But some people did make you feel uncomfortable. I remember in school once during sports selection, everyone was talking, laughing and then someone asked me my name and the atmosphere changed suddenly. I felt a sense of repulsion from the others. You remember small things like this and you realize people don't accept you as part of this country. However, I don't want to leave,

even in the US people are discriminated against for being Asian. You just have to live with it. I was too young to realize that there was some discrimination—my friend was offered a job if he joined the RSS. It still hurts that a mosque was demolished and nothing was done about it.

During the riots, Salim was a child.

I remember they threw bottles at our building. We had to leave and go to my uncle's place. The riot has affected us a lot. We had to shift to a ghetto from a mixed locality in Mazgaon. We stayed near the docks for a while and we moved to Mohammed Ali road—my mother was firm she would only stay in a Muslim area. Opposite our building was a big colony. They used to throw things at us and we were an easy target as our building was full of Muslim families. I saw them steal a metal gate, now they have put it up at their entrance. You still have those memories.

Salim interacts with a lot of people in his job, but he finds Gujaratis hate Muslims.

You can sense it in the way they talk to you. I read about Khwaja Yunus, a young engineer who was picked up for the train blasts in Mumbai in 2002 and who later died in police custody. I feel this could happen to me too.

His mother Alifiya (name changed), 47, who has studied till first-year college, says:

I saw what happened, the burning, the looting and we did not get any help from the police. They stole our stuff, even the gate was taken away. I cried a lot.... I could not eat and I knew people were dying. There was fire all around and so much smoke we could not see. I have four sons and one was five months old. I saw police beating small children. I went to a Muslim area.

I did not want my sons to be taken away. The problem is we were on the edge of the colony—that caused all the trouble. After those riots, on every 6 December we used to be tense and my children used to ask what will happen? It's very worrying every time. Now I have this new house, it's in Mazgaon, but in a Muslim part—I feel very safe here. The police shot people in their homes. I could not sleep then and even now I get very little sleep. After the riots, I moved to an area which was very congested. This was a middle-class area and it fitted with our budget. I feel safer in my community and even my friends agree it's better. I feel the common person is not communal, they are taught to be like this. I sold my old house to a Bohra and then for seven years lived on Mohammed Ali street—after that I did not have the courage to live in a Hindu *mohalla*. Now one girl comes to take tuitions—when she comes here she does not wear a *tikka*, she gets very scared, but she needs the money. I will not leave India, it is not Bal Thackeray's *dahej* that he should kick us out. You are terrorists burning Indian property. People who did this are roaming free. I never thought such riots would happen. I can't forget all this—I can hear screams, smell the fires. We were saved because my husband was a businessman and he had contacts. All my neighbours have gone now. Now, the place where I used to live is full of Bohras—they pay Bal Thackeray for their safety. My son had to pay ₹ 2,500 for his passport, otherwise they said we won't give it.

The sense of discrimination continues, though there is a feeling of safety as they are living in a Muslim area. Alifiya cannot understand why the girl who comes to give tuitions feels insecure. After all, the place she lived in was the place from where their building was attacked. She also understands that the two communities need to live together, but the fear is paramount, the fear that riots can happen again and the fear that they will have nowhere to go.

Like Alifiya, Leena Shinde also moved into what she considers a safe area. She now works for a private firm in Mahim and has raised her son, then in the 10th standard, with great difficulty. In 1992–93, she was living with her husband's family in Dharavi. Her husband Narendra has been missing since 3 January 1993.

I had just delivered a boy 14 days ago and I had gone home for delivery. Narendra used to work in an orchestra—he was fair and tall. My sister used to stay in Kandivali and Narendra had gone there for a function. The last anyone saw him was in the rickshaw—he was seen off by my brother-in-law. We don't know what happened after that. He was 26 at that time; I was just married for over a year. I lived with my in-laws for many years with my son. Now, finally, my friend has got me this job. My in-laws did not help me at all and I had two brothers, but they also did not help. I used to stay on rent, but I just bought a house. I was 23 at that time. My mother looked after me for nine months and then I started working on small jobs. My parents found it difficult as they too were not in a good condition. My in-laws did not give me any money. I got my husband's death compensation after 10 years. If I had got it immediately it would have made such a difference. I applied so many times, ran around so much, so much red tape. I had gone to meet so many people I got so fed up. Then Teesta Setalvad helped me a lot. Where I live now, there are mostly Hindus—so there is no tension. I was there on 6 December 1992 in Dharavi and the riots were quite bad. I was very scared; then my father brought me back home. We stayed in an area that had both Muslims and Maharashtrians. The Muslim families are still there—we had told them not to go. I feel all Muslims are not bad—only some, those who riot.

Leena used to work for ₹ 1,200 a month, now her salary is about ₹ 4,000.

I am worried about my son. He's in the tenth class now. I have been through some very bad times. One Sena corporator paid my son's fees for two years. I got help from various people for a while. But even now I get scared when I hear about a bomb blast. I don't send my son too far but he goes to a Muslim area for classes. I am anxious till he returns—what if it starts again? After the riots I had TB and my health was very poor.

My job is close to my house, so I have time to look after my son. I prefer to stay in Mahim, I think it's safer. In Dharavi, I feel there can be a bad impact on children if we stay in a mixed community. Here it's mostly Hindus so it's better. There are no Muslims here at all. I feel wherever there are Muslims as in a mixed area, it is scary.

The police cannot find my husband. My in-laws searched for so long in hospitals, in the morgue, and they even went to Nashik. At that time we had told him to stay back home but he left. We really did not think this would happen. He was such a nice guy, he had a tattoo on his hand and he used to dance in an orchestra. My son looks like him he was fair too.

Leena has managed to put her life back on track, but her trials have remained hers alone. She has managed with little support and done her best to educate her son. Yet, the riots have left a deep impression on her about safety and she like others who move into ghettos feel safe there.

Those who lived in areas dominated by their community have not left. Even though they moved out for a while during the riots, they have returned to start their lives again. In Bainganwadi, a small area on the edge of the creek, which is used as a municipal dumping ground, both Hindus and Muslims have lived together and even after the riots they continue to do so. Just before Bainganwadi, on the dumping ground road is Kamla Raman Nagar. Noorjehan, wife of Altaf Hussain Sheikh lives in Kamla Raman Nagar. Altaf came to Mumbai in 1949 and used to work in the docks. Now retired, he has a cold drink stall. She remembers that many people were missing after the riots. The mother of four girls and two sons, she was nine-months pregnant when she went to a relief camp at Musafirkhana. She remembers the police firing at their windows. 'We went without *chappals*. I was pregnant at that time and even earlier when there were riots we had to leave this place. We had two rooms here and we so terror stricken; there was firing in our lane too.' After the riots they came back. 'We never thought of going away. There must be some alternative for us otherwise where can we go? We were harassed so often—police would come and ask for our men. Police only indulged in arson and in this lane two boys were missing', she remembers.

> Now I feel there is a lot of hatred between the two communities, people think Muslims are bad. People have funny ideas about us. But we have stayed back in India, Hindustan is our home. Political parties are responsible for this—why are only Muslims held guilty? We get the hurt and also the blame. There is a general stereotype about us that we are bad people. After the riots it has worsened.

Her daughter Shahjahan lives in Nashik.

> People tell me that we are dirty. I think you should approach this issue from both angles. People are being tutored—all we want is to progress, how can we study if we are blamed for all evils? We don't get jobs—even highly educated people among us don't get jobs.

She was married at 16. The other issue raised by her sister Salaha, who lives in Shivaji Nagar, is that when they go to hospitals, people tell them to stop having children: 'They tell us we have too many children.' Shaheen says 'if we don't get jobs we can create them. My husband is in the oil business, he is not educated. He has managed to fend for himself.' She says she feels safe in a mixed area. 'If there are only Marathis, then I feel insecure. However, I see that people prefer their own area—I am happier in a mixed locality. That's how we can get to know each other. This is the only way to end these differences.' Shahjahan's husband left her eight years ago. She has three children. 'I fought so much for money,

LOSS OF LIVELIHOOD

but he refuses to pay. I feel in a different community we would have got justice.'

In a sense, Altaf's daughters echo the wide-ranging perceptions people have about the Muslim community and how they have learnt to grapple with it. A little ahead of where Altaf lives is the *chawl* he rebuilt after the riots. Bainganwadi is on the edge of a swamp, an unattractive smelly place, but home to hundreds of people. The entire *chawl* was burnt down in the riots and later rebuilt with the help of people like Altaf and Fazal Ali Shaad of the Bombay Aman Committee. The 40 rooms were razed to the ground. Now, the rows of *chawls* border the dumping ground and a large pond behind has almost been filled up with garbage. A new wall has sprung up separating partially the ground behind and the *chawl*. Abid Ali Ansari says:

> I saw my own house burning. We spent so many years in the *maidan* behind and the houses were rebuilt after 1999. People had no clothes even at that time. Three boys in their teens were missing from this *chawl*. All three are believed to be killed by the police and dumped into a van.

There was no riot here, residents say—the police came, picked up the men, shot a few, and then set the place on fire. There were only a handful of Hindus here, the rest were Muslim. Some Hindus live here still, though all have not left. Nasima says that her husband was saved by Aruna, their neighbour:

> We all helped each other—there was no issue of Hindu–Muslim here. No one complained about living here. We are Hindustanis first. They killed us because of politics. *Siyasaat mein koi imaan nahi.* It took so many years to rebuild our home and we lived in the open for at least over three months.

Zeenat Sheikh who lives in Kurar village was 16 at the time of riots. She stays in a mixed locality and wants to move out.

We were six brothers and sisters. When the riots started, we came and lived in a camp for eight days. There were so many people from Kurar village. There was curfew here and we went to live in Vasai with my sister and after that we went to Latur. Only my parents stayed back. We were afraid for my three brothers. People were killing all the men. It's a Hindu-dominated locality and we were initially safe. Our houses were not destroyed. But later, people started singing Hare Rama Hare Krishna and said remove all the Muslims. For 20 years we lived there. My father was a tailor. My neighbours said don't go, so we stayed back. But in Laxman Nagar, the *khadim* of the *masjid* was killed and the holy book was burnt; after that incident many Muslims left. Now mostly Hindus live there. People sold in distress and left and did not come back.

Zeenat studied up to the fifth standard and works as a domestic help. She has three children and her husband is a drunk. She lives with her mother.

So many people's homes were taken over and at that time we were scared of our *izzat*. Now we don't want to live there. At Ramzan it's difficult, my neighbours play loud *bhajans* and we want to move out. I feel in a mixed locality children get influenced badly. There is a lot of provocation between the communities. I feel something will happen and there will be riots. The Sena can still cause trouble.

Clearly, Zeenat does not believe in the merits of living in a Hindu-dominated area. She is highly insecure, but cannot leave as she really has no means to move out and barely ekes out a living. All these examples show that there is no single pattern to people wanting to live in ghettos or move out. However, there is some sort of dynamics operating here, which is moving back and forth in memory or in physical reality.

LOSS OF LIVELIHOOD

Like Zeenat, who still is thinking of moving out, Mehtab moved into a ghetto from a mixed area. Mehtab was born in Devi Pada in Borivali, which saw some really terrible rioting—a woman was raped, killed, and burnt there. Mehtab has now shifted to Pathan Wadi in Malad where he earns a living by renting out a few rickshaws. He was in the eighth standard at that time.

> After the riots, we went to Kurla for a while and had decided not to stay at Devipada. We sold our house for ₹ 2 lakhs; it was a loss. At that time my father was working in a company. We had just built this house. On 6 December when the Babri Masjid was demolished, they broke our door. We had been living there for 20 years and I don't remember how we got to Kurla to stay with our relatives. My uncles and their children also left. Most of the Muslim families there had to leave. They burnt our house, our vehicles, and took away our things. We came later to a camp here. We thought that area was free of tension and nothing would happen.
>
> How could I ever go back and live there? How can we play with each other? Things were very different after the riots. These people destroyed our homes. We bought our own place here [in Pathan Wadi] and I later went to college at Andheri and studied till the twelfth [standard]. We are safe here it is our area. Before riots we had an integrated society. I still believe a mixed colony is a good thing always. Given an option I don't mind living in a mixed locality. Now I don't have contact with Devipada, there are two Muslim families still there.

Mehtab says:

> ... there is a difference in growing up in a place and suddenly going to live there. Now there is a lot of mistrust and misgivings among the two communities. I am in business I have to

trust people. I have gone back to Borivli for training as I want to start a tile business. In that sense, there is mutual trust. Our neighbour in Devipada was a good man, he helped us, but he too was scared. We had hidden for a while with other families, but in the end we had to leave. I remember we had an auto, it was burnt and we did not get any insurance.

Often people who ran away during the riots came back and found things had really changed. Some stayed back because they had no options like Zeenat. In Kandivali East, Sagar Society, people moved out in large numbers from Pathan Wadi. There were 40 to 50 families here and after the riots many left. Fifty-year-old Saeeda Bi is one of the few Muslims in this area. This is her story:

> My son earns now and my three daughters are married. My husband Ansar Khan sells bangles in Borivli. After the riots, for nearly two months we were in Mumbra and in the meanwhile all our things were stolen and we had to leave. Many people were killed here—they were the original people who had come here and helped others settle here. The whole place was completely destroyed. When we came back we had to rebuild our homes from scratch. We were so worried all the time. I was the first to come back and three families more came after that. The rest left forever. We had nowhere to go really, which is why we came back. We lived on rent for a while in another place and we really did not have the courage to come back here. People kept telling us not to go back, what if something happens? But it was our *majburi* [helplessness] that we came back. People are so scared of riots. There are more Hindus now—first they did not talk to us, now things are better. I don't know who burnt and killed, but there were eyewitnesses who gave names. I remember Alibhai, he was the trustee of the local *masjid*; he and his son were killed and his whole family has moved out. His family don't come here even to visit, they have terrible

memories. After the riots I started rebuilding the house in February. Citizens for Peace raised the money for us and about 75 to 80 people who lost their houses were given money.

Now, Saeeda has only one Muslim neighbour and she feels that there are not too many problems. Her main worry is her house, which gets flooded every monsoon. There was 4 feet of water in 2007. How have her feelings changed after the riots?

It was a Marathi who helped us escape. So many people helped us, kept us in their homes. We were told to hide and that Muslims would be killed. I wondered why? We used to go for their weddings and we had good relations. Why did we become so evil? Now it's many years, we have forgotten, but we do get scared. I want to leave but the question is where can we go? I feel we should let the past go. Now the area is no longer called Pathan Wadi. It's as if that entire past was erased.

Saeeda cannot forget that it was a Marathi lady who helped them escape. She smiles and says:

She kept us in her house till the police came—we had to sneak out so that other people did not see that these people had helped us. Here some things are subtle—people don't go to Muslim shops. I run a small shop now but don't keep too many things. People don't buy that much. *Jaat-paat dekhte hain hamare yahan* [they see where you come from, your caste, community].

She has low expectations, lives in fear, and does not keep too many things in the shop. She wants to move out but cannot. Her son is a graduate and her three daughters have been to school.

Like her, Parveen Begum, 40, who lives in Zainab ki Chawl, Prem Nagar, Jogeshwari, has little choice but to live there.

I have stayed here for 25 years and came here when I was married. My husband Habib Ahmed used to teach driving. I have two boys and a daughter. I am still staying in my in-laws house. I used to stitch clothes and bring up children.

Her son Zaheer is in second-year BCom (when I met them in 2007) and also works part-time. He does not like to stay here as it is a ghetto. He prefers to hang around with his friends in malls. Parveen has managed to educate her children. 'Many times I felt like leaving this place, but I cannot afford to go anywhere else. When the children were small I was not scared of Hindu–Muslim fights. Though this is a Muslim area there are a lot of fights.'

She stays in a low-ceilinged spacious house. She has studied up to the seventh standard.

> I feel my children should not suffer, so I educated them. My daughter has to get married. I would like to stay in a good place where people are nice. For eight to ten years, I struggled to live and now they earn so I don't have to work. There were some Hindu families here, but I think they left. My husband was shot dead—he was very young then. Allah is generous so I managed to raise my children. There are so many problems. I have a lot of loans—the school fees were paid by the government till the fifth or sixth standard, but it stopped after that. I took a lot of loans for my children's education; now they are after me to repay the loans. There is a lot of tension. Only those who suffered know what their lives have been and how things have changed. I got no help or support from any social organization.

Parveen is also worried about her daughter's marriage. She has very little money and she starts crying when she talks about it. Her helplessness comes through clearly.

Others who live in ghettos fear for their lives. They know that they can be targets if riots occur again. In Yasin Mistry ki Chawl, Ghatkopar, which is over 60 years old, Syed Jaani Syed Kasim and Mohammed Hanif vividly remember the riots. Hanif says:

> This *chawl* is over 60 years old. Many of us were born here. There were 120 rooms and more Muslims lived here. There are six or seven places you can enter inside. In the *chawls* outside there are mostly Hindus. We were surrounded by a mob and they came looking for me with swords. There was no chance of escape. Luckily the fire brigade came though—my room was burnt—but my life was saved. My wife Sultana had left earlier to my home in Ratnagiri and the other women were taken to nearby relief camps. They used to attack all night and early morning we got away.

Jaani went to hospital and later to Mumbra in a relief camp.

> I still have sword marks on my back. We came back some weeks later and the whole *chawl* was empty—it was looted—my door was burnt. We lost all the property, but we got ₹ 5,000, which was not enough. We did think of leaving—now we are only 15 of us left. It was so well planned, the attacks, that we did not dare go out. We hid in our houses for days not even daring to go out for treatment or stitches. It took two or three years to get back on track. We are in the jewellery business and we lost all the raw materials. First the Gujarat businessmen said they did not want to deal with us. Our main clientele is Gujaratis and Marwaris and they turned hostile. It was a wretched time for us.

Sultana Hanif Galsurkar says:

> We are scared even now supposing there is a riot—we don't buy too many things. Supposing it all happens again. It is scary even now—they burnt our Koran. I left all my children's

clothes—my son was six months then—they did not even spare that. Finally, it was Naseembhai (the local MLA and now Minister Arif Naseem Khan) who said don't leave. The fear is there though. There is no one to protect us. No one wants riots again. All those who rioted Allah has punished them—but after Gujarat we feel anything can happen. We thought some reaction would take place here. We are in constant uncertainty and threat. I feel the culprits have to be punished or else they will get a chance to do the same thing again. I feel now only *uparwala* will give us some relief. We were specially attacked because we were in the Congress; the Sena–BJP targeted us because we voted for the Congress. My father was in the Congress. We really wanted to leave, but we stayed back.

Not everyone stays back only in a Muslim ghetto. Hamid Khan (name changed) lives in a Hindu settlement in a group of *chawls* near Thakurdwar, south Mumbai. He lives in a stone, double-storied structure owned by a Hindu and that was what saved his house from being burnt as the owner lived on top. In K Nagar, his is the only Muslim family. The riots forced his entire family, about 15 to 20 of them, to flee to Pune and they came back only about 20 days later. Syed Wadi, which is adjacent, was burnt and their house was wrecked. Their car was charred and there was a small family-owned envelope-making factory just behind their house, which was also finished.

> These people used to call my mother 'Ma'. At that time they took so much care to only burn our houses and shops. We filed so many complaints, but got no cooperation. My parents had a huge reputation in this area and everyone knew them. When the mob came at night we thought someone would help. We waited till morning, then we realized that no one will help us and we left. As soon as we reached Pune we got the news that the car was burnt. My car was new, it was just two months old and we had it insured.

> We had to fully rebuild the place. After that I insured the house. At that time we lost ₹ 5 lakh. Even after coming back we did not stay at nights in this house—we took a rest house in Nagpada on rent and spent the nights there. There was a lot of insecurity. When we came back after the riots, the neighbours fell at our feet and they said it was not their fault, but the work of outsiders. After the riots, meetings were held for relief for peace, but at that time the *mahaul* [atmosphere] was different, people were determined to do something.

Sitting in his high-ceilinged well-appointed house, 60-year-old Khan is not happy with talking about the past.

> We were four brothers and I was the only one working. The others had a business. We heard about these *maha aaratis* and there was a lot of tension. When the mob came, they found only one family, they waited till morning and so we managed to escape. We had no enemies here and every year for Janmashtami there was some programme and the make-up of Krishna was done here. Our family had a great contribution to the cultural activities in this area. What was the challenge in destroying our house? After the bomb blasts, people have come to their senses. Muslims should not be treated like this. The blasts changed the psychology, it will not happen again.

Khan is confused about the reason for the riots. After he came back, people kept asking him why he continued to live here.

> I used to say so proudly that I was the only Muslim and I had no cause for complaint. After the riots, when I came back, I would have said proudly that I was defended by the community, but I told my neighbours you lost that one chance to protect us. That will stay with me forever. I reinvented myself, my life, after that. I don't feel I am not part of this whole society. Why all

this happened is a question mark. At that time, some politics prevailed and suddenly tomorrow was not safe. I told everyone to leave Mumbai, in those days it had become unsafe. On the day we left for Pune, I had my salary; I bought nearly 50 to 60 train tickets and took people with me. Police harassed us when we reached Pune and someone from here had to call and inform the cops we had fled for our own safety.

Khan feels the riots and the blasts have stabilized the relations. He is happy now.

> What's gone is gone. Mumbai is like that. There was no real reason for this to have happened. It was all politics. I still have the pictures of that destruction. I believe in God, whatever will happen, will happen. I still have no problems with my neighbours. I called them for my daughter's wedding. They respect us and we have some social relations.

Though he feels his neighbours shamed him during the riots by not protecting his family, he does not blame any community.

> I only blame my destiny. It has happened and things are over now. Eighty per cent of my friends are still Hindu and some from the Sena. I don't ever want to go to the Muslim area and live there. Police pick up people from such areas, I am happier in a mixed area. In 1993, I bought a flat in Mira Road in case something happens and you have to move there. Two years ago I sold it off. None of us wanted to go there and live so far away and I wanted the money for Haj. I am a God-fearing man I believe in God above everything. No religion says you kill someone.

Like Khan, Samar Khadas, a journalist, continues to live in a Hindu–Marathi locality. In a sense, growing up there has shaped his perceptions as a Muslim and made him more conscious of that.

LOSS OF LIVELIHOOD

I live in a Hindu Marathi locality in Sion in a housing board colony. I did not know we were Muslims and once when I was three or four years old my best friend told me I was a Muslim. I asked him what is that? I felt I was not part of them for the first time. Then I asked my father what is a Muslim—he was a member of the Praja Socialist Party and he said it's all the same, there is nothing like Hindu or Muslim. My neighbour one day asked me if I had pierced my ears, then I asked my mother why this was not done and she said we did not do it.

He was not trained in Arabic or Urdu and did not have a typical upbringing, though his relatives in Chiplun are practicsing Muslims. His constant encounters added to his insecurity.

I started getting very scared about the fact of circumcision—the fact that Muslims get it done and others don't. I was worried about going to public toilets. Once, in class, the teacher was explaining the Gita and I raised some questions. My father has been in Left of the Centre politics and I used to overhear many discussions on the caste system and discrimination. After this, the teacher used to call me 'Jumma Ke Jumma' implying that I bathed only every Friday. In the history class I was the most disturbed. I felt my ancestors did wrong things and I had an inferiority complex that I was a Muslim. It was in my subconscious. When the Pakistan cricket team won, people would say your team had won, they could call me '*landya*'. I feel if I lived in a ghetto I would not have got that complex, I would have been more confident.

There was no Shiv Sena presence in his colony. There were 90 families and only two Muslims.

In the riots of 1992 and 1993, many people changed towards us. We did not have any real problems, but my family went to

Chiplun and my dad to Thane. I was in the University at that time and everyone there supported me well. There was a lot of reassurance. My mother used to visit riot-hit areas and try and help people, and my colony people used to abuse her. My neighbours who were supposed to be secular changed after the riots. They asked my mother why should these people go for *namaz* when the riots were on. The other Muslim family was attacked and *goondas* burnt their bike. They blamed the whole thing on that family saying he was an eve teaser, etc. Once a mob had come to the colony and I felt very vulnerable.

However, after the riots, his inferiority complex changed.

I felt more confident—I felt it was not such a bad thing to be Muslim and we should not get scared. I joined my father's business and there also I found that people abused Muslims. Then I started reading and writing and I read a lot about religion, I read the Koran in Marathi. Once, in my office, where I work, there were complaints that there was no water in Bhendi Bazar and my colleagues said why do people need water there, they don't bathe—there are lot of stereotypical things that are said as jokes. Once, someone in my office asked if I would reconvert to Hinduism. I said yes, but what about my caste—if I get a Brahmin certificate, I will re-convert I told him. I became more aggressive because of all this.

To overcome all this, Samar joined a Left cultural group, which helped him understand social movements in Maharashtra and reading Phule, Ambedkar, and a lot of Marxist writing, apart from the history of the Communist movement, helped him see the contradictions for what they were.

Muslims are not enemies of Hindus, but the upper castes don't want them to ally with lower-caste Hindus. I was attending a meeting when 9/11 happened and I heard a social activist say these Muslims have gone mad. No one even knew at that time who was really responsible. I had an affair with a Hindu girl and she was told by an activist that this was not a good idea as both of us had different cultures. Even a senior socialist came home and said Muslims have to change reading the *namaz* five times a day and marrying four wives if they want to improve.

What horrified him was that after the riots people changed.

My best friend also said Muslims should be killed—one of my junior classmates was involved in rioting and he had killed someone. People said they were scared to enter Muslim areas—I get scared to go both into Hindu and Muslim areas. Things really changed after 9/11, even those Left of the Centre accepted that Muslims are involved in terrorist activities. That is because their leadership is from a certain class and caste. When you oppose these things you are targeted as a Muslim. When I wrote against the World Social Forum, a leading journalist wrote that I was a SIMI and Lashkar-e-Tayyiba man. No one questioned that or supported me. My entire family is in Left politics, how can he say such a thing? My identity is also being created for me—earlier I used to give *gaalis* [abuses] to Muslims, to Pakistan. People say why do you burst crackers when Pakistan wins—they call Muslims *desh drohi*. I say so far all the spies who have sold secrets from India are all Brahmins, do you call all of them *desh drohis*?

Samar and his family did not leave the house despite problems. He says, 'I don't think we can live in a Muslim area. We did have worries that even now something can happen. I married a Hindu and I've decided not to circumcise my son. We were tense after Gujarat too.' Being tall and bearded, he often gets caught by the police and is frisked. Once, he was 'mistaken' for a Kashmiri terrorist, and even showing his press card did not help. His colleague and friend too was caught. He was not a Muslim, but they thought he was an accomplice!

As a community, people on the one hand have sought safety in numbers, but at the same time have also decided to stay in their old homes, which are not in ghettos and it is sometimes a conscious choice. This has an important message. While the saffron ideology has been promoting a culture based on the purity of religion and race, and is totally against Hindu–Muslim marriage, Mumbai is an example of how this is not true. Though there are ghettos and people are scared, the situation is not hopeless. For centuries, different communities have been living in India. Whether you blame the British for their divide-and-rule policy, or the Hindutva ideology for driving a wedge between communities, people have had the last laugh. Even during the riots, there were many people who helped each other, hid people from mobs, and rescued women and despite the terror, showed exemplary courage. As Sanjeev Agrawal narrates in the following interview, people acted despite propaganda and did not allow their feelings to be swayed. One other common aspect among the people who were affected in the riots was the fact that, in some cases, Hindus helped them escape, hid them in their houses, or bought stuff for them. In many cases, people were warned by their Hindu neighbours to leave for their safety. In some societies, Muslims were protected by their neighbours. Thirty-eight-year old Sanjeev Agrawal, who lived in a colony in Antop Hill, which saw some of the worst rioting, testifies to this. Originally from Haryana, his grandfather came here when he was 16 to study. He and his father were both born in Mumbai.

> Dad was a civil engineer and we used live in Sardar Nagar in Sion Koliwada. It had seven buildings and there were 108 families and every building had three or four Muslim families. Our colony had only one entrance and it had a stone wall around it. In the evenings, all of us, both Hindus and Muslims, used to gather down with whatever weapons we had, sickles, sticks, swords. I did not have any weapon, just the stick where my mother used to hang clothes. We divided the group into sections

and we guarded the society. The whole idea was to protect ourselves. At that time only my mother and I were home. There were lots of rumours that a young mother with a belt of bombs was going around and rumours of jeep loads of people coming to attack. At that time, there were big red lights on top of the buildings and if something happened in the vicinity these red lights would flash. Our gathering every evening to defend ourselves was more fun. People gave us food and we would snack all night and there would be rumours that someone was coming and there would be some action—we would all rush to the gate. This would happen two or three times in the night when we would stop eating and run with our weapons to the gate.

As Sanjeev and many of those who set up 'vigilance' squads at that time found, there was no Muslim horde at their gates. But Sanjeev admits that as the tension grew, people started talking 'anti-Muslim things'. However, people were united and used to guard the buildings together. Antop Hill was burning and people had stopped going out in the day time. He says that all the belongings of their Muslim neighbours were shifted to various houses. He recalls:

We had to keep resisting big groups of young men who would come and ask where the Muslims lived. A few of them moved out. Once, when I was going to buy bread, I saw a Maruti van being overturned and being burnt, the cops next to me were watching the whole thing and did nothing. Later, we heard that the van had people with AK 47s and they were going to the transit camps. That was the turning point for me; after that I was terrified and did not go out. Our colony was very close-knit, yet things got out of hand. A huge mob came in the day and we could not stop them. They ransacked the Muslim houses—we had already asked the Muslims to leave or stay with us like Hindus. I saw belongings being flung down and burnt and they kept asking where are the families. We said we did not know. The whole thing was targeted against Muslims, after this the police came. The mob was 100–200 strong and furious and armed.

The Shiv Sena was dominant in the area and the *shakha* was right next to the colony.

We guessed that something would happen. A lot of young folks like me started thinking anti-Muslim. We all used to talk about what we saw and read and all that created an impression that Muslims were in the wrong. The army vacated the nearby transit camps full of Muslims and when the trucks passed us we could hear them give anti-Hindu slogans. The police had to use tear gas so that nothing would happen and Muslims in the trucks kept saying we'll finish you all, etc. It was the first time I experienced tear gas and we heard people say we'll come back and take revenge and they abused Hindus. We went through a phase of anti-Muslim feelings but that died.

His mother remembers that they took out the name plates of Muslims in the society. She too attributes all this to politics. Among the people I met, there was always this allusion to the politics behind the riots. This was an effort to further marginalize the community, they felt.

Bipan Chandra (2004: 18) observes:

Communal violence forces even secular persons to organize self-defence on communal lines and to join hands with communal forces to defend their lives and property. It arouses in a flash all the hidden, passive communal elements in the personalities of the mass of the people. In fact, the major purpose of those who inspire and organize communal violence is not to reduce the number of the other religious community or genocide or impoverish it through loss of property. This cannot be done till the state takes up the task a la Nazi Germany. That is nearly impossible today. The purpose is to create situations which communalize the mass of the people.

Nothing could be truer of this than what happened in Mumbai.

Syed Sultan, who lives in Naya Nagar, agrees that the riots were about politics: 'Politicians mislead people. However, common people are not interested in riots, they just want to earn a decent living.' After the riots, over 80 per cent Muslims left the housing society where he used to live.

> My neighbours were Kutchis and I still have good relations with them. In Hindu areas there is an unsaid rule that Muslims should be given no place. People don't want Muslims. There is a sense of separation after the riots. Muslims are a no-no in many places. I don't see the same rules for Christians.

Syed is acutely aware of the role played by the police.

> The issue is that the police caused the riots in some places. The doers are not punished. But I believe from the start if there was some sympathy, this would not have happened. Muslims are trusting. Advani says if the Supreme Court rules in their favour only they will accept the decision—such people should be punished. People here don't accept the Constitution. We are suffering because we are tagged with being Islamic. Even the Prophet has been called a terrorist. Islam is a revolutionary religion and that's why the capitalists are opposed to us. Initially I felt there was a division after the riots but later I realized people don't discriminate. People understand each other very well.

He feels this segregation is because the government and the political forces do not want that exchange of ideas between two communities.

They want to keep us out of the mainstream—people can talk and clear their doubts, this is exactly what the powers that we don't want. I feel the government does not want that degree of cooperation among the communities. It's not easy to spread peace—it's easier to create divisions. People know only their rights not their duties. There has to be a deeper understanding of your actions and the distance between the two communities has to be addressed.

A small businessman like Izhar *bhai*, who lost his factory in the riots, is also bitter. Izhar says:

People changed after the riots. They did not speak to me or want to help, they had seen nothing. Things have changed a lot after the riots. People want to live in their own community. This has increased after the riots. There is a kind of partition. Only for Hindus, only for Muslims. This will cause more division. '*Hukumat*' [the rulers] is doing this.

Clearly, there was increased polarization and a move to live in ghettos after the riots. This marginalization of the community and discrimination is a serious area of concern. As filmmaker Madhusree Dutta points out, the ghettos are not only Muslim, even Hindus are ghettoizing themselves into secluded areas for their safety and other considerations.

Salim Jaffer Sheikh, who lived in the Hindu-dominated Tulsiwadi and later moved to Mumbra, still does not believe it was a Hindu–Muslim riot. 'The Hindus were given shelter by us. It was a small group of people from the RSS and the Shiv Sena, the Bajrang Dal, who caused trouble. Everyone else was secular', he says. However now everything has changed. Recently, he was called to Tardeo Police Station in connection with a dowry death case, where he had ratified a dying declaration when he was a special executive magistrate a long time ago. He could not be present in court to give evidence as he was away in Ahmednagar. Despite telling the police he was away, they issued a non-bailable warrant against him and when he finally went to the police station on return, the police shouted at him and said if he acted like this they would put him inside and charge him in the 11 July serial bomb blast case.

He said:

> The worst impact of the riots is that I have lost faith in the Mumbai police. I still have faith in Hindus and have very good relations with them. I blame politics for those riots and I feel they wanted to remove those slums from there and make way for posh buildings.

7

PERCEPTIONS OF JUSTICE

In Cold Blood

As you enter Tahir Wagle's pink-walled house, the photograph of young Shahnawaz stares at you from the corner of a framed calendar. He was an 11th-standard science student of Elphinstone College when he was shot dead, watched by his mother and sister, below his house at Pathan *chawl* behind the Ehle-e-Hadees Masjid in Mazgaon in south Mumbai. Since 1993, his father, Tahir Wagle, has tried to file a case against the policemen who allegedly killed his son. Wagle stands in his balcony on the second floor and points down. 'See, this is where he was shot. My daughter could see the whole thing from here', he says. Below, there is a narrow passage between his building and the mosque. The passage curves down to the main road.

Wagle, who wanted his son to join the merchant navy, like his grandfather, says:

In this country, those who shoot deer get punished, not those who kill human beings. *Insaan se jyada hiran ki keemat hai* [Deer have more value than human beings]. My son's status is lower than that of a deer. I have yet to get any answers from the police after all these years. They say my son was a terrorist and was indulging in rioting.

'I had told him go to London and appear for his exams', he says. He has two daughters, one of them died in 1983 in a drowning accident in Ratnagiri. The other daughter Yasmin was eyewitness to the killing of her brother. Wagle was away on the day the incident happened.

On the morning of 10 January 1993, a huge posse of policemen entered Pathan *chawl* and rounded up 70-odd men. Shahnawaz was pulled out of his house and taken down by the police. Yasmin, then 18, and her mother screamed for help and from their balcony, saw the police putting a bullet into the boy. They ran down, but by then the van had moved away, leaving behind a pool of blood. Wagle, on his return, went to Byculla Police Station and claimed his son's body. 'They had dredged out the bullet from his head, so that there is no evidence', he says.

He went repeatedly to lodge a complaint, but no one was willing to record it at Byculla Police Station. 'They always fobbed me off saying my son was a rioter', he recalls. 'I ran around for 14 years, would they have given me 14 hours if I had killed a cop?'

With the revival of the riot cases, Wagle has submitted a letter to the Mumbai Police, which called him to record his statement in August 2007. 'I know all the policemen who were there. They have all been promoted', he says. 'At least their promotion should be stopped and a case should be registered against them.' He is determined to fight for justice. 'I know some day there will be a decision on this case. I have nothing else to do but carry on my struggle', says 58-year-old Wagle.

The *Srikrishna Commission Report* (Srikrishna 1998: 25–26, Volume II) says:

There is one incident which is very serious in the view of the Commission and amounts to cold blooded murder by the police. Between 11 to 11:30 hours on 10 January 1993, after having arrived at Pathan Chawl, the police forcibly entered the premises of the Muslims and started picking them up. They entered the residence of one Hasanmiya Wagle [Tahir], terrorized the wife of Hasanmiya and his daughter Yasmin at the point of rifle, picked up Hasanmiya's 16-year-old son Shahnawaz and dragged him out, all the while kicking him and assaulting him with rifle butts. Yasmin Hasan Wagle saw Shahnawaz being taken towards the police vehicle, when one of the constables standing behind him shot him from behind, almost at point blank range. Immediately, the policemen dragged the body by the feet and dumped it in the vehicle and took it away. Yasmin and her mother came down later and saw that the spot where Shahnawaz was shot down has a pool of blood.

The Commission later accepted the evidence of Yasmin and also directed the Commissioner of Police to make an inquiry into this 'grisly' incident. However, the Commission says that despite the overwhelming evidence, which, in the opinion of the Commission, clearly indicts the police for cold-blooded murder of Shahnawaz, the Deputy Commissioner of Police assigned to conduct the inquiry, has adroitly white-washed the affair and recorded the finding that the statement of two or three witnesses could not be safely relied on and that Yasmin or other witnesses had never reported the incident to the police. The inquiry report also said the evidence of Muslim witnesses was unreliable.

Calling it a brazen cover-up, the Commission strongly felt this was a matter of which the government must take a very serious notice and have it investigated by an impartial agency and take strict action against the guilty persons. However, all these years after the submission of the Commission's report, the police did nothing. It is only now that Wagle's statement was recorded by the Byculla Police Station.

> Ours is a Muslim area; there were no riots here, but the police came and created all the problems. There is only one Hindu woman who lives here. We had told her not to go—*Izzat ka khopra ho jayega* [we will lose all respect]. When the police came to take her away for her safety she refused to leave.

Wagle affirms that there were no Hindus to fight with here. 'The fight was between the cops and Muslims. The police said don't go by the uniforms, we are Sainiks underneath. My wife is now silent—she knows no one will hang for her son's death.' His neighbour, Shantabai Gawli, has been living here for 30 years and her husband for longer. 'Why should we leave this place? Police did the riots, we have no ill will', she says.

Like Tahir Wagle, who has been fighting all these years, the two brothers Izhar and Rafique Ahmed Khan, too live with personal loss and injustice. From Antop Hill one has to walk down a long tar road to enter the slum where the brothers live now. It is a ramshackle place, but Izhar will not trade it for any other. Tears flow freely from 54-year-old Rafique Ahmed Khan's eyes. 'When I heard the factory was attacked, the first thing I asked was where are my sons?' Rafique, along with his brother Izhar, 58, owned Star Metal Works, a small factory in Worli in central Mumbai. It was Sunday—his children and some other relatives had gone to visit the factory. They never returned. He said:

> When my children did not come for lunch, I was worried. I sent someone to look for them, but he was not allowed to go near the factory. It was night when I called the police and only next morning could we go inside the factory, which was completely wrecked.

On 10 January 1993, a mob attacked the electrical lamination factory and burnt it down. Nine people including two of Rafique's children, Abdul and Shah Alam, aged 12 and 14, died in the fire. Five others who died were related to the family. Now, there is no sign left of their factory.

A building stands in its place. Rafique and Izhar stay in Bharati Kamala Nagar, a slum in Antop Hill, where they run a telephone booth and sell construction materials. Rafique used to live in Adarsh Nagar—near the factory. He says: 'I decided to move close to where my brother lived. If we have to die, let it be together. It took four days for us to meet at that time.'

Though a complaint was filed at Worli Police Station and nine people were arrested under the TADA, they were acquitted four years later, says Izhar bitterly:

> I was in court the day that happened. We had collected the evidence so painstakingly. I even managed to get an eyewitness— one of the workers who saw what happened and managed to escape. I got him to come all the way from Uttar Pradesh and made sure he was protected. He even identified the culprits. But the police messed it up.

The factory was worth ₹ 10 to 12 lakh, but they sold it for a pittance. In 1978, the brothers who hail from Azamgarh had put all their money into it. The money from the sale did not cover their losses or their debts. 'We got ₹ 4,000 for our burnt factory from the government', says Izhar with a cynical grin. He sits in a small telephone booth, which was his house once. The memories of those days are fresh. 'When the culprits went free, it broke my heart. We have not got justice', said Izhar. 'Things changed overnight after the riots. It was if we had no friends. No one was willing to support us or give evidence in our case', he adds.

'Things are back to normal now', says Izhar, but there is one major difference. 'People want to live with their own community. There is a kind of partition and this is going to create more problems.' He is not very optimistic about the government's claims that it will implement the *Srikrishna Commission Report*. 'We have little hope of justice now', he says morosely.

Did he ever think of leaving the city? Izhar says:

PERCEPTIONS OF JUSTICE

Bombay chodenge, Hindustan chodenge [we will leave Bombay, we will leave Hindustan], where can we go finally? *Jo hoga so hoga* [what will be will be]. We went home after six years of the riots. What will we do back home? The land is poor quality, there are no jobs, *ghar bhi nahin hai* [there is no house either]. We never imagined that this would happen here. We had excellent relations with everyone. All said don't worry. We lived in such a good atmosphere. We had no enemies—it just happened suddenly. We did not get any help from anyone. If the Sikh riots cases can be reopened these riot cases should be too.

Izhar worked hard to make the case good. The Sena had gheraoed the court and there was a lot of pressure not to press charges by the relatives of the accused. The second witness failed to identify anyone. A bitter Izhar says:

We were asked if we wanted to stay here only [a veiled threat], but there was no effect on us—we got everything together, but the police investigation was poor and it was because of the police that this case failed. Police were with the rioters. We called so many people at night; there were no lights in the area and we had no courage to go alone. The police came only the next day at 9 am. The whole of the next day we took out the bodies. There were 13 people who lived and worked there. No one came to stop the fire.

He also says: 'After all this, now, we have lost courage. We also did not know about the Srikrishna Commission—we had met so many people including then home minister Chhagan Bhujbal and we sent letters to the President.'

For young Asma Bano Ansari, who had just come to Mumbai in December 1992, life started in the city in a shocking manner. 'I had got married 15 days before the riots broke out. My father-in-law, elder brother-in-law, brother-in-law's son, and his grandfather were burnt to death—they used to often stay over in the timber godowns at night.' I barely met her before she blurts this out. The years have not dulled the shock for Asma and her family. Her husband Naseemuddin Ansari sits in the small row of timber shops near Ghatkopar station. Opposite are the more glitzy furniture showrooms, something Ansari can never aspire for. The whole place was burnt, he recalls.

> It was on 12 December 1992. We got to know at 2 am. There were four shops—my father, elder brother, used to sleep here often. My cousin and his grandfather were there too. One person who managed to escape told us. The road was jammed from everywhere and we could not get to the place. No one was arrested and I don't remember a police case being filed.

> We are three brothers now—the other two are younger than me. My elder brother was managing the business. I had come newly to Mumbai and I did not know much. My mother and sister-in-law came here collected the compensation and went back. They don't live here. I thought this was a safe area—I thought riots happened in other places, not here. Even now we do get scared that it will happen. After that no one stays in the shops. We lock the place and leave. We keep less expensive goods and we can't give people what they want.

Things have also changed around this place.

> Earlier there were lots of slums and people had less money; they used *halka maal* [light wood]. Now so many buildings have come up. They don't want our cheap stuff. Now we live in a makeshift way—we can't rebuild because of the uncertainty that we may be kicked out any minute. We did try to meet so many people and even the chief minister, but that was the day the serial blasts happened on 12 March 1993 and everything went for a toss.

Each of the shop owners got ₹ 5,000 for the five shops and ₹ 2 lakh per head for the deaths. He adds:

> But we don't know who burnt all this down. We had at that time stocks worth ₹ 5 to 6 lakh. That one incident has ruined us forever—we never got back on track. Even today, we are under a litigation, we have a shop that is in shambles—we don't have the money to make it look good. We don't even have the means to move somewhere else.

These old timber godowns were started in 1945 and it was all run by his family members.

The ramshackle timber shops are on the road in front of a building which is lying unused. The builder wants them out as they ruin his frontage. The flats have no takers because of the problems of access. Since 1984 the builder has filed a case against them in the small causes court and no decision is yet been given in the matter. Ansari says:

> We will never know what happened that night; there can be so many reasons. However, we are being evicted from here and there are many cases pending. We can go only if they give us an alternative. We used to pay the rent, but after the riots, he stopped taking the rent. We even sent a cheque, which he returned. He is not ready to give us an alternative place. Everyone lost lakhs of rupees—we got ₹ 5,000 in return, how can we set up shop properly?

Next door, Nasrulla Ansari says all the five shops had plywood and *jungli* wood. Since 31 years he has been running this shop.

> When the fire broke out, all lost lakhs of rupees and we have never returned back to normal. We had no insurance even. We had nothing to eat for days. It was scarier in the *chawl*. This was a peaceful area, we never felt insecure. It's mainly a Gujarati area. After the riots we stayed awake all night there was a lot of fear.

In Jawahar Nagar, a mixed locality, both communities coexisted peacefully till the riots broke out. Raisa Bano's mother and her three brothers were burnt to death in the riots in Mumbai. She was staying in Antop Hill with her husband after marriage. Her husband works as a taxi driver. Raisa, 48, says:

> In Jawahar Nagar, there were lots of Hindus. My mother was living there for nearly 50 years. She had many rooms there. Of the three brothers, only one was married. At first they were all registered as missing. We waited 11 years for the compensation. The police told us what is the guarantee that they have not run away. My mother too was registered as missing. We later found her fingers and some teeth, which was my brother's. My sister-in-law Anisa escaped because she left with her children for a safe place. They did not spare my family. My brothers were killed and set on fire. Even my mother—the police did nothing. We knew the Shakha Pramukh, my brothers used to sit with him. No one helped us.

The tears and the long silences say it all:

> My daughter lives in Mumbra, her husband is in Muscat. They all grew up here—I have two sons. Before the riots I felt safe in a mixed area, now I feel a Muslim area is safe. There was no problem at all there and in Jawahar Nagar we all knew each other. I also lost property and had to sell two of the rooms we owned. The rest are not paying me rent and they threaten me when I ask. They even sent armed *goondas* to my house to threaten me, my husband and children.

Raisa's entire family perished in the riots. It is something she can ever forget.

> I loved my brothers so much. I was ill when the riots happened I could not walk. Later I got breathing problems and cried very

often. It was my children who gave me so much support. But I have so much pain in my heart I cannot forget it. I learnt about my sister-in-law Anisa's whereabouts from a committee—I came to know of the incident three or four days later. We had given some names, but no one was arrested till today.

Not far from the place where Raisa lives now, is perhaps one of the worst affected places during the riots—Prateeksha Nagar. This was a series of transit camps in central Mumbai where people stayed while their houses were being rebuilt by the government. However, many of them sub-let these houses and many Muslims lived there before the riots, some for over 20 years. It was one of the worst-affected areas in the city and the army had to escort truckloads of people out at the height of the riots. People were stranded for three days before they were rescued. Ibrahim Sheikh, 43, is a taxi driver since 1994. Since 14 years, he and 40 others from his community have been running from pillar to post for housing. Now, they live in government tenements and wait for a permanent solution to their problems of shelter.

When the riots broke out he was working in Saudi Arabia. His wife Khurshida, says, 'I was living with my in-laws and there were eight of us. When the riots broke out, the Masjid was destroyed and our houses too. People ran helter-skelter and it was the end of the world.' Her son was still-born and she was recuperating from her delivery in December 1992 when she was forced to flee. 'We went to Kurla to live with some friends for some months. We went from transit camps to other people's houses. We were sub-tenants in the transit camp and had no real claims', she says.

Ibrahim explains:

> First Ziauddin Bukhari [a politician] settled us in Jogeshwari and he had promised us homes. We lost almost ₹ 1.8 lakh of goods in the house. It was my sister's wedding on 6 December and we had to postpone it. We lived for a while in the Jogeshwari transit camp and then we were kicked out. The state housing authority official, then it was D. P. Madan promised to

resettle us, but he was transferred. We are kicked around like footballs. We met so many politicians like Naseem Khan and Yusuf Abrahani, but it was of no use. The place where I am now is also temporary. I have a slip disc now and had a heart attack in 2003. Now am not going anywhere even if I die. I drive a taxi for my livelihood, but it's very erratic now. The Maharashtra Housing and Area Development Authority finally told us we'll get houses if we pay the market rate of ₹ 1,700 a sq foot. How can we afford this? They wanted to show that they were giving us houses, but we were not taking them. It's all uncertain. So many years after the riots we are still running around.

Khurshida says:

I have five children. We can be removed anytime. After the riots, we could not go back to Prateeksha Nagar as the local people, mostly from the Sena, said they would not allow Muslims to come back. We had to be escorted out with the army's help—things were so bad there. People were burnt alive, houses ransacked, women assaulted. We lived together for so many years. Our Hindu neighbours hid us when the mob came.

Zeenat Qureishi has not forgotten those awful days. For her, a time of happiness—her brother's wedding—was also a time of great sorrow.

I used to live in Sion Koliwada. I had gone to Prateeksha Nagar for my brother's wedding. My brother Mohammed Hanif, 25, who worked in Saudi Arabia, was married and two days later he was killed. My whole family had gathered for the wedding. We had also taken some rooms on rent. Hanif was drinking tea when the mob came and attacked my mother—he assaulted them and tried to run away and we all ran till we were rescued by the military. They killed him and left him on the road. My elder brother was being taken by the police to hospital when they saw this body on the road—it was my brother. He died in the hospital. I feel they poisoned him. At least we got his body back; many people were not getting bodies. While we were being escorted out stones fell on us, without the military we would be dead.

Her brother Meraj and the rest have been fighting for all these years for justice, apart from their struggle for housing. Now, since nine months, many of them live in MHADA houses—small, poky rooms. Jamaluddin, who has been leading the fight for housing, says while the government has claimed it has allotted them houses, there is no proper allotment letter.

We were supposed to be given homes in 2002 but now they are saying we have to pay money. Some people live in huts, some are on rent—we also paid some middlemen for these houses. It's a long and tragic story. Now only Allah can help us, there is no sympathy for us as riot victims. We did not even get the ₹ 5,000 for loss of property. Why are we the sacrificial lambs?

He adds:

Now they want each of us to pay ₹ 5 lakh—we said we'll give it in installments, even that is not being agreed upon. They tell us how long will you be riot victims? The government has accepted that we should get free houses, we are ready to pay in installments, but who is listening. Fifty-six families were homeless in Prateeksha Nagar. Now about 40 are left of that lot.

Many families have had to deal with loss of their homes, loss of lives, and insecurity of shelter and income. In Farooq Mapkar's case, he was wrongly accused of rioting when he himself was a victim of police firing. Farooq was acquitted by the session court in 2009. Since 16 years, Farooq, both a victim and an accused in the firing, has been running around for justice. Farooq, who works as a security guard in a cooperative bank, has been trying to get an offence registered against Nikhil Kapse and other policemen responsible for the firing. Fed up with waiting, 41-year-old Farooq filed a writ petition in the Bombay High Court in 2007, demanding the lodging of a First Information Report (FIR) against the police who shot at people in Hari Masjid. In response, the state government has finally agreed to a CBI investigation in his case.

Farooq was one of those injured when police opened fire at Hari Masjid on the afternoon of 10 January 1993. 'We had all gathered for *namaz* and people were milling around the mosque when the firing took place', Farooq says. He too got a bullet injury in his left shoulder, but instead of being taken to the hospital, he was put in jail for 15 days. 'The bullet was removed on 27 January', he recalls after he was let out on bail. The irony does not end there. Farooq is one of the 57 persons accused by the police of mob violence. According to the chargesheet filed by the police in 1994, there was private firing from the mosque and later the mob went to a house 1 km away and burnt it, killing one man. Shakil Ahmed of Nirbhay Bano Andolan, who is an activist and Mapkar's lawyer, said that all the 57 persons were charged with murder too. The case was pending for 10 years. 'I have already suffered so much', says Mapkar.

In 2004, the case was shifted to a fast-track court in Sewri, where it was finally heard before sessions judge, C. M. Salunkhe. However, Ahmed points out that during the hearing, one of the witnesses, Shravan Killari, testified in court that he was injured in police firing. However, the court, when recording this, dropped the word 'police'. 'I objected to this and there were a lot of issues about my intentions. Finally, the judge separated Farooq's trial as a result of this', explains Ahmed. He said that this separation of the trial was illegal and the judge issued no directions as to how the trial would proceed in Mapkar's case. Finally, on 4 February 2006, the court acquitted most of the people in the case. In the meanwhile, some had died and the rest were untraceable, and only 30-odd persons were acquitted by the court due to lack of evidence. Even in that judgement no directions were given about Mapkar's case.

After an application was made by Ahmed, it took over eight months for the case to come on board. The new judge, in July 2007, ordered the police to file a separate chargesheet in Mapkar's case since his trial was separated.

The *Srikrishna Commission Report* has documented the Hari Masjid case in detail. It said that one of the policemen, Nikhil Kapse, was not justified in opening fire and his conduct was violent. Kapse, who has been promoted since then, was exonerated in a departmental inquiry and even the Special Task Force (STF) that was set up to look into the riots cases gave him a clean chit. Mapkar says he was not even summoned by the STF to give evidence.

In 2001, Ahmed filed a petition in the Supreme Court demanding action against 31 policemen involved in the riots who have been named in the *Srikrishna Commission Report*. The case is still going on. The Commission has said that in the Hari Masjid case, the version of the police is unbelievable and has been fabricated to support the unjustified firing of large numbers of rounds, which resulted in killing six Muslims. It also held a policeman Nikhil Kapse of unjustified firing and inhuman and brutal behaviour during the incident. It is only in 2009 that the CBI is probing the role of Kapse and other policemen and that too in a rather lackadaisical manner. The Maharashtra government sought a stay on its own order demanding a CBI probe, which was granted by the Supreme Court in August 2009. However, later, the apex court finally ordered the CBI to conduct the inquiry, much to Mapkar's relief.

8

CONCLUSION

Nationalism, communalism, secularism, 'pseudo-secularism', terror, 'Islamic' terror, 'saffron' terror, Hindu *Rashtra*, riots, blasts—form a spectrum of ideologies and events which continue to dominate the sociopolitical scenario in this country. In the late 19th century, in response to the Christian missionaries, the Arya Samaj and other groups sought to give Hinduism a more reformative tone and, yet, each time the British created laws, which would do away with heinous traditional Hindu practices such as early marriage, there was a backlash from revivalists who felt the imperial power should keep out of their religion. In the complex theatre of religion, tradition, and the need to be progressive, emerged a nationalism that was tinged with a dominant Brahminical ideology. By the time the RSS came on the scene in the 1920s, India was already seething with cow protection movements, Ganpati festivals, and public displays of religious fervour, which were not in existence earlier. Religious processions caused riots between Shias and Sunnis, but now the riots were between Hindus and Muslims. The reclaiming of public space

CONCLUSION

through religious processions and public displays of religion marked the beginning of the 20th century. This, coupled with the electoral reforms, which devolved power to the provinces and the communal award, led to demands for a separate country causing a deep divide right from the grassroots level.

Even as the trauma of Partition gripped the Indian subcontinent, communal riots became another bane. Each time religious processions, disputed temples or mosques were among the issues. The 1980s saw the movement to build the Ram temple at Ayodhya at the site of a mosque, a classic confrontation. The religious fervour of the days preceding the Ram Janmabhoomi movement will haunt the country for a long time. That was a time when secularism was attacked, pseudo secularism was used freely to target those who did not support the Ram temple and the Hindu *Rashtra*, as envisaged by the RSS. A close observer of those days, the late Prime Minister P. V. Narasimha Rao (1992: 48) says in his book:

> Most of the religious leaders in the country somehow got subsumed in the BJP outlook, with the result that neither the country's ancient ethos of sarva dharma samabhava, nor its modern Constitutional version of secularism, was projected effectively in non-communal terms. Religiosity and communalism subconsciously (in some cases consciously and deliberately) were made to look almost identical. This was a great tragedy in a country where for centuries on end samanwaya (harmonization) among several strands of thought and faith had remained the main preoccupation among leaders of the evolving society—enveloping, in its stride, numerous historical and political events of conquest and absorption. The BJP's pseudo-religious movement could not have sustained itself on a purely religious plane; it needed a political reaction, to flourish politically. I cannot escape the uneasy feeling that we Congressmen (while in government) supplied it with just that. We also let our own religious susceptibilities go by default, with the

same subconscious inhibition that any expression of religious sentiment on our part, even if we felt it strongly, would be seen as 'non-secular'. As a result, the BJP became the sole repository and protector of the Hindu religion in the public mind.

The Congress seemed ineffective in containing the surge of Hindutva and was helpless as the Masjid was brought down. While the BJP later was lukewarm on the construction of the Ram temple after it came to power, it was an issue every time there were elections. For the *aam admi*, the prospect of hunger was more serious than a temple at Ram's birthplace, yet the RSS and the VHP persisted with sporadic attempts at *kar seva*. Just as the Shiv Sena sought to represent the Hindus in Maharashtra, the BJP and the Right wing sought to create a national Hindu identity using Ram and the construction of the Ram temple as the focus. The RSS is not about to let go. Kanungo (2003: 270–71) says at the end of his book:

> In the past, the RSS has demonstrated strategic flexibility responding to the diktats of realpolitik, at the same time, it has also taken refuge under militant ideological rigidity during times when it has been in political wilderness and isolation. The RSS, therefore, will retain and consolidate its pivotal place in Indian politics rather than renouncing power so easily. After all, this is a hard earned effort of millions of dedicated and devoted swayamsevaks for the last 75 years—from Hedgewar to Sudarshan. The RSS will continue is tryst with politics to establish a Hindu hegemony and convert India into a Hindu Rashtra.

Central to the issue of creating a communal divide is a philosophy that Hindus and Muslims cannot live together.

Today, it seems, that organizers of communal violence are working towards another major objective: to force segregation

CONCLUSION

on Hindus and Muslims so that persons belonging to a religion stop living in religiously mixed localities and ... confined to separate parts of cities and clusters of villages. The purpose, in particular, is to ghettoize the minorities, as happened in Bombay after 1993, in Gujarat since the 1980s and in other places where major riots have taken place. (Chandra 2004: 18)

Globally, 9/11 served to create a worldview on Islamic terror. Writers like Samuel Huntington in *The Clash of Civilizations and the Remaking of the World Order* have advanced a sweeping, though popular, discourse. He says, for example, '... and the most dangerous conflicts are those along the fault lines between civilizations' (1997: 28). He goes on to say '[t]he world is indeed anarchical, rife with tribal and nationality conflicts, but the conflicts that pose the greatest dangers for stability are those between states or groups between different civilizations' (1997: 36). While the perceived Islamic threat is very real for Americans, as Huntington points out quoting various studies, in India too it is a strong perception.

Madhav Sadashiv Golwalkar, who headed the RSS after the death of its founder Dr Keshav Baliram Hedgewar, has been explicit in his *Bunch of Thoughts* (Golwalker 1966). The RSS, founded in 1925, and its affiliates have projected Muslims as invaders or outcastes.

> We, in the Sangh, are Hindus to the core. That's why we have respect for all faiths and religious beliefs. He cannot be a Hindu at all who is intolerant of other faiths. But the question before us now is, what is the attitude of those people who have been converted to Islam or Christianity? They are born in this land, no doubt. But are they true to its salt? Are they grateful towards this land which has brought them up? Do they feel that they are the children of this land and its tradition and that to serve it is their great good fortune? Do they feel it is a duty to serve her? No! Together with the change in their faith, gone are the spirit of love and devotion for the nation. Nor does it end there.

They have also developed a feeling of identification with the enemies of this land. They look to some foreign land as their holy places. They call themselves Sheikhs and Sayeds. Sheikhs and Sayeds are certain clans in Arabia. How then did these people come to feel that they are their descendants? That is because they have cut off all their ancestral national moorings of this land and mentally merged themselves with the aggressors. They still think they have come here to only to conquer and establish their kingdoms. (Golwalkar 1966: 127)

Hindutva ideologue Vinayak Damodar Savarkar was anti-caste, yet he opposed Hindu–Muslim marriages. He says (Savarkar 1935: 86):

In the present stage of human progress and the current peculiar situation in the Hindu Nation, one limit should be followed without exception as far as intermarriages are concerned. While there is no cause for concern if Hindus marry amongst themselves without any caste considerations no one should cross the ambit of Hindutva and marry Muslims, Christians and the like. So long as the Muslim desires to remain a Muslim, the Hindu too must remain a Hindu. It is extremely harmful to our Hindu nation if a Hindu marries a non-Hindu without bringing that girl or boy into the Hindu fold. It is only when the adamant non-Hindus swear by humanism and merge their Muslim identity into humanism that the Hindu too will abide by humanism and leaving aside considerations of caste, religion and country shall follow the ties of humanism only. But it will be against humanism if Hindus show such misplaced generosity at this point in time.

The thoughts propounded by Golwalkar and Savarkar are popular even today. It is the bedrock of the Hindutva philosophy adopted by the BJP. The Shiv Sena's system of *shakhas* or branches/local units, has evolved from the RSS. The doubting of the Muslim's allegiance to this country,

CONCLUSION

the antipathy to Hindu–Muslim marriages, the suspicion that the Muslim is anti-national, has grown over the years, and the repeated terror strikes have served to strengthen this image. The destruction of the Babri Masjid was an act of cleansing, to set right all the historical wrongs. The temple for Ram became an election issue taking the BJP to its first ever victory in the general elections. The 1992–93 riots in Mumbai were a reaction to that well-planned destruction. 'The conflict over the Babri Masjid in Ayodhya is part of a larger right wing Hindu political project to reclaim the "national culture" from its enemies—Muslims, but also secularists and Westernisers' (Pandey and Samad 2007: 29).

In 2008, riots in Dhule, a town in north Maharashtra, shattered peace of over 40 years. There was a deliberate attempt to destroy communal peace and one of the issues before the riots was a marriage between two people from different communities. Later, religious processions were stoned, temples and mosques were attacked, and Muslims were singled out and beaten up. People had to move to camps for shelter. Immediately, there was a talk of building separate homes for Hindus and Muslims, who had lived side-by-side for so many years. Riots are followed by displacement and then the element of living in separate townships or ghettos comes up. Mumbai already had places where Muslims lived separately. History shows that Hindu–Muslim tension is not new to Mumbai or the Indian subcontinent. Mumbai's first communal riot dates back to 1893 and, since then, there have been several riots in the Bombay Presidency and even during and after Independence. In 1893, many had to flee the city. At that time too, it was a highly charged atmosphere and the movement for cow protection had polarized the communities. Post-Independence, Maharashtra was witness to a number of communal riots. In Malegaon, riots broke out in 1967 and, later, in 1970, riots took place in Bhiwandi, Jalgaon, and Mahad, and in 1984, in Bhiwandi again and parts of Mumbai. Temples and mosques, religious processions, and petty disputes have snowballed into major reasons for bloodletting even before independence in 1947. The process of ghettoization could have started in those days, when people moved out to seek safety in their own community. There was propaganda against both communities, calls for boycott, which later found its echo in the Shiv Sena's core of beliefs, and in the Gujarat riots after Godhra in 2002. In addition, pre-Partition, the formation of the Muslim League, and the demand for a separate nation for Muslims inflamed relations between the two communities as never before.

Bipan Chandra (2004: 44–45) says:

> Hindu communalism remained weak before 1947, and, in fact, till 1984, possessing no real mass support because it was not able to harness religious fervour. It did not talk of protecting the interests of the Hindus and their culture or sanskriti. But this was not an emotive enough slogan. Hindu communalism did get aroused on the issue of the cutting of a peepal tree or the killing of a cow, or the selling of beef, or a Hindu girl marrying a Muslim boy, or a quarrel between a Muslim and a Hindu shopkeeper, or some other local issue.
>
> Same was the case with Muslim communalists before 1938 when it had no mass base and was mainly confined, except in periods of communal tension to Muslim landlords and sections of the middle classes. It was from 1938 onwards that M A Jinnah and the Muslim League leadership began to place increasing emphasis on religion and religious zeal and use religious symbols. Above all, Muslim communalism acquired massive support during the 1940s by arguing that Islam would be in danger in a united and secular India, and Pakistan would embody the renaissance of Islam.

Post-Independence, secularism has progressively become a casualty. Mushirul Hasan writes in 'Legacy of a Divided Nation' (Hasan 2007: 136):

> Nehru's optimism was finely balanced against the painful recognition that forces of secular nationalism were badly bruised at the dawn of Independence and that partition signified the failure of the Congress liberal socialist combine to keep the

nation's fabric intact. Gandhi was aware of this harsh reality. So were leaders of diverse political backgrounds, who while rejoicing in the freedom that had crowned their efforts, saw their lifelong mission being dissipated in those terrible days. The pageantry and ceremony over, free India was confronted with a troubled legacy, as also with the need to devise a strategy to deal with religious minorities, specially the Muslims who stayed put in the country of their birth.

The Constitution recognized the inherent multiracial and cultural tradition of India and its past, which was a tolerant one. Hasan (2007: 139) writes 'secularism did not find a place in the preamble till 1976 when the 42nd Constitutional amendment made India a "Sovereign, Socialist, Secular Democratic Republic"'. Yet, its broad principles were embodied in the Constitution, especially in the articles dealing with fundamental rights.

> It was possible to draw important lessons from a Constitution that defended and safeguarded India's pluralism and multi culturalism. Yet separating religion from public life or distancing the party and government from non secular causes was not the Congress agenda after Nehru. Hence the feeble secular response to communalism, as also the compulsion to derive political mileage from Hindu symbols, traditions and institutions. (Hasan 2007: 263)

Citing the Shah Bano case, he says, 'Meanwhile the Congress was busy wooing and pandering to the religious sentiments of Muslim orthodoxy. It did so to ensure that the religious reverses suffered by the party in by elections were not repeated nationally.' (Hasan 2007: 263)

In fact, the famous Shah Bano case, which led to the Muslim Women's Bill in Parliament and the opening of the Babri Masjid gates, are not unconnected as journalist Neerja Chowdhury explains in her article (Chowdhury 2006: 221–24):

The hue and cry raised by the All India Muslim Personal Law Board against the Shah Bano judgement and the result of the by-election and the Assam elections in December 1985 appear to have convinced the prime minister that the Muslims had moved away from the Congress (I) and that the remedial action was necessary. While Mr. Rajiv Gandhi was promising Muslim leaders even an ordinance to override the effects of the Shah Bano judgement at the end of last year, Vishwa Hindu Parishad led religious leaders were lobbying Hindu MPs in Delhi on the opening of the doors of the Ram Janmabhoomi temple which Muslims claim as their Babari Masjid. A policy of appeasement of both communities being pursued by the government for electoral gains is a vicious cycle which will become difficult to break.

The rulers of the state and the overwhelming majority of the ruling class in India are basically Hindus and are steeped in Hindu cultural practices even in their daily personal routine, says A. R. Desai (1984: 20) in his paper 'Caste and Communal Violence': 'They have very astutely generated and strengthened the climate for upper caste Hindu cultural tradition as a dominant and superior national, spiritual, moral, cultural ethos and are spreading it as identical with secular ethos.' Desai also points out that communal violence is more visible in urban areas. 'Further a peculiar cut throat economic competition is also visible as an underlying force in a number of these communal upheavals.' According to Kuldip Nayar (1984: 21, 22) till 1980, 5,000 cases of communal disturbances were recorded. From the 1960s, the incidents of communal violence have taken place at an accelerated rate (1984: 22).

The RSS and, later, the Shiv Sena formed in 1966 in Mumbai, increasingly gave rise to an anti-Muslim rhetoric. Mumbai, for instance, a trading and working-class city, was home to a number of Muslims. The Shiv Sena's rise to power involved targeting business; first, it was the south Indian Udipi hotels and, later, the Muslims. Today, the city still calls itself cosmopolitan, but it has had to deal with many dents along

CONCLUSION

the way. The rift between the two communities may have seemingly healed, but there is resentment fuelled by a lack of justice, loss of livelihoods, personal grief, and loss. When I meet people affected by the riots, I can see how they perceive things. From their perspective of loss, the city has changed immeasurably and it can never go back to what it was. Yet, people have reconciled in many ways to their situation.

The Shiv Sena enjoyed the confidence of the Congress when it started. The Congress saw the Sena as a check on the Communist parties and what resulted was the nurturing of a cadre that would come in handy in 1992. Jayant Lele (1996: 202, 203) has a word of caution.

> The opportunism of the mainstream political parties professing secularism is often blamed for the continuing strength of proponents of hindutva, such as the Shiv Sena. There is ample evidence to show how factionalism within the ruling Congress Party often gave the Sena a new lease on life. It would be inadequate, however, to rest one's analysis on these factors as the explanation of the Sena's viability. An encompassing explanation must focus on the shifts occurring in the material basis of its diverse constituency, its changing interests, and the different signals the ideology of hindutva transmits to various sectors of its support.

For those affected by the riots, reconciliation has come without the truth being acknowledged. Moreover, there is no attempt to understand the factors that drove the violence and redress those issues which are splintering communities. Ordinary people are sharp to realize that there is an enormous political stake in all this. As more than one person has pointed out, the ruling class encourages this policy of divide-and-rule and the segregation of communities helps their vote banks. The political establishment benefits from this division and the helplessness of a community, and the threat of marginalization is like the sword of Damocles hanging over it. The lack of justice and equality is almost deliberate just so they can be the targeted beneficiaries of largesse in the form of minority affairs programmes and scholarships. Many Muslims said that they did not need the Sachar Committee to tell them about their own poverty and backwardness. Now, a political issue is being made out of the implementation of the report.

The reasons for the backwardness and helplessness are not being addressed in the first place. As a result, the reconciliation, post riots, with their lives is at a deeply personal level and there is little political attempt to breach this communal divide. Political parties pay lip service to secularism, and nurture people as their voters. At a time when Muslims were disillusioned with the Congress, the Malegaon blast investigation, which led to the arrest of suspected Hindu Right wing activists, including a Sadhvi and an army officer, changed perceptions. All terror attacks were not to be laid at the door of the Muslims. However, the case is under trial still. The political class manipulates the community and Malegaon is another string it can pull for votes. While the Shiv Sena and BJP government, which was in power after the riots from 1995–99 was not expected to punish its own people, nothing prevented the subsequent Congress and NCP governments from doing so.

The Congress–NCP have been elected to power in Maharashtra for the third time in 2009. Since the last 10 years or more that they have been in power, these two parties have made a mockery of their own manifesto, promising the implementation of the *Srikrishna Commission Report*. The special courts, which were set up, did not deal with the really serious cases. Also, the time lag has affected the spirit of many. It is a case of too-little-too-late. The state has to show that the law can be applied irrespective of religion and it is this intent that is singularly lacking. Senior customs officials who abetted the arms and explosives landings, which facilitated the serial blasts of 12 March 1993, were not spared. Why not show the same seriousness for the riot cases?

There are some common threads that emerge from the various interviews—the lack of justice, the lingering sense of loss, alienation, and perceptions of what has happened to the city. Some have been able to get on with their lives, put their business back on track, but for others it has meant a downward trend both economically and socially. Crucial to this are the perceptions of security when one lives in a ghetto and outside.

There is a continuing sense of persecution—every time there is a blast, Muslim areas are targeted and men are picked up. Even after Ajmer, Hyderabad, and Malegaon (in 2006), when blasts took place near mosques, it was again the Muslims who were arrested. There is a sense of disbelief and distrust. People feel they will never get justice and only Allah will help them. This belief in divine retribution is intensified by the fact that there is no justice on earth. There is a huge loss of faith in the government and the judiciary and the political parties, specially the Congress. A lot of people I met said that rioters were punished with death in accidents or died of AIDS. I suspect this may not be the case. But this is how people have reconciled with the reality that there will be no justice for them in ways they can expect.

Also, some of the people I met, spoke of how the blasts of 12 March 1993 in many ways had 'equalized the effects of the riots'. One person said: 'The blasts came as a signal that you cannot treat Muslims like this.' After the blasts, many Muslims said that the attitude of the majority community changed. Many said now there will never be riots because the blasts showed that the Muslim community cannot be a soft target. Even if they did not support the killing of innocent people or the criminal minds behind the blast, some people voiced a sense of justice. This is a chilling conclusion, but even educated people spoke of this. They also referred to the worsening situation after the events of 9/11 in the USA and India's proximity to Israel.

The main issue after the riots was the loss of livelihoods, which was not compensated for. A mere ₹ 5,000 was provided for the loss of property or houses. There was very little community support to get back on track. However, many have tried to come back and have succeeded, but these cases do not make up for the bulk of what has happened to the community—they have been shown their place as second-class citizens, neither liable for support nor justice. And being poor, many of them may not even be part of Mumbai's dream to be a world-class city.

People who lived in 'mixed' areas find it difficult to live in ghettos, but they seem to have no choice. It is forced ghettoization, as journalist Huma Khan points out. The perception that Muslims are a threat is only reinforced; it has not gone away. A few groups are fighting for justice for riot victims. As Zeenat Shaukat Ali, professor of Islamic Studies, at a public hearing in Mumbai on 5 September 2007, told the National Commission for Minorities: 'Why should people come and demand justice, it is their right'.

Dil toot gaya, abh saha nahi jaata (the heart is broken, one can't suffer anymore) are oft repeated phrases. The Gujarat riots too have reinforced the belief that Muslims will never get justice. Some of the people I spoke to said they will not get jobs, and even if they do, they are looked at with suspicion. With the police, there was no question of confidence. Despite all this, many prefer to live in Mumbai. As Izhar *bhai* says: 'Where will we go? And how much will we keep shifting?' Or they say: 'Now what can happen, the worst is over.' Gujarat created more of a fear psychosis—it also added to the divisions in society and the fear that something will happen again.

It is the single-minded pursuit of justice that has kept alive people like Tahir Wagle, whose son was allegedly shot dead by the police. In many of the riot cases, no complaints were ever filed and no one was arrested. People were dissuaded from filing complaints or speaking up by the police. In some cases, they do not even want to file complaints for fear of retribution. People feel if nothing was done till now, it will never be done and, also, politically, they feel betrayed by the Congress. The interviews show a wide range of feelings and thoughts—there is a deep sense of loss and people cannot understand why the riots took place. People have suffered from mental ailments, shock, and trauma and have had to leave homes leading to dislocation and insecurity of shelter, food, and jobs. There is alienation and isolation from the majority community, and huddling together in ghettos, reluctance to talk or meet on this issue, and a feeling of lethargy and hopelessness. There is tremendous loss of confidence in society, in the judiciary, police, and even

CONCLUSION

in the media. When I met some of the people, often it is the first time they talked about their experiences and it is with a sense of numbness. They cannot empathize with anyone because their own experiences are terrible and nothing stands above that.

The events in Mumbai and its aftermath raise many questions. It also draws attention to the question of identity. The spread of the Shiv Sena ideology has led to a general perception that Muslims deserved the riots. Instead of being perceived as the victims, the Muslims were seen as the aggressors. People really feel that the Sena saved the Hindus in the city and the city itself from Muslims. So well entrenched is this belief that many also believe the bomb blasts occurred first and then the riots. Muslims are dirty, live in ghettos, have many children, the men marry four times, they do not bathe, they are violent—these are some of the commonly held beliefs and nothing is being done to dispel them. As the historian Bipan Chandra says in a personal interview (October 2007) that the basic issue is that people react only after a riot has occurred and then lament about the lack of justice. However, once communalism is widespread in society, everyone is affected. Even secular people feel a twinge and feel they must support the majority community. In that sense, secularism is a spectrum, it is a question of degrees, he feels. The people who are spreading this corrupt ideology are not punished, it is not enough to merely punish the culprits in the riots. There is no real strong stand or fight against communalism. Rioters are condemned, but not the ideology that is leading to this. A lot of communal prejudices are now accepted.

The rise of Hindu militancy has put the Muslim community on the back foot and each time they have to reassert their own patriotism and identity as Indians. Every time there is a blast Muslim organizations rush to condemn it, but yet there is a feeling that this is not being done. The other issue is the question of riot victims. Every time one mentions riots, people ask what about the blast victims? Are they not victims too? What has happened to them? They too did not get any money. Often, when the Mumbai riots are mentioned, people are quick to point out that the

Muslims caused the serial bomb blasts. The two are linked as even Justice Srikrishna has pointed out in his report. Yet, justice to riot victims cannot be obliterated by the argument that Muslims are terrorists and do not deserve any sympathy. To instigate riots and kill is a serious offence, just as terrorism is a crime and it must be treated as such. There can be no excuse for mass murder. The guilty have to be punished. There is a predominant feeling that Muslims are terrorists, which is why the discrimination against them has intensified in the minds of the common person. It is only after the Hindu terror network was exposed that the BJP and Sena started talking about terror being a crime and not an affiliate of a particular religion. Very true, but BJP politicians add, in the same breath, that all terrorists caught so far have been Muslims.

For the Sena and its followers, the illusion that Muslims and Bangladeshis are a threat, has to be kept alive. No one is underestimating terrorism or the gravity of terror threats to Mumbai or the country. It is a city which has already witnessed a spate of bomb blasts right from 12 March 1993, some of them unsurpassed in heinousness and brutality. Terrorism has to be tackled at its root, the solutions are at a political level. Yet, an entire community is tarnished because of global and local perceptions of Islamic terror. Every arrest, every bomb blast creates a fear psychosis and reinforces the terror threat. It is something that will never go away. On 5 November 1982, 44 Muslim MPs, including those belonging to the ruling Congress (I) submitted a memorandum to Prime Minister Gandhi:

> Today communal violence is turning more and more into police action against the Muslim minority. Today the victim is being projected as the aggressor, as a rebel, and as a traitor. Today Muslims are arrested in hundreds and tortured, their limbs are broken, the privacy of homes is violated, their property is destroyed, their place of business is put to flames and their place of worship are desecrated, all with the connivance and support of the so called guardians of law and order. (Noorani 2006: 196, 197)

Little has changed after all these years.

The entire government machinery is working to keep policemen out of the purview of punishment. The Sena defends the police every time saying taking action will demoralize the police force. The government too is quite chummy with the Sena and has no intentions of prosecuting Thackeray or any of the Sainiks involved in the riots. Though the government makes noises about punishing the guilty, in reality nothing will happen. In the absence of a strong political alternative for Muslims, the Congress is complacent that it will get their votes.

In Mumbai, it is difficult for Muslims to buy houses, as Huma has said, or get houses on rent; housing societies too are known to refuse Muslims flats. There are exceptions as has been pointed out earlier. But, what does this mean for a society as a whole? Our inclusive philosophy has been narrowed down to such a level of discrimination and things seem to be getting worse. As other people I met have said, inherently, there was no bias against Muslims. In various places, people protected each other and said their Hindu neighbours had helped them. Many also said that the mobs, which attacked them, consisted of strangers. They also attributed the riots to political motives. Yet, what has caused it is the chief insecurity they are going through. What if it happens again? Who will help them? What will be their future? People do not buy expensive goods or stock their houses for fear of riots, they cannot expand their shops and businesses, they live in ghettos for safety, they are afraid if a bomb blast happens, they know it is their community which will be targeted. Students experience discrimination in colleges, people who manage to get jobs feel there is a wall around them. Despite all this, there is a sense of forgiveness that Allah is the final arbiter. This is the truth that people live with. However, unless there is an attempt to forge a larger political framework to understand the forces of communal violence and its impact, this sense of despair will be self-defeating.

There is really very little difference between the Congress, which claims to be secular, and parties like the Sena or the BJP. A far cry from the days of Nehru and Gandhi, as Bipan Chandra (2004: 31) puts it:

Unfortunately the spectrum of Indian politics which shunned communalism in toto has been gradually getting narrowed down. It is not only in corruption and the nexus between politicians, bureaucracy and *goonda* gangster elements that the general degeneration of Indian politics has been finding expression. It also expresses itself in a soft approach towards Hindu, Muslim and Sikh communalism. This flabbiness and opportunism are in deep contrast with the sturdy approach of a Jawaharlal Nehru or Mahatma Gandhi. Nehru, for example, would make no compromise with communalism, whatever the electoral consequences. 'So far as I am concerned', he was to declare in 1954, 'I am prepared to lose every election in India but to give no quarter to communalism or casteism.'

The Malegaon blast case of 29 September 2008 was a major election plank in the 2009 Lok Sabha. Politicians like Sharad Pawar took a tough stand that no community must be targeted for terrorism and terror had no religion. Beautiful words! Mr Pawar struck a chord in the Muslims and whenever he campaigned in the state, he made it a point to target Gujarat Chief Minister Narendra Modi and his politics. After polarizing the Maratha votes, by making a strident demand for reservation for poor Marathas, the NCP was clearly aiming to consolidate the Dalit and Muslim votes. Taking a leaf out of the Congress book, Pawar made promises about reservations for the poor and backward, including Muslims. The government showed great promptness in investigating the Malegaon blast, but there were other blasts before, in Nanded for instance, that clearly show the involvement of Hindu Right wing groups. These cases are stagnating in court since 2006. The political establishment fears a Hindu backlash and it clearly does not want to take a stand that can be viewed as strident.

The Congress has played a Machiavellian role in its wooing of Muslims. It is almost a cruel joke. It supports the community, lures them to vote for it, and then stops short of all its promises. Then again during election time, it casts its net around, giving several sops, hoping to garner support. Muslims, in some parts of the country, have resisted these attempts, but not on a collective level. The community is conscious of the manner in which it has been used, but it is caught in a cleft stick. Its alienation makes sure that any political support is welcome, even if it is poll-related. The sense of defeatism must be turned around into a political articulation of rights for equality and justice. This is a fight that is universal and not of a single community. As equal citizens, they have a constitutional right to justice and fair treatment. No one can take that away. It is time to regain that lost ground with conviction, however slowly and painful it may be. India is a pluralistic society and the attempts of certain groups to develop a single national identity have to be resisted. Governments, instead of wooing communities, must focus more on problem-solving and not cash in on helplessness and insecurity. While there have been some attempts at dialogues between communities, the time has come for taking this forward in a serious and planned manner. Secularism is not a joke as the saffron parties are making out, it is the foundation of the Indian state and no one must be allowed to trifle with it, especially at the cost of people's lives.

Despite the series of communal riots, Mumbai has always been hailed for its cosmopolitan spirit. People and their actions have often belied the saffron propaganda to some extent. Communities have always existed together in the past and they will continue to do so in the future. The philosophy of hatred too has been rejected more than once by the Indian people. However, after the riots, I saw that people had accepted the Sena as a legitimate defender of the Hindus. The Sena had prevented the invasion by Islamic hordes and even educated people believed this. That was the moment the city changed for me. Suddenly, I saw Mumbai from a populist viewpoint. A tiny island being valiantly defended by the Sena against a mythical Islamic invasion. People had set up vigilance squads against the Muslims, but no one came. Terrified Hindus voted for their saviour and made the Sena's day when it came to power in 1995 in the state. The saffron combine has not managed to repeat that victory though. Weakened by rivalry and the exit of key party members like Chhagan Bhujbal, Narayan Rane and the formation of the MNS by Raj Thackeray, the Sena needs to reinvent itself, and its main challenge now is to regain control over the BMC, elections for which are due in 2012.

Over the years, the militancy of terror groups with the alleged backing of Pakistan has become more barbaric and unabated, setting the scene in a way for a militant 'Hindu' response. The 2008 Malegaon blast arrests of Sadhvi Pragya Thakur Singh and other conspirators and their reasons for setting up Abhinav Bharat point to a revival of terror tactics as envisaged by Veer Savarkar, as Jaffrelot (2009) has pointed out. Another group, the Sanatan Sanstha, along with the Hindu Janjagruti Samiti, have been charged with perpetrating blasts in Maharashtra and the Sanstha again in Goa and Maharashtra. This is an indication of things to come. In this vicious cycle of 'action and reaction', the burning problems of the country like the situation in Kashmir, the building of the Ram temple, which are changing once again the notions of communalism and nationalism, remain unresolved. In the face of this explosive political situation, which is festering, it is the common people who will continue to suffer. The battles are being waged at the level of ideology and political one-upmanship, but the victims as always will remain mostly the poor as the interviews have shown in the preceding chapters. In the greater glory of achieving a political end, either the Hindu *Rashtra* or the separation of Kashmir, hundreds of lives will be sacrificed. In an interview (Menon 17 January 2009) with Mahmood Mamdani, he says that the answer to violence cannot be more violence, sometimes the best answers may not be the way out or they may have to be set aside for an amicable solution. Historically, there are reasons for a separate Hindu and Muslim nationalism evolving in this country and Partition only made that sharper. For Indian Muslims, India was home, yet their allegiance was always questioned. The Right wing has played no small part in this by taking the Ram temple issue to new heights of cultural nationalism.

In the case of Mumbai, over a century, the city has vastly changed, both in terms of its geography and population. From a cluster of seven islands, Greater Mumbai is spread over 468 sq km, while the Mumbai

CONCLUSION

Metropolitan Region (MMR) extends over 3,887 sq km in adjoining Thane and Raigad districts. Mumbai has a population of 11.91 million (Census 2001, Maharashtra Economic Survey 2009–10), while MMR has 5.90 million (Basic statistics, see MMRDA website www.mmrda-mumbai.org). Poised to become a global financial hub, it is easy to miss the reality beneath the city's dizzying pace of growth. Though ghettoized in parts, in Mumbai, people have not allowed themselves to be defeated by a divisive philosophy. There are many examples of people helping each other during the riots and there are a great many stories of courage. That is what must give hope for the future.

Mumbai has become a fragile city, very breakable, and yet the fissures are underneath—over it is the gloss of unity and toughness. Mumbai is, in reality, a breakable city. It is another matter that it joins up very fast. When we speak of Mumbai as a safe city it is a very relative perception—it depends on where you live, which community you belong to, your gender, how much money you have, where you are located socially, economically, and even politically. But it is a city that takes everyone into its generous fold—few go hungry here and few will have no shelter. It is a crazy sprawl of humanity. The city too is a survivor; it has survived so much exploitation, expansion, and reclamation. As a city, it has given its people qualities of that inherent survival.

For those affected by the riots, the city has changed forever in some ways. There is a different canvas of memory juggling with the reality of their existence. I think it is that old comforting canvas of hope and enterprise that lets them survive here. The fissures exist, the fear exists, and comfort lies far away like a distant cloak. Once, the possibilities were endless in the city, now, that has shrunk. Choices and aspirations are all dictated by where one comes from, religion, most importantly, life has come to be defined by parameters outside one's control. That is what Mumbai has become. Resurgent yet restrictive, unbreakable yet broken. In the grand sweeping cityscape, with all its bright lights, glitz, and glamour, everything has always had a place. Increasingly, that space is being squeezed for the poor and for the poor Muslims and other marginalized groups, more so. The city is on the threshold of futuristic development—the poor will have very little space in that scheme of things. Builders have taken over the city, edging out communities, as can be seen in Thakurdwar, for instance, and for Muslims the choices of where to buy houses are very narrow. In some places, what the riots could not do, the builders have achieved. Riot victims too have to contend with changing scenarios—shifts in residence, reduction of aspirations, and a continuing fear of violence.

The canvas then is of various illusions, of broken dreams, of identities conferred on you. There is a band-aid of togetherness, while the real sufferers bleed in silence. Three strong strains run through the stories of riot victims. Stifled aspirations, alienation, and injustice and displacement. There is a shock that the riots took place, that the city became divided and the growing acceptance that things will not get better. Instead of healing wounds, the rift is widening. People were left to recover on their own, scrabble around for their survival, and dumped in a sense that has marginalized them further. There are heartening stories like the Mahila Shakti Mandals, of how people helped each other during the riots, of how some have resisted ghettoization, and the healing touch if any has come from within. That is where Mumbai's fragility lies—in the silence of the neighbour, in the closed doors and averted eyes, and in the minds which are made up.

Yet, people will continue to come and live here because of the hope it offers in many ways. Mumbai is a city of contradictions. If there is great despair, there is also great hope. If there is ghettoization, there is also camaraderie. If there is hunger, there is a way to defeat that hunger. That is where the greatness of the city lies. And those who come to live here understand that.

APPENDIX

Cases against Bal Thackeray during the Riots of 1992–93 and before

In December 2004, I had filed an application under the Right to Information(RTI) Act, 2005, asking for copies of police cases against Shiv Sena chief Mr Bal Thackeray and what action was taken in those cases. I also wanted to know the status of the cases and if they were withdrawn, and copies of documents saying so. This is in the context of the post-Babri Masjid demolition riots of Mumbai between December 1992 and January 1993 when some cases were filed against Mr Thackeray for his writings in *Saamna*, the Shiv Sena newspaper that he edits.

The request was made to the Mumbai police who referred the matter to Special Branch I. The public information officer (PIO) in his first reply on 22 December 2004 itself said the matter had nothing to do with his office. Less than a month later, he said that my request was denied under Section 8 of the RTI Act. There was no reasoning given and no mention of the specific clause under Section 8. Under Section 19 (5) of the Act, the onus to prove that a denial of a request was justified shall be on the Central Public Information Officer or State Public Information Officer as the case may be.

Under the Act you are allowed two appeals. The first appellate authority in a letter on 24 January 2006 said my appeal was rejected under sub section 4, of section 24 of the RTI Act, and the 'Special Branch' of all Police Commissionerates does not fall within the ambit of the Act. This order too I challenged and this time my appeal came up a year later on 17 April 2007 before the Chief Information Commissioner (CIC), Maharashtra, Mr Suresh Joshi.

During the hearing, the PIO of Special Branch clearly said that the Branch was not dealing with the cases about which I had asked for information. The CIC in his order dated 20 April 2007, said that exemption from providing information to the Special Branch could pertain to those matters dealt with by the Special Branch. Since the matter itself is not being dealt with by Special Branch, the Police Commissioner should decide as to which police station would deal with my RTI application.

The CIC's order had said that it was a clear case of not marking the application to the correct authority who can give the information. The order also noted that the PIO had initially returned this application saying the subject matter does not pertain to the Special Branch. If this was the position, it is not understood how the same PIO has rejected the application, it said.

The CIC's order said that the PIO, Special Branch, and Appellate Officer both erred in dealing with my request as by their own admission, they were not the correct authority to deal with this application and appeal. He directed the application to the Commissioner of Police, Mumbai, who should decide as to who will deal with the application within 10 days.

In a reply dated 19 May 2007, the PIO of the Mumbai police commissionerate sent me a reply detailing eight cases filed against Mr Bal Thackeray, Shiv Sena chief and editor of *Saamna* between October 1992 to December 1993. The cases were filed between 20 January 1993 to 1 October 1993. In four cases, the chargesheets were filed on 30 July 1993. All these four cases were withdrawn from the court at Dadar.

In two cases, the chargesheets were filed after the stipulated time period. And the remaining two cases have been closed for lack of evidence.

No further details were available. The reasons for cases being withdrawn or closed as well as the case papers in the form of chargesheets or FIRs cannot be made available, the PIO said under Section 8 (g) of the RTI act. This section relates to information, the disclosure of which would endanger the life or physical safety of any person or identify the source of information or assistance given in confidence for law enforcement or security purposes. Again, there was no reasoning of how this section applies. In my first appeal I said that if the cases are in court then they are in the public domain and if there is a danger to the life of the person who has filed the case, that aspect can be kept a secret, but there cannot be a blanket denial of information.

On 12 July my appeal was heard by the First Appellate Authority, the Deputy Commissioner of Police (Operations), Mr Ashutosh Dumbre, who after giving the matter a patient hearing decided that Section 8 (g) was valid as raking up the matter could cause communal unrest and pose a threat to the life and personal security of many people. He accepted the PIO's argument that there would be unrest among Shiv Sainiks and denied me this information once again. The PIO had also contended during the hearing that since the 1993 blasts sentencing was in progress, there was tension in any case which was also upheld.

The RTI Act of 2005 was meant to be a landmark in ensuring transparency of governance and people would have a tool to get information denied to them otherwise. This application was filed as a test case under the Act to see how the law really worked. My second appeal was heard by the CIC on 30 November 2009. Mr Joshi again heard both sides and in his final order of 8 October 2010 said:

> In furtherance of the order given on the earlier appeal of Shrimati Menon on the same subject on 17.04.07, information about when chargesheet was filed against Shri Balasaheb Thackeray, the present information like withdrawal of cases has not been given under section 8(1) (g). Therefore the applicant has come in appeal. After hearing both sides, it is now decided

that if the court has given the decision on the withdrawal of cases, then the text of the request made by the government for withdrawal of cases and the copy of the decision of the court be given to the applicant.

Mr Joshi allowed the appeal and directed the PIO to give the information within 15 days of receipt of the order.

However, on 8 November 2010, the PIO of the police commissioner's office said the order was sent to Special Branch I for replies, since the matter had nothing to with them. On 11 November 2010, the Special Branch I PIO sent a letter back to the commissioner's office saying the subject of the appeal was in not their domain. Finally on 25 November 2010, the PIO at the police commissioner's office sent me a letter stating that they have asked for the relevant information and they will provide it when they get it.

The replies to my RTI started coming in from 18 January 2011. The first installment on 18 January 2011 contained information from Dadar, Mahim and Shivaji Park police stations.

In Dadar police station, there is a list of 14 cases registered under Sections 153 A, 295 A, 143 to 149, 427, 447, 117, 505 (1) and (2) of the Indian Penal Code (IPC).

Of the 14 cases, three cases were closed under A summary (case closed for filing a false or baseless FIR), two cases on 31 December 1991, and one on 26 December 1991. In four cases, Mr Thackeray was acquitted after being charged under Section 153 A of the IPC by the court on 18 October 1996.

In two cases the court closed the cases filed under 153 A invoking section 468 (2) (c) of the Code of Criminal Procedure (CrPC). In three more cases the matter was closed after C summary (no evidence in the case) was accepted by the court. In one case, approval for C summary filed by the investigating officer is pending in court. In one more case, the case under 153 A is pending since the government is yet to give approval for Mr Thackeray's arrest. In cases of prosecution under Section 153A IPC, the permission of the state is required.

Mahim police station, there are three older cases. In one case, Mr Thackeray was acquited on 15 November 1990. In an old case of 1984, under Section 153 A, the papers of this case are old and torn and so it is unclear what action was taken.

In another case, of 1991, also under 153 A, 143 to 149, 326, 324, 114, of IPC, after the chargesheet was filed, the case was committed to the sessions court at Bandra on 27 September 1998. On 6 April 2004, the case was withdrawn after directions from the state government. No reason for withdrawal has been given.

There are two cases at the Shivaji Park police station. In one case of 2002, under Section 153 A, the government is yet to give its approval to file the chargesheet in court. The matter is pending. In another case involving defamation, of 2004, the accused Mr Thackeray was not arrested even though a chargesheet was filed in court and the matter is sub judice.

In Gamdevi police station—via a letter dated 30 December 2010—the police said it came to know in 1984 a case was registered under Section 153 A, 295 A of IPC but it has no information on the current position about these offences and there is no information in the records and so it cannot be furnished.

Crime Branch

Even before the riots, there were cases filed against Mr Thackeray but they seem to have gone nowhere. According to the records under RTI, the Crime Branch unit 3, (in a letter of 12 January 2011) states that two cases were registered against Mr Thackeray at Azad Maidan police station on 28 March 1988. The government ordered the Crime Branch unit 3 to investigate these cases on 30 March 1988. According to the investigation, there was plenty of evidence under Sections 153A, 153 B and 505 (1) (c) of the IPC and the Police Commissioner asked permission from the Secretary, Home Department, to file a case in court against Mr Thackeray in a letter on 9 June 1988. After that on 3 February 1995, the Additional Commissioner of Police Crime

Branch sent another letter requesting speedy clearance to file the case in court. On 13 April 2000, the Additional Chief Secretary, Home Department, asked for all the police cases against Mr Thackeray which had to be committed to court. Accordingly on 25 April 2000 police inspector M. M. Kulkarni of Crime Branch unit 3 submitted the papers to Special Branch I. After this there is no permission forthcoming from the government till now, the RTI letter said. Till the government permission is received, the charge sheets cannot be filed in court and the cases remain pending.

Some Relevant Sections of IPC and CrPC

- Section 468 of CrPc: Bar to taking cognizance after lapse of the period of limitation which can range from six months to three years depending on the punishment.
- Section 153A Indian Penal Code (IPC): Promoting enmity between different groups on grounds of religion, race, place of birth, residence, language, etc., and doing acts prejudicial to maintenance of harmony.
- Section 153B IPC: Imputations, assertions prejudicial to national-integration.
- Section 295 A: Deliberate and malicious acts intended to outrage religious feelings of any class by insulting its religion or religious beliefs.
- Section 501 IPC: Printing or engraving matter known to be defamatory.
- Section 502 IPC: Sale of printed or engraved substance containing defamatory matter.

BIBLIOGRAPHY

Advani, Lal Krishna. 2008. *My Country My Life*. New Delhi: Rupa & Co.
Ali, S. Ahmed. 2002. 'Urs, Mumbai Police Keep Tryst with Sufi Saint', *Indian Express*, 22 December. Available online at http://www.indianexpress.com/storyOld.php?storyId=15261 (last date of access: 15 June 2011)
Aloysius, G. 1998. *Nationalism without a Nation in India*. New Delhi: Oxford University Press.
Ambedkar, B. R. 1941. *Thoughts on Pakistan*. Bombay: Thacker and Company Limited Rampart Row.
Anand, Javed. 1993. *Damning Verdict: Report of the Srikrishna Commission Appointed for Inquiry into the Riots at Mumbai during December 1992, January 1993 and the March 12, 1993 Bomb Blasts*. Sabrang Communications and Publishing Pvt. Ltd.
Anderson, Benedict. 1991. *Imagined Communities Reflections on the Origin and Spread of Nationalism* (revised edition). London: Verso.
Barve, Sushobha. 2003. *Healing Streams: Bringing Back Hope in the Aftermath of Violence*. New Delhi: Penguin Books.
Blitz. 1945. 'Goonda Raj', *Blitz*, 6 October.
Bombay Sentinel. 1945. 'Vesper Notes', *Bombay Sentinel*, 2 October.
Bombay Sentinel. 1945, 'Communal Riots from P. V. Krishnan', *Bombay Sentinel*, 4 October.
———. 1945, 'Morning Free from Incidents', *Bombay Sentinel*, 12 October.
Butalia, Urvashi. 1998. *The Other Side of Silence: Voices from the Partition of India*. New Delhi: Penguin Books.
Chandra, Bipan. 2004. *Communalism: A Primer*. New Delhi: Anamika Publishers and Distributors (P) Ltd.
Chitre, Dilip. 2007. *Namdeo Dhasal, Poet of the Underworld, Poems 1972–2006*, selected, introduced and translated from the Marathi. New Delhi: Navayana Publishing.
Chowdhury, Neerja. 1986. 'Shortsighted Move to Appease Communities', *The Statesman*, 1 May 1986, in A. G. Noorani (ed.), *The Muslims of India*, pp. 221–24. New Delhi: Oxford University Press.
Desai, A. R. 1984. 'Caste and Communal Violence', in Asghar Ali Engineer (ed.), *Communal Riots in Post-Independence India*, Hyderabad Sangam Books.

Dossal, Mariam. 1996. *Imperial Designs and Indian Realities: The Planning of Bombay City 1845–1875*. New Delhi: Oxford University Press.
Edwardes, S. M. 1923. *The Bombay City Police: A Historical Sketch 1672–1916*. London: Humphrey Milford, Oxford University Press.
———. 1924. *Crime in India*. Humphrey Milford, Oxford University Press.
Free Press Journal. 1945. 'Electioneering Handicapped Mr Patil's Appeal', *Free Press Journal*, 1 October.
Freitag, Sandria, B. 1980. 'Sacred Symbol as Mobilizing Ideology: The North Indian Search for a "Hindu" Community', *Comparative Studies in Society and History*, 22: 604, 606.
Golwalkar, M. S. 1966. *Bunch of Thoughts*. Bangalore: Vikrama Prakashan.
Government of Maharashtra affidavit to Supreme Court, 16 January 2008.
Griffiths, Sir Percival. 1971. *To Guard My People: The History of Indian Police*. London: Ernest Benn Ltd, Bombay: Allied Publishers Private Limited.
Gupta, Dipankar. 1982. *Nativism in a Metropolis: Shiv Sena in Bombay*. New Delhi: Manohar Publications.
Hansen, Thomas Blom. 2005. *Violence in Urban India, Identity, Politics and the Post Colonial City*. New Delhi: Permanent Black.
Hasan, Mushirul. 2007. 'Legacy of a Divided Nation', in *India's Muslims: An Omnibus*. New Delhi: Oxford University Press.
Heuze, Gerard. 1996. 'Culture Populism: The Appeal of the Shiv Sena', in Sujata Patel and Alice Thorner (eds), *Bombay: Metaphor for Modern India*, pp. 213–47. New Delhi: Oxford University Press.
Huntington, Samuel. 1997. *The Clash of Civilizations and the Remaking of the World Order*. New Delhi: Penguin Books.
Inder Singh, Anita. 2010. *The Origins of the Partition of India 1936–1947* (The Partition Omnibus edition). New Delhi: Oxford University Press.
Indian Daily Mail. 1932. 'Riot Averted by the Police, Hindu Muslim Clash', *Indian Daily Mail*, 18 March.
Jaffrelot, Christophe. 1999. *The Hindu Nationalist Movement and Indian Politics 1925 to the 1990s Strategies of Identity Building Implantation and Mobilisation (with Special Reference to Central India)*. New Delhi: Penguin Books.
———. 2009. 'A Running Thread of Deep Saffron', *Indian Express*, 29 January. Available online at http://www.indianexpress.com/news/a-running-thread-of-deep-saffron/416409/ (last date of access: 15 June 2011)
Kanungo, Pralay. 2003. *RSS's Tryst with Politics from Hedgewar to Sudarshan*. New Delhi: Manohar.

Katzenstein, Mary Fainsod. 1979. *Ethnicity and Equality: The Shiv Sena Party and Preferential Policies in Bombay*. Cornell University Press.

Khalidi, Omar. 2006. *Muslims in Indian Economy*. New Delhi: Three Essays.

Kosambi, Meera. 1996. 'British Bombay and Marathi Mumbai: Some Nineteenth Century Perceptions', in Sujata Patel and Alice Thorner (eds), *Bombay: Mosaic of Modern Culture*, pp. 3–24. New Delhi: Oxford University Press.

Kothari, Miloon and Nasreen Contractor. 1996. 'Planned Segregation Riots Evictions and Dispossession in Jogeshwari East', Report prepared by Youth for Unity and Voluntary Action (YUVA).

Lele, Jayant. 1996. 'Saffronization of the Shiv Sena: The Political Economy of City, State and Nation', in Sujata Patel and Alice Thorner (eds) *Bombay: Metaphor for Modern India*, pp. 185–212. New Delhi: Oxford University Press.

Maharashtra State Archives Department, Elphinstone College, Mumbai. Files sourced from Home Department Speical on Riots, Mumbai, various documents and reports.

Maharashtra State Gazetteers Department. 2001. *Gazetteer of Bombay City and Island, Volume 2*. Cosmo Publications.

Mahratta, Home Department Special File No. 844-H-VIII, Maharashtra State Archives Department, Poona, 4 July 1941.

Masselos, Jim. 2007. *The City in Action: Bombay Struggles for Power*. Oxford University Press.

Menon, Meena. 2008. 'Nanded Case: Of Lost Leads and Shoddy Investigation', *The Hindu*, 3 November.

Menon, Meena. 2009. 'The Way of Truth and Reconciliation', (Interview with Mahmood Mamdani), *The Hindu*. 17 January, Chennai edition.

———. 2009. 'The Long and Winding Road', *The Hindu*, 5 December.

Nair, Smita. 2010. *The Indian Express*. 15 September, Malegaon, Ajmer, Hyderabad edition.

Nayar, Kuldip. 1984. 'Caste and Communal Violence', in Asghar Ali Engineer (ed.), *Communal Riots in Post-Independence India*, New Delhi: Sangam Books.

Noorani, A. G. (ed.). 2006. *The Muslims of India*. New Delhi: Oxford University Press.

Padgaonkar, Dileep. 1993. *When Bombay Burned*. UBS Publishers' Distributors Ltd.

Page, David. 2010. *Prelude to Partition, The Indian Muslims and the Imperial Systems of Control 1920–1932*, The Partition Omnibus. New Delhi: Oxford University Press.

Pandey, Gyanendra. 2008. *The Construction of Communalism in Colonial North India*, The Gyanendra Pandey Omnibus, Second Edition. New Delhi: Oxford University Press.

Pandey, Gyanendra and Yunas Samad. 2007. *Fault Lines of Nationhood* (series editor David Page). New Delhi: Lotus Collection Roli Books.

Patel, Sujata and Alice Thorner (eds). 1996a. *Bombay: Metaphor for Modern India*. New Delhi: Oxford University Press.

———. 1996b. *Bombay: Mosaic for Modern Culture*. New Delhi: Oxford University Press.

Patel, Sujata and Jim Masselos (eds). 2003. *Bombay and Mumbai: The City in Transition*. New Delhi: Oxford University Press.

Punwani, Jyoti. 2002. 'The Carnage at Godhra', in Siddharth Varadarajan (ed.), *Gujarat: The Making of a Tragedy*. New Delhi: Penguin Books.

———. 2003. '"My Area, Your Area": How Riots Changed the City', in Sujata Patel and Jim Masselos (eds), *Bombay and Mumbai: The City in Transition*. New Delhi: Oxford University Press.

Purandare, Vaibhav. 1999. *The Sena Story*. Mumbai: Business Publications Inc.

Rao, Dipak. 2007. *Mumbai Police Urbs Prima in Indis*. Mumbai: Silver Point Press.

Rao, P. V. Narasimha. 1992. *Ayodhya 6 December*. New Delhi: Penguin Viking.

Rowena Robinson. 2005. *Tremors of Violence: Muslim Survivors of Ethnic Strife in Western India*. New Delhi: SAGE Publications.

Sachar Committee Report. 2006. *Social, Economic and Educational Status of the Muslim Community of India: A Report*, Prime Minister's High Level Committee, chaired by Justice Rajendra Sachar, Cabinet Secretariat, Government of India.

Sadhwani, Yogesh. 5 May 2010. 'Dislodged Muslim Man Gets Support from Sena, MNS', *Mumbai Mirror*, 5 May.

Sarkar, Tanika. 2001. *Hindu Wife, Hindu Nation: Community, Religion, and Cultural Nationalism*. Permanent Black.

Savarkar, Vinayak Damodar. 1935. 'Hindutvache Panchapran or the Spirit of Hindutva', *Samagra Savarkar Vangmaya*, 3: 86.

Sen, Amartya. 2006. *Identity and Violence: The Illusion of Destiny*. Allen Lane.

Srikrishna, Justice B. N. 1998. *Srikrishna Commission Report: Volumes I and II.* Government of Maharashtra.

Sunthankar, B. R. 1993. *Maharashtra 1858–1920.* Popular Book Depot.

Swami, Praveen and V. Venkatesan. 1999. 'Above the Law', *Frontline*, 13–26 March, 16(6). Available online at http://www.hinduonnet.com/fline/fl1606/16060420.htm

Tarkunde, V. M. Fubruary 1996. 'Supreme Court Judgment: A Blow to Secular Democracy', *PUCL Bulletin*, 19 January. Available online at http://www.pucl.org/from-archives/Religion-communalism/sc-judgement.htm (last date of access: 15 June 2011)

Thackeray, Raj (ed.). 2005. *Bal Keshav Thackeray: Photobiography.* Chinar Publishers.

The Bombay Chronicle, 1936, 'Shaukat Ali in Fighting Mood at Peace Committee: Talks of Congress Bullying the Muslims and Grave Apprehensions', *The Bombay Chronicle*, 2 April.

———. 1936. 'Hope of Sabha Mandap Dispute Settlement: Free and Frank Talks in Search for Peace ... Leaders Appeal to Warring Sections', *The Bombay Chronicle*, 17 October.

———. 1945. 'Three Killed and 25 Injured in Clashes in Golpitha', *The Bombay Chronicle*, 27 September.

———. 1945. 'Why Magnify Hooliganism into Communal Riots', *The Bombay Chronicle*, 5 October.

———. 1945. 'Unmistakable Signs of Returning Normality', *The Bombay Chronicle*, 8 October.

———. 1946. 'Home Minister Tours City Riot Areas', *The Bombay Chronicle*, 16 September.

The Indian Peoples Human Rights Tribunal. 1993. *The Peoples Verdict: An Inquiry into the December '92 and Jan '93 Riots in Bombay.* Conducted by Justice S. M. Daud and Justice H. Suresh

Thapar, Romila, Harbans Mukhiya, and Bipan Chandra. 1981. *Communalism and the Writing of Indian History.* New Delhi: Peoples Publishing House.

Tindall, Gillian. 1992. *The City of Gold, A Biography of Bombay.* New Delhi: Penguin.

Upadhyay, Shashi Bhushan. 1989. 'Communalism and Working Class—Riot of 1893 in Bombay City', *Economic and Political Weekly*, 29 July: 69–75.

Vora, Rajendra and Suhas Palshikar. 2003. 'Politics of Locality, Community and Marginalization', in Sujata Patel and Jim Masselos (eds), *Bombay and Mumbai: The City in Transition*, pp. 161–82. Oxford University Press.

Yang, Anand A. 1980. 'Sacred Symbol and Sacred Space in Rural India: Community Mobilization in the "Anti-cow Killing" Riot of 1983', *Comparative Studies in Society and History*, 22: 580, 588.

INDEX

Aagaz, 91
Abhinav Bharat, xc, lxxxix, 240
Advani, L. K., xliv, lxiii, 101, 105
   Ayodhya movement, lxxiii
   Rath Yatra, lxxiii
Age of Consent Bill 1891, lxii
Akali Dal, lxxi
All India Congress Committee (AICC), 79–80
All India Hindu Mahasabha, 81. *See also* 1945 riots
Anandamath, lxi
Anjuman-I-Islam, 31
anti-Sikh riots, lxxi, 82
Anti-Terrorism Squad (ATS), lxxxix, xc
Anusuya *chawl*, 105
Aryabhiviniya Aur Govilap, 26
Arya Samaj, liv
   Hindu nationalism (*see* Hindu nationalism)
   shuddhi programme, lx
Ayodhya
   symbol of struggle between genuine secularism and pseudo secularism, lxxiv
   target of Hindu revivalism, xlii
Azamgarh district, cow slaughter in, lv

Babri Masjid demolition, xli
   Ram Lalla idols, xlii
   Thackeray addressed after, xliv
Bajrang Dal, 206
Bakri Id, 35

Bandra suburban station, 123
Banias, 4
Basantpur riots, in Bihar, lv–lvi
Behrampada, 124–126
   changes over years, 126–129
   changing relations between Hindus and Muslims after riots, 174
   Hindu community in gullies of, 178
   impact of riots, on retail clothing, 166
   residents assistance, to 2006 bomb explosion victims, 123
   residents living in ghettos, 177
   riots of 1992–93, 124
      impact of, 175–177
   Srikrishna Commission report, 123
benevolent dictatorship, 14
Bengal
   Hindu revivalism in, lxi
   militant nationalism in, lxii
bhakti, modern forms of
   deshbhakti (*see* Deshbhakti)
   Rambhakti (*see* Rambhakti)
Bharatiya Jana Sangh, lxv
Bharatiya Janata Party (BJP), xxii, xliv, lxv, 223
   alliance with Shiv Sena, xlvii
   gathering of support, from *vanvasis*, lxvi
   Janata party programme, lxv
Bhujbal, Chhagan, 20, 213, 239
Black quarter. *See* Mumbai
Bombay. *See also* Mumbai
   founding father of, 4

Hindu–Muslim clash, in 1893, 4
population of, 3
Portuguese landing in, 1
twentieth century maps of, 2
Bombay Aman Committee, 189
Bombay Chronicle, 67, 80
Bombay (Emergency Powers) Whipping Act 1933, 68
Bombay Girni Kamgar Union, 81
Bombay Milch Cattle Owners Association, 70
Bombay Pradesh Congress Committee, 77
Bombay Presidency, communal riots between Hindus and Muslim, history of, xlv
Bombay Society for the Preservation of Cows and Buffaloes, 24. *See also* Cow Protection Movement
British Bombay, diversity of, 7
British Broadcasting Corporation (BBC), 105
Byculla Temple–Mosque dispute, 1936
agitation by Muslims, over *sabha mandap* construction, 62–63
attempts to fire Laxmi Narayan temple, 68
Bombay [Emergency Powers] Whipping Act 1933 (*see* Bombay [Emergency Powers] Whipping Act 1933)
calling of reinforcements, by Commissioner of Police, 67
causalities during, 68, 71
censure motion against mayor, 64
Central Khilafat Committee meeting, 63
demotion of, old *sabha mandap*, 64
dispute over *sabha mandap*, 62
express letter from head police office, 61–62
Hindu Samrakshak Mandal, revival of, 67
Hindus and Muslims leaders appeal in, *Bombay Chronicle*, 67
invitation to *ulemas*, 71–72
Muslim Peace and Relief Committee
issuance of fatwas, 69–70
meeting with Mohammed Ali Jinnah, 69
Muslims petition before chief presidency magistrate, on *sabha mandap* construction, 66–67
opening ceremony of *sabha mandap*, orders for, 71
origin of, 65
Urdu posters appeal, to Muslims, 71

Central Khilafat Committee, 63
Centre for the Study of Developing Societies (CSDS), xix
Cheetah Camp, xxxiii
Chidambaram, P., li
Citizens Relief Committee, 77
clashes in 1990s, history of, 36–39
Communal Award, lxxxiii
Communalism, lvii, 222
communal violence, 204
Communist Party of India (CPI), xliii, 81. *See also* 1945 riots
Congress–NCP, elected to power in 2009, 232
Congress Party, xxv, 229
Congress secularism, lxxi
constructive retaliation, 23

INDEX

Cow Protection Movement, xlv, xlvii, lii–liii
  Arya Samaj, liv
  efforts in north India, lv
  Hindu community, mobilization of, lxxx
  and Hindu revivalism, liv
  riots of 1893, 22–27
  cultural identity, transformation of, lxix–lxx

Dayananda Saraswati, liii, lv
deshbhakti, lxii
desh drohis, 201
Dharavi, xxxiii, xxxv
Dharma Sansad, lxxii
Dhule riots (2008), 227
Divya Marathi, 177
Doordarshan, 112
Durga Bhavan, 182–183
Dutt, Sanjay, 166
Dutt, Sunil, 166

Elphinstone College, 208
Emergency Whipping Act of 1941, 79–80
European quarter. *See* Mumbai

Fernandes, George, xliv
Forbes list, lxxxviii. *See also* Ibrahim, Dawood
Fort Town. *See* Mumbai
Free Press Journal (FPJ), 9, 79

Gandhian socialism, lxv
Gandhi *chawl*, xxxviii
  incident of, 86–91
Gandhi, Indira, lxxi, 236
Gandhi, Mahatma, lxvii, lxxxix, lxxxv

Gandhi, Rajiv, 230
Gaorakshak Sabha, 24. *See also* Cow Protection Movement
garbhadhan tradition, lxii
Gaurakshak Sabha, 31
Gaurakshini Sabha, liii. *See also* Dayananda Saraswati
Ghatkopar blasts, li
ghettoization process, 227
Girni Kamgar Union. *See* Red Flag Union
Godhra massacre, xxxii
Godse, Nathuram, lxxxix
Golwalkar, Madhav Sadashiv, lxiv, 225
Greater Mumbai Police Band, 7–8
Green terror, li
Gujarati, 34
Gujarat riots (2002), 228

Hari Masjid case, xxxiv, 221
Hedgewar, Keshav Baliram, lxiv, 225
Hindu community, lviii
Hindu cultural nationalism, lxi
Hinduism, lix
Hindu Janjagruti Samiti, xc, 240
Hindu Mahasabha, xlii, 39
Hindu nationalism, xlvii
  roots of, lvii
Hindu Rashtra, li, 222
Hindu Rashtra Dal, xc, xci
Hindu Samrakshak Mandal, 67
Hindustan, 79
Hindustan ki Awaz, 150
Hitler, 14
Hukumat, 206
Hunter Committee Report, lxxxi

Ibrahim, Dawood, lxxxviii

257

Indian Daily Mail, 47
Indian quarter. See Mumbai
Inquilab e Jadid, 79
Inter-services Intelligence (ISI), lxxxviii
Iqbal, 79
Islamic terror, xci, li

Jogeshwari riots (1974)
　assault of Mohamed Azada, by Muslims, 85
　Gandhi chawl incident, 86–91
　　revisiting of, 91–97
　Jogeshwari police station, 83
　madarsa creation by Muslims, 84
　migration from Jogeshwari, 97–107
　Society for Awareness, Harmony and Equal Rights (SAHER) (see Society for Awareness, Harmony and Equal Rights [SAHER])
　special branch report, 83
Joshi, Manohar, xliv, 8

Kamathi gully, 178
Kapse, Nikhil, 221
Karkare, Hemant, lxxxix
Kar Seva, xlii, lxxiv
Kasab, Ajmal, xl, lxxxviii
Kasaiwada, 136, 177
　Hindu basti in, 179
　population in, 181
Kesari, 22
Khilafat, 79
Khilafat Movement, lxvii
Konkan migrants, xxxviii

Lashkar-e-Tayyiba, 201

Madarsa, 84

Madhya Hindu Samaj, lxxvii
Maharashtra Control of Organised Crimes Act (MCOCA), xc
Maharashtra Housing and Area Development Authority (MHADA), 86–87, 219
Maharashtra Navnirman Sena (MNS), 18, 240. See also Thackeray, Raj
　debut in Lok Sabha elections, 19
Mahila Mandals, 147–150
Makhdoom Baba Sandal Greater Bombay Police Committee, 7
Malegaon riots, 227
Malegaon terror attack, li, xc, 238
Marathi manoos, 19–21
Marmik, 9
maulanas, 182
maulvis, 182
Mazgaon, population of Muslims and Christians, 181
Memon, Tiger, xlix, lxxxviii. See also Serial bomb blasts (1993)
militant Hinduism, xlvii
militant Hindu nationalism, lxiv, 81
Modi, Narendra, 238
Mohalla Committee Movement Trust, xxxiv
mohalla committees, xxxiii–xxxiv
Mohammed Ali Jinnah, 69
Montague Chelmsford reforms (1932), lxvii, lxxxii
　trends in all-India politics, lxxxiii
Morley–Minto Reforms (1919), lxxxii
Muharram festival
　dispute between Khoja community members, 33
　and riots, 35–36

INDEX

Mukim survival, 150–152
Mumbai
  as cosmopolitan metropolis, 3
  literacy rate, in suburbs, xxxvi
  Marathi speaking population, 3
  multicultural aspect of, 7
  Muslims of, 4–5
  population of, xxxv–xxxvi
Mumbai riots (1992–93)
  background to riots, l
Mumbai Unbreakable, xxii
Mumbra, refugees in, 177
Muslim businesses, after 1992–93
  riots, xxxv
Muslim community, xx
Muslim fanaticism, lxvii
Muslim League, xliii, lxxxvi, 39
  British and Congress tactics,
    lxxxvii
  demand for, sovereign Muslim
    state, lxxxvii
Muslim nationalism, ideologues of,
  lxxxiv–lxxxv
Muslim Peace and Relief Committee,
  69
Muslim separatism, lxxxvi
Muslim terror, xx, li
Muslim Women Bill, 229
Muslim Women (Protection of Rights
  on Divorce) Act, 1986, lxxii
Mussolini's Balilla movement, xci
My Country My Life, lxiii

namaz, 16, 109, 112, 150, 200–201
Nationalism, 222
Nationalist Congress Party (NCP),
  21, 183
nation, definition of, lxxx
Naupada

changes over Years, 126–129
Hindu families in, 166
Khatun Bi story, 129–131, 147
revisiting of old memories,
  131–132
residents assistance, to 2006 bomb
  explosion victims, 123, 166
riots of 1992–93
  impact of, 175–177
settlement of, 123
Srikrishna Commission report, 123
Naya Nagar
  base of VHP and Shiv Sena, 113
  formation of closed communities
    in, 108
  impact of 1992–93 riots, 117
  infamous for suspected terrorists,
    108
Majid
  award for best teacher, 111
  Punjabi neighbours of, 110
  shop put on fire, 109
  middle-class dream, 108
  real estate business, 113
  refugees in, 120, 177
Nehru, Motilal, lxxvii
New Nirman *chawl*, 174
26 November terror strike (2008),
  xxxix
  Anti-Terrorism Squad (ATS) (*see*
    Anti-Terrorism Squad (ATS))
  death sentence to Kasab, xl
  reaction of Muslim groups, xl

Parsis
  and Hindu
    riots in 1832 between, 33
  and Muslims
    riots in 1832 between, 33

259

riots in 1874 between, 34–35
partition, community of survivors, for, xxxii
Pathan *chawl*, 208
Shahnawaz
   assault by policemen, 209
   cold-blooded murder of, 210
Patil, Vasantrao, xliv
Pawar, Sharad, xliv, 238
post-Babri Masjid demolition riots
   arrest of Sarpotdar, xxiii
   creation of new colonies, xx
   division between Hindus and Muslims, xix
   impact of, xxxii
   on journalists, xxxvii
   Maharashtra chief minister decision, to create special courts, xxv
   Muslim businesses after, xxxv
   Srikrishna Commission, appointment of, xxi
   suspect on Muslims, xx
   tendency among media, xxxviii
Praja Socialist Party (PSP), xliii, 10
Prayag Hindu Samaj, lxxvii
pseudo-secularism, 222
Public Works Department (PWD), explosion in 2006, xci–xcii
Punjabi Hindu Sabha, lx

Radhabai *chawl*, xxxviii, 88
Rambhakti, lxii
Ram Janmabhoomi movement, xlii, xliv, 223
Ram Jyot Yatras, lxxiii
Ram Lalla, xlii
Ram temple, xlii, 223
Rane, Narayan, 239

Rao, P. V. Narasimha, xxv, 223
Rashtriya Swayamsevak Sangh (RSS), 206
   Indian terrorist societies, lxiv
   Khilafat Movement (*see* Khilafat Movement)
   origin of, lxv, 225
   shakhas, xliii, lxii, 11
   agenda of cultural nationalism, lxv
   upper-caste Brahmin, dominance of, lxiv
Rath Yatra, lxxiii, 101
Red Flag Union, 40. *See also* 1929 riots
refuge, xix
Report of the Inquiry Commission, 1929, 39
Representation of the People Act, 1951, 12
1893 riots, 27–33
1929 riots
   Bombay Textile Mills, general strike in, 40
   Inquiry Commission Report, 41–42
   communal vote, 46
   Lord Irwin impact, 45
   second phase of, 43–44
1932 riots
   beginning of
      demolition of tomb, 48–49
      Mohammedan tombs, 48
      order of Home Member, 50
      placing of Hindu idols, 49
      press note from director of information, 48
      translation of Marathi leaflet, issued by Sanatan Hindu Dharma Pratipalak Sangh, 53

details of, 54–61
warning to editors, 61
1937 riots, 72–75
1938 riots, 72–75
1941 riots, 75–79
1945 riots, 79–81
1984 riots
  Cheetah Camp (*see* Cheetah Camp)
  impact on young Bombayites, xxxiii

Saamna, xxxviii, 16
Sachar Committee Report, lxxxi, 232
Sadhu Sansad, lxxii
Sadhvi Pragya Thakur Singh, li, lxxxix, 240. *See also* Malegaon terror attack
saffron terror, li
Sanatan Hindu Dharma Pratipalak Sangh, 53
Sanatan Sanstha, xc, 240
sanghathan campaign, lx
Sangh Parivar
  Ram bhakti, role of, lxxii
  saffron terror, xlii, li
Sant Bhindranwale, lxxi
Sarpotdar, Madhukar, xxiii
Secularism, 222
secular nationalism, lxxv–lxxx
serial bomb blasts (1993), xx, xxxvii
Shah Bano case, lxxii, 229–230
Shaikh, Anisabi Yusuf, 121
Shias and Sunnis, riots during Muharram festival, 35–36
Shiv Sena, xxi–xxii, xxxviii, 204, 206
  base at Naya Nagar, 113
  degeneration of, 20
  Hindu identity creation, lxviii

Maharashtra–Karnataka border issue, xlv
militant Hinduism, xlvii
origin of, xlv, 230
participation in Ram Janmabhoomi movement, xliv
rada culture of, 19
rise of
  adoption of Hindutva, 10
  agitations against communities, 14
  alliance with BJP, xliv, xlvii, 10
  Babri Masjid demolition, 16
  blood donation camp, 9
  connection with RSS, 11
  focus of, 9
  Joshi, Manohar (*see* Joshi, Manohar)
  in Konkan region, 21
  raising of pro Pakistani Muslims issues, at Durgadi Fort, 14–15
  sons of the soil approach, 15
  Srikrishna Commission Report, Joshi views on, 11–12
  Thane Municipal Corporation election, 10
shuddhi programme, of Arya Samaj, lx
Simon Commission, lxxxii
Singh, Manmohan, lxxi
Society for Awareness, Harmony and Equal Rights (SAHER), 93
Special Task Force (STF), xxii, 221
Srikrishna Commission Report, xx, xxii, xxiii, xxvi, xlviii, 209–210
  Gandhi *chawl* incident, 90–91
  Hari Masjid case, 221
  rejected by Sena–BJP government, l
Students Islamic Movement of India (SIMI), 119–120, 201

suburban local trains, terror strike on July 2006, xxii
Suleiman Usman Bakery case, xxiii–xxiv

Terrorist and Disruptive Activities (Prevention) Act (TADA), xxi, 90, 212
Thackeray, Bal, xliii, xxi, xxxviii, 9, 21, 116, 185
Thackeray, Keshav, 9. *See also* Shiv Sena
Thackeray, Raj, 19, 240
Thackeray, Uddhav, 9, 19
Thakurdwar community, disappearance of
  Badi home and residents, 152–158
  Choti *Badi*, 164–165
  Salma Agha story, 158–164
The Times of India, xxi, 22, 111, 174

Tilak, Bal Gangadhar, lxviii

Vajpayee, Atal Bihari, xxvi, lxv
Vande Mataram, lxi–lxii, 183
vanvasis, lxvi
Videsh Sanchar Nigam Limited (VSNL), 118
Vishwa Hindu Parishad (VHP), xliv, lxvi
  base at Naya Nagar, 113
  blast at Neemuch office, xci
  formation of, lxv
  Sadhu Sansad (*see* Sadhu Sansad)

White Town. *See* Mumbai
World Social Forum, 201

Yasin Mistry ki Chawl, 194–195
Youth for Unity and Voluntary Action (YUVA), 88, 91, 94

ABOUT THE AUTHOR

Meena Menon is an independent journalist and former Deputy Editor with *The Hindu*, which she quit in 2015. She is the author of *Reporting Pakistan* (2017) and co-author of *A Frayed History: The Journey of Cotton in India* (2017). She has been a journalist since 1984 and has worked with *Bombay* magazine, United News of India, *The Times of India*, and *The Hindu*. In 2004, she published *Organic Cotton: Reinventing the Wheel*. Prior to this, she co-authored *The Unseen Worker: On the Trail of the Girl Child*, published in 1998. She has received many fellowships and writes on politics, development, health, and human rights.

COPYRIGHT PERMISSIONS AND ACKNOWLEDGEMENTS

The frontispiece from Namdeo Dhasal's poem 'Concomitantly: December 6' has been reproduced with the kind permission of S. Anand (Publisher, Navayana Publishing, New Delhi).

Some of the material in this book was first published in *The Hindu*. In addition, I have sourced other articles from *The Hindu*. Mr N. Ram, Editor-in-Chief, *The Hindu*, has kindly granted permission for the use of the articles and material for this book.

Extracts from the following books have been used with the written permission of the authors.

Aloysius, G. 1997. *Nationalism without a Nation in India*. New Delhi: Oxford University Press.

Pandey, Gyanendra. 1990. *The Construction of Communalism in Colonial North India*. New Delhi: Oxford University Press.

Hasan, Mushirul. 2007. 'Legacy of a Divided Nation', in *India's Muslims: An Omnibus*. New Delhi: Oxford University Press.

Dossal, Mariam. 1996. *Imperial Designs and Indian Realities: The Planning of Bombay City, 1845–1875*. New Delhi: Oxford University Press.

Lele, Jayant. 1996. 'Saffronization of the Shiv Sena: The Political economy of City, State and Nation' in Sujata Patel and Alice Thorner (eds) *Bombay: Metaphor for Modern India*. New Delhi: Oxford University Press.

Palshikar, Suhas and Rajendra Vora. 2003. 'Politics of Locality, Community and Marginalization', in Sujata Patel and Jim Masselos (eds) *Bombay and Mumbai: The City in Transition*. New Delhi: Oxford University Press.

Kosambi, Meera. 1996. 'British Bombay and Marathi Mumbai: Some Nineteenth Century Perceptions', in Sujata Patel and Alice Thorner (eds) *Bombay: Mosaic of Modern Culture*. New Delhi: Oxford University Press.

Gupta, Dipankar. 1982. *Nativism in a Metropolis*. New Delhi: Manohar Publishers.

Jaffrelot, Christophe. 1999. *The Hindu Nationalist Movement and Indian Politics: 1925 to the 1990s Strategies of Identity Building Implantation and Mobilisation (with special reference to Central India)*. Penguin Books.

———. 2009. 'A Running Thread of Deep Saffron', *Indian Express*, 29 January.

Samad, Yunas and Gyanendra Pandey. 2007. *Fault Lines of Nationhood*. New Delhi: Roli Books.

Upadhyay, Shashi Bhushan. 1989. 'Communalism and Working Class: Riot of 1893 in Bombay City', *Economic and Political Weekly*, July 29.

Kanungo, Pralay. 2003. *RSS's Tryst with Politics from Hedgewar to Sudarshan*. New Delhi: Manohar Publishers and Distributors.

Advani, L.K. 2008. *My Country My Life*. New Delhi: Rupa and Co.

Barve, Sushobha. 2003. *Healing Streams, Bringing Back Hope in the Aftermath of Violence*. New Delhi: Penguin Books.

Butalia, Urvashi. 1998. *The Other Side of Silence: Voices from the Partition of India*. New Delhi: Penguin Books.

Publishers

Verso, London

Anderson, Benedict. 1991. *Imagined Communities Reflections on the Origin and Spread of Nationalism* (rev. ed.), pp. 6 and 12.

Jha, D. N. 2002. *The Myth of the Holy Cow*, pp. 19–20.

Permanent Black, New Delhi

Sarkar, Tanika. 2001. *Hindu Wife, Hindu Nation: Community, Religion, and Cultural Nationalism.*

Hansen, Thomas Blom. 2005. *Violence in Urban India: Identity, Politics and the Post Colonial City.*

Three Essays, New Delhi

Khalidi, Omar. 2006. *Muslims in Indian Economy.*

Cambridge University Press, UK

Freitag, Sandria B. 1980. 'Sacred Symbol as Mobilizing Ideology: The North Indian Search for a "Hindu" community', *Comparative Studies in Society and History*, 22: 604 and 606 © Society for the Comparative Study of Society and History, published by Cambridge University Press, UK, reproduced with permission.

Yang, Anand A. 1980. 'Sacred Symbol and Sacred Space in Rural India: Community Mobilization in the "Anti-Cow Killing" Riot of 1893', *Comparative Studies in Society and History*, 22: 580 and 588 © Society for the Comparative Study of Society and History, published by Cambridge University Press, UK, reproduced with permission.

Penguin, New Delhi

For quotes from Rao, P. V. Narasimha. 2006. *Ayodhya, 6 December 1992.*

For quotes from Punwani, Jyoti. 'Carnage at Godhra', in Siddharth Varadarajan (ed.) *The Making of a Tragedy.*

Curtis Brown

Tindal, Gillian. 1992. *The City of Gold: A Biography of Bombay*. New Delhi: Penguin. Reproduced with permission of Curtis Brown on behalf of Gillian Tindall Copyright © Gillian Tindall.

Oxford University Press

Material from the following titles has been reproduced with the permission of Oxford University Press India, New Delhi.

Page, David. 2010. 'Prelude to Partition: The Indian Muslims and the Imperial System of Control, 1920–1932', *The Partition Omnibus*.

Singh, Anita Inder. 2010. 'The Origins of the Partition of India 1936–1947', *The Partition Omnibus*.

Noorani, A. G. (ed.). 2006. *The Muslims of India*.

Punwani, Jyoti. 2003. '"My Area, Your Area": How Riots Changed the City' in Sujata Patel and Jim Maselos (eds) *Bombay and Mumbai: The City in Transition*.

Masselos, Jim. 2007. *The City in Action: Bombay Struggles for Power*.